P. R. Hunter

GW00992237

may

3

A Century of Gardeners

A Century of
Gardeners

BETTY MASSINGHAM

faber and faber

First published in 1982
by Faber and Faber Limited
3 Queen Square London WC1N 3AU
Printed in Great Britain by
BAS Printers Limited, Over Wallop, Hampshire
All rights reserved

British Library Cataloguing in Publication Data

Massingham, Betty
A century of gardeners.
1. Gardens—Great Britain—History
I. Title
712'.6'0941   SB466.G17

ISBN 0 571 11811 9

To Adam

The river drew her that day as it did every day; overlooking it she watched the ducks swimming in it, saying to herself: 'Virgil does not speak of the beauty of ducks swimming in a river, the softness of their voices and their round, black beautiful eyes so intelligent, but I should not have known how beautiful they are when swimming in a river if I had not read Virgil, and might well have lived my life out from birth to death without knowing that ducks swam with their pert tails turned up to the sky. It is strange that he should have no words about water-lilies, yet he taught me to see their great leathery leaves ...

GEORGE MOORE
Heloise and Abelard

Contents

Illustrations

Acknowledgements

Many people have assisted me in the compiling of *A Century of Gardeners* with their advice, their hospitality, their permission to use material in which they own the copyright and their offers to read through the manuscript. Some of them have become friends. To name them all individually would involve a list running to several pages, so I would like to take this opportunity of thanking each one of them for their kindness and help.

For permission to include copyright material my publishers and I thank the following authors (or their representatives), publishers and agents:

Mr J. C Medley for the extract from: George Moore *Heloise and Abelard* (Heinemann, 1928); Russell Page for extracts from *The Education of a Gardener* (Collins, 1962); George F. Chadwick *The Works of Sir Joseph Paxton* (Architectural Press, 1961); Betty Massingham *Turn on the Fountains* (Gollancz, 1974 and permission of Curtis Brown Ltd., London); William Robinson: *The Wild Garden* (1870), *The English Flower Garden* (1897), *Gravetye Manor* (1911), *The Virgin's Bower* (1912) (John Murray); Mrs Francis King: *The Well-Considered Garden* © 1915 Charles Scribner's Sons, © renewed 1943 Mrs Francis King (New York: Charles Scribner's Sons, 1915), reprinted with the permission of Charles Scribner's Sons, *The Beginner's Garden* © 1927 Charles Scribner's Sons (New York: Charles Scribner's Sons, 1927), reprinted with the permission of Charles Scribner's Sons; Mrs Francis King *From a New Garden* (Alfred A. Knopf, 1930); E. A. Bowles *My Garden in Spring* (Thomas Nelson,

1914); Sir Basil Arthur, Bart., for extracts from *The Letters of Lord and Lady Wolseley 1870–1911* (Heinemann, 1922) and *The Life of Lord Wolseley*; William Keble Martin *Over the Hills* (Michael Joseph, 1968); Eleanour Sinclair Rohde *Herbs and Herb Gardening* (1936) and *The Scented Garden* (1931) (Medici Society), *The Countryman* for an article by Eleanour Sinclair Rohde; Jason Hill (Dr F. A. Hampton) *Wild Foods of Britain* (A & C Black, 1939), (with X. M. Boulestin) *Herbs, Salads and Seasonings* (Heinemann, 1930, permission from A. D. Peters & Co.); Helen Van Pelt Wilson (and Leonie Bell) *The Fragrant Year* (Dent, 1951); Vita Sackville-West *Pepita* (reprinted by permission of Curtis Brown Ltd., London, on behalf of the Estate of Vita Sackville-West), and *The Garden* (1946) and *Vita Sackville-West's Garden Book* (1968) (Michael Joseph); Christopher Hassall *Edward Marsh—A Biography* (Longman, 1959, permission from David Higham Associates).

My publishers and I should also like to thank the following for permission to reproduce the illustrations:
Royal Horticultural Society (1, 3); BBC Hulton Picture Library (2); J. E. Downward (4, 21); Victor Gollancz Ltd (5); Country Life Ltd (6, 8, 29); Mr and Mrs J. Wolley Dod (10, 11); Mrs John Eden (13); Mr N. J. Prockter (15); Directors of the National Portrait Gallery (16); Trustees of the Tate Gallery and Miss Marguerite Steen (19); Mrs Berkeley (20); Morton Aboretum (22, 23); Trustees of the British Museum (25); Michael Joseph Ltd (30, 31); Dr and Mrs John Farrer (32, 33); Miss Irene Shepheard-Walwyn (34); Mrs F. A. Hampton (36); Mr Nigel Nicolson (38).

February 1982   B.M.

Foreword

This Century of Gardeners is not a rigid hundred years—it starts approximately at 1850. In making a selection from among so many possibilities, I can only apologize to readers for what may seem to some to be surprising omissions. My own personal choice has been made with some difficulty.

A friend most kindly gave me his own short list of gardeners; it contained no names familiar to me, but I could not resist looking some of them up. There was, for instance, the Revd. Henry Ewbank, sometime vicar of St John's, Ryde, Isle of Wight, who 'had a garden', and who died in 1901. This was, after all, a time for good clerical gardens.

Next on the list came the slightly improbable name of William Edward Gumbleton (1840–1911), who fitted nicely into the date period and seemed unusually eccentric, particularly where the use of his umbrella was concerned. Mr Gumbleton had a collection of rare and newly introduced plants at his Belgrove garden on the main island in Cork Harbour and he showed little patience and a good deal of anger with other gardeners who cared for a plant not just for its rarity value but because they loved it.

For instance, on a visit to the National Botanic Gardens, Glasnevin, with Edward Woodall of Scarborough (an English gentleman and respected friend of Miss Gertrude Jekyll), Mr Gumbleton attacked 'with his flailing umbrella' a plant which he considered inferior, destroying it completely. Sir Frederick Moore recalled sadly that 'Gumbleton had destroyed plants in other gardens . . . usually with an angry ejaculation of "tush" at each swipe of the umbrella.' This was the fate of any (in his opinion) inferior plants.

As this is a collection of short biographies of people who are of interest in their own right and not solely because of their garden-making, I should like to mention Baroness Burdett-Coutts, not known so much for gardening as for philanthropy. Although her personal gardening experience is thought to have been negligible, her influence among the poor and deprived, encouraging them in the love of nature and the countryside and in growing plants in cities, has been impossible to assess.

She was known more for her generosity in signing numerous cheques than her own skill in wielding a trowel, but her interest in gardens, churchyards, open spaces and rural activities as well as her prizes to young people for essays, which encouraged their enthusiasm for such things as growing vegetables and planting seeds and caring for them, had a wide influence.

There must be a mention of two of the greatest names in contemporary gardening, Major Lawrence Johnston of Hidcote in the Cotswolds and the second Lord Aberconway of Bodnant in North Wales. Not only did Lawrence Johnston design Hidcote— as though that was not enough—he also designed Serre de la Madonne, near Menton, France. Lord Aberconway was not only the creator of Bodnant but was President of the Royal Horticultural Society from 1931–53.

There is also Mrs Margery Fish of East Lambrook Manor, author, after her retirement from a successful career in London, of many excellent gardening books. Her ideas were derived largely from cottage gardens, their design and planting, in which there has recently been such a revival of interest. Her garden in Somerset is maintained very much as it was in her lifetime and attracts many visitors throughout the year.

In choosing the gardening people for this book I based my selection on those who have interested me as people, not just as gardeners. (I have found that it is not always the obvious interests or hobbies which tell us most about the person).

These 'people' were not just gardeners but trustees of the plants discovered and brought safely back from across the world and today, although we have to adapt to certain conditions of contemporary life, we are also such trustees. We owe it to the memory of those great gardeners of the past to care for our plants, to appreciate them and display them to their best advantage. This is being done, especially in the larger estate gardens, many of them, such as Bodnant and Hidcote, belonging to the National Trust, and open to the public.

Sometimes contemporary life produces harsh and difficult things for us to contend with and perhaps it is these which more than ever today give us the desire for quiet and peace. 'So', as Russell Page writes in *The Education of a Gardener*, 'time becomes an important aspect of garden design in more senses than its mere passage through the seasons . . .' He goes on:

> There seems to be time only to look, note and look away. Outside pressures distract; nourishment for our mind and feelings becomes ever more meagre. It is a gardener's pleasure, as it could be the designer's privilege, to break this crazy rhythm, to change and break the rush of time, and make the garden a quiet island in which a moment has a new meaning.

Sir Joseph Paxton

1801–1865

His name at Chatsworth is chiefly associated with
the remarkable palm-house he designed, which was
begun in 1836 and finished in 1840. 'This palm-
house, which was 300 ft. long, 123 ft. wide and
67 ft. high, was regarded as one of the most
remarkable achievements of the age, for in it a
tropical garden could be enjoyed even in the depth
of winter. . . .'

Loudon's Encyclopaedia of Gardening

Designer of the glass pavilion (later to become the Crystal
Palace) at the Great Exhibition of 1851 and co-founder of the
Gardeners' Chronicle, among a diversity of other interests and
achievements—these alone are not small claims to fame. But
Joseph Paxton was also the Member of Parliament for Coventry
for eleven years, his name was synonymous with Chatsworth, he
took an active part in the development of the railway system with
the Stephensons and was placed in charge of road transport in the
Crimea. No wonder *The Times* obituary described him as 'a man of
genius' and 'the greatest gardener of his time'.

Paxton was born in the year 1801 at the small village of Milton
Bryant in Bedfordshire. From the age of fifteen he worked as a
junior gardener at Battlesden, near Woburn, for Sir Gregory
Page-Taylor. He left there to work in the Woodhall gardens near
Walton, Hertfordshire, returning after a time to Battlesden for a
further two years, and going on to Wimbledon to work for the
Duke of Somerset. When he was twenty-two he secured a position
in the newly-opened gardens of the Horticultural Society,
adjoining Chiswick House. It was here that he was noticed by the
Duke of Devonshire who was impressed by his skill and
knowledge to such an extent that when, in 1826, the Duke
required a new head gardener, he offered the job to Paxton at a
weekly salary of 25s with a cottage thrown in.

Paxton's account of his arrival at Chatsworth, early on a May
morning, according to the *Handbook to Chatsworth and Hardwick*, is
practical and to the point but it also has a poetic touch:

1 Designer of the Crystal Palace, Sir Joseph Paxton, from a portrait by Octavius Oakley

I left London by the Comet Coach for Chesterfield; and arrived at Chatsworth at half-past four o'clock in the morning of the ninth of May, 1826. As no person was to be seen at that early hour, I got over the greenhouse gate by the old covered way, explored the pleasure grounds and looked round the outside of the house. I then went down to the kitchen gardens, scaled the outside wall and saw the whole of the place, set the men to work there at six o'clock; then returned to Chatsworth and got Thomas Weldon to play me the waterworks and afterwards went to breakfast with poor dear Mrs. Gregory and her niece; the latter fell in love with me and I with her, and thus completed my first morning's work at Chatsworth before 9 o'clock.

Anyone who could fit the opening bars of their life's work—a lasting marriage and a great garden—into a few hours and then record them in two or three sentences must surely be capable of something valuable to come. The greatness was there undoubtedly, but it was amplified by the vision of Paxton's employer. Together they made the gardens of Chatsworth exceptional. Gardeners were sent out with the pioneers to distant parts of the world to bring back rare plants, especially orchids which were becoming increasingly popular. An arboretum containing 1,670 trees was planted and a fountain constructed which sent water over 200 feet into the air. Then there were the glasshouses covering an acre of ground. It was not surprising that Chatsworth became famous.

Somehow Paxton found spare energy for journalism and in 1831 he started the *Horticultural Register*, emulating the example of Loudon's *Gardener's Magazine*, which was first published five years earlier. In the first years of their acquaintance these two gardeners were highly critical of each other's ideas and work—Loudon visited Chatsworth in 1831 and opened an article in his *Gardener's Magazine* with the words: 'Chatsworth has always appeared to us an unsatisfactory place.' He commented on the use of timber where he would have used iron in conjunction with glass. However, the two men had in reality much in common and after a few years we find Paxton contributing to Loudon's magazine and Loudon, in 1839, acknowledging the great changes in the Chatsworth gardens owing to the 'talents and exertions' of the Duke of Devonshire's head gardener. When Loudon died in 1843 it was Paxton who helped to contribute financial aid for his widow.

In 1841 Paxton was a co-founder with John Lindley of the *Gardeners' Chronicle*. The early editions brought before the public a need for better training and pay for working gardeners and especially called attention to the Gardeners' Benevolent Institution which for many years continued to be one of the journal's main concerns.

There were many important visitors to Chatsworth, some of whom have recorded their visits either in diaries or letters. Among them were Mr and Mrs W. E. Nightingale with their daughters Florence and Parthenope (Flo and Parthe). They were invited for a visit to meet HRH the Duke of Sussex in August, 1842, and entertaining was arranged on a grand scale with the house full of 'Howards, Cavendishes, Percys, Greys, all in gala dress with stars, garters, diamonds and velvets . . .' So wrote Mrs Nightingale to Miss Mary Clarke. Describing the forerunner of the Crystal Palace she went on: 'An omnibus plied at the gates of Chatsworth every evening to take those who could not walk so far to the monster conservatory, which covers an acre of ground, and where groves of palms and bananas are making all haste to grow to their natural size.'

2 Victoria regina, *the gigantic water-lily, in flower at Chatsworth. As this engraving shows, the huge leaves could support the weight of a child*

A few years later, in 1849, Agnes Loudon and her mother visited Chatsworth while staying with friends at Derby. It is not surprising that Paxton's generous spirit showed itself again on this occasion when he presented Loudon's daughter with a fine bouquet, as a token of regard for her famous father. On a tour of the glasshouses they were shown the Amazon water-lily, *Victoria regina*, with its enormous leaves, measuring over five feet across, on which a child could safely stand.

This had been discovered in 1837; it had in fact been found earlier but no records had been taken. It was reputed to have flowers which measured at least a foot across. Some years afterwards seeds of this plant germinated at Kew, and Paxton, managing to procure a plant for Chatsworth, also managed to persuade it to flower in November 1849.

Owing to the size and rarity of the Amazon water-lily, it had been essential to construct a special glasshouse, to be called the Great Conservatory, large enough for the lily to thrive. Arising from this construction, Paxton conceived the idea for the domed glass building at the Great Exhibition in Hyde Park in 1851, known to everyone as the Crystal Palace: for this he was knighted.

'For this he was knighted.' It is easy enough to write these few words but difficult to interpret them into the hard facts of discovery and invention made by this brilliant man. There were so many problems to overcome in this comparatively new and recent use of glass, and this is emphasized by Professor G. F. Chadwick in his book. *The Works of Sir Joseph Paxton*. He writes: 'The glass used by Paxton in the Great Conservatory was in itself a considerable technical achievement.' He goes on to explain:

Although Paxton's ridge and furrow system remained the same in principle as before, he wished to enlarge the span of each sash bar and to avoid overlapping the glass. An improved method of making broad or sheet glass had been introduced into England from France by Robert Lucas Chance, the Birmingham glass manufacturer, in 1832 and this, the cylinder process, had been further refined by Chance to a point where sheets three feet long and ten inches wide could be supplied in quantity. Paxton visited Chance and he advised the use of the new three foot length, 'but to this I could not assent', wrote Paxton, 'as I observed that since they had so far advanced as to be able to produce sheets three feet in length, I saw no reason why they should not accomplish another foot; and if this could not be done, I would decline giving the order, as at the time, sheet glass was altogether an experiment in horticultural purposes.' Paxton was right: Chance found that it was possible by skilful blowing to make sheets four feet long, and Paxton got all the glass he needed.

The technical details read like some enchanted poem, giving lists of fascinating objects stretching far beyond one's imagination. 'The actual contents of the Great Conservatory at the height of its fame would occupy almost a catalogue', writes Professor Chadwick, 'there were tropical birds, gold and silver fish in the pools, and large crystals and rock-ores were displayed.' On the Queen's visit to Chatsworth in December 1843, it took 12,000 lamps, 'placed along the ribs' to light the huge glass building, and the Duke of Wellington is reported to have said, of this same visit: 'I have travelled Europe through and through, and witnessed many scenes of surpassing grandeur on many occasions, but never did I see so magnificent a *coup d'oeil* as that extended before me.'

A letter from the Duke of Devonshire giving a description of the opening day of the 1851 Exhibition is quoted by Miss Violet Markham, granddaughter of Paxton. He writes: 'I was satisfied for Paxton, and so must he have been when at the mention of his name Victoria turned towards him and made a gesture of approbation. . . . After the Queen had left I descended from the gallery where my capital place had been to parade the architect about. . . .' They overheard people saying 'Look, look, there's Mr. Paxton', in a loud voice, and then, more gently, 'There's the Duke of Devonshire.'

The Duke of Devonshire and Joseph Paxton enjoyed a relationship of trust on the one hand and devotion on the other. This developed into a close friendship which lasted for the rest of their lives, and the Duke came to depend more and more on Paxton's friendship, companionship and advice. In letters to his wife—he had married Sarah a few months after meeting her on his first day at Chatsworth—Paxton wrote at length on his impressions of Paris, where he was collecting seeds with the Duke, and on another and later tour of Rome, Venice, Verona, Vicenza, Padua, where he travelled in the Duke's party. Plants were not neglected and in Malta three dozen orange trees were bought for the Chatsworth greenhouses.

Paxton was an architect as well as a gardener, and he laid out parks, gardens and suburbs, designed large houses or added extensions, as well as building the many glasshouses for which he is now famous. He was interested in scientific discovery and development—particularly as Chairman of the Midland Railway for some years until his death—and it is significant that an important consideration of the Sydenham site for the Crystal Palace grounds, to which the Great Exhibition building was moved from Hyde Park, was that it was of easy access to the Brighton line. The original prospectus mentions that the Palace would have a railway station inside the building.

Behind the genius there was a kindly man with the interests of his many friends at heart and time was found to help them if they were in need, in spite of all these activities. After his death in 1865, *The Times*, whose obituary I quoted earlier, emphasized this aspect of his character: 'Friendship was a plant which he loved to cultivate wherever it would grow—among the nobly born if they sought him; among literary men and artists, with whom he had close and cherished relations; among the great captains of industry, who appreciated and were proud of him; but most of all among younger men than himself whom he could help or cheer on their path through life.'

Samuel Reynolds Hole

DEAN OF ROCHESTER
1819–1904

I read every book I could find on the rose. . . . if I
heard of a garden in which roses were grown, I
went to see—they were few and far between in
those days, but I had youth and horses on my side
and I drove any distance. And thus I became a
rosarian.

REYNOLDS HOLE
QUOTED IN BETTY MASSINGHAM,
Turn on the Fountains

The early nineteenth century in England was a time of awakening
among rose-growers, many of them working men whose small
home-built glasshouses were as precious to them as the greater
works of Paxton to the Duke at Chatsworth. There were various
stories of hardship willingly endured in order to produce good
roses. One enthusiastic grower, whose garden was more than a
mile away from his house, often walked there and back before
work, during his dinner hour and again after work in the evening.
There were cases known of blankets being taken in cold weather in
order to keep the frost out of these small glasshouses—blankets
which were needed by the family to keep them warm and could not
easily be spared.

Among roses arriving in this country there had recently been
introduced from China the sweet-scented white Macartney rose
and the Banksian roses—the double yellow coming over in 1824.
Catalogues were beginning to appear and in a letter to Thomas
Rivers, dated April 1836, J. C. Loudon writes: 'It is singular that
when I received your letter, I had just sent to the printers . . . a
sort of synopsis of your Catalogue of Roses, which I hope will be
gratifying to you, as well as being of service in a business point of
view.' Mr Rivers published his *Rose Amateur's Guide* in 1837,
which was followed by William Paul's *The Rose Garden* in 1848;
these books quickly established themselves as rose-garden
classics.

These were the times when Reynolds Hole was born in
Ardwick, Manchester, in December 1819, and was taken as a baby

to Caunton, near Newark, where the Hole family had been established for many years. Caunton was, and still is, a small unspoint Nottinghamshire village through which the Caunton Beck winds its unhurried way. It was here of which Hole writes that, as a boy intent on archery, he went down 'to the brook for the stiff, straight reed', which he 'shortened into arrow form'. Archery became a keen interest in his life. He reports practising with his father at the targets and later, as an adult, becoming a member of the Royal Sherwood Archers.

He recalls an early love of wild flowers and also of collecting plants for the garden. But there was a natural lapse during his later schooldays when other interests came along—'the busy occupations of our manhood, and the dazzling attractions of the world'.

3 Rosarian Samuel Reynolds Hole, Dean of Rochester

He had gone up to Oxford with his head full of horses, hunting, archery, charades, pretty girls and cricket—all very right and proper; but he writes later of the powerful influence of the Oxford Movement, of Newman's Sunday afternoon sermons at the Church of St Mary the Virgin, which he often heard as an undergraduate, and of his own allegiance to the preaching and ideas of Dr Pusey.

In her diary for the year 1844 his mother (among mention of village happenings, archery meetings, etc.) lovingly records her only son's latter days at Oxford—his BA degree in May, his ordination at Lincoln Cathedral in September and his appointment as curate at Caunton. On 29 September she writes: 'Our dear son did the duty for the first time and got through it very well indeed. His sermon was excellent and very much liked.'

The first rose show at which Reynolds Hole was asked to judge was arranged by local workers near Nottingham for an Easter Monday when roses in flower could only have been grown under glass. As he was not at that time a rose-grower himself, the invitation must have come as something of a surprise. Some years later he gives a frank account of the event and one is reminded that the writer then had no roses in his own garden. Apparently he only agreed to judge the show with some reluctance because at first he thought it must have been a joke—roses, after all, are not usually out at Easter. On returning home from the show, however, feeling humbled and almost hypocritical, he at once wrote off 'for an assortment of *roses in pots*'.

The romance of that April show of roses is told, with a lightness of touch which is endearing, in the second chapter of *A Book about Roses*. It is followed by various chapters on conditions, planting, selection, etc., and by tributes to the early rose-growers. In 1846, when Reynolds Hole first joined the ranks of enthusiasts, the most distinguished names were Mr Rivers of Chiswick, Mr Adam Paul of Cheshunt, Mr Wood of Maresfield and Mr Lane of Berkhampstead. Of these four it is Mr Paul's name which is best remembered today in some of the most widely grown of all roses: 'Paul's Scarlet' climbing rose, one of the best in colour and most reliable in its manner of growing, 'Paul's Himalayan Musk', and 'Paul's Lemon Pillar'. For the young curate the fever of rose-growing began with a dozen trees, then a score and then a hundred. From that hundred he eventually reached a thousand and, in time, up to four thousand. These were all grown at Caunton on his father's land. He writes of this period: 'My good old father, whose delight was in agriculture, calmly watched not only the transformation of his garden, but the robbery of his farm with a quaint gravity and kindly satire, that not doubting for a moment the lucrative wisdom of applying the best manure in unlimited quantities to the common hedgerow briar, he ventured, nevertheless, to express his hope that I would leave a little for the wheat.'

4 *'Paul's Scarlet' climbing rose, a favourite of Reynolds Hole and still popular today. The 'Reynolds Hole' rose was later developed by Paul's nurseries*

Having surrounded himself with roses, Reynolds Hole felt that this was a flower which should have a show to itself, because there were already carnation shows or dahlia shows, tulip shows and auricula shows, At Stoke Newington there were chrysanthemum shows and there had even been held a gooseberry show. What about the roses? And so in the April number of *The Florist* magazine in 1857 there appeared a suggestion from Mr Hole, now vicar of Caunton, that a Grand National Rose Show should be held, near some central station. Referring to this enterprise, he wrote: 'And I must confess that, when I had made this proposal to the world, I rather purred internally with self-approbation. I felt confident that the world would be pleased.'

But the world made no sign. Weeks went by and still there was no response. However, he was not the sort of man to be sunk in despair without making an effort to improve the situation, and so wrote round to a few of the chief rosarians asking them a simple question: 'Will you help me in establishing a National Rose Show?' The replies came back as soon as the mail could bring them, answering in the affirmative, offering willing help and giving their full support to the idea. The vicar records that, in his delight, he rashly whistled while he was shaving and it was 'a bloody business'.

A meeting was arranged and held in London at Webbs Hotel, Piccadilly, where first a good meal was ordered and consumed and then the work began. Messrs Rivers, Turner and Paul were the backbone of his support. It was decided to hold a Grand National Rose Show about the beginning of July 1858, each person present subscribing five pounds towards a fund. A further meeting was arranged, details discussed and the Rose Show was on its way. This had all been achieved between men, some of whom had only met together for the first time, who at once felt a bond of interest between them. Such is the friendliness of plant-lovers.

Turning this matter over in the train as he 'went rushing down the Northern Line' on his homeward journey, Hole confirmed his long-felt ideas on the value of friendship between lovers of flowers and gardens.

Were it my deplorable destiny to keep a toll-bar on some bleak, melancholy waste, and were I permitted to choose in alleviation a companion of whom I was to know only that he had one special enthusiasm. I should certainly select a florist. Authors would be too clever for me. Artists would have nothing to paint. Sportsmen I have always loved; but that brook, which they will jump so often at dessert or in the smoke-room does get such an amazing breadth—that stone wall such a fearful height—that rocketing pheasant so invisible—that salmon (in Norway such a raging, gigantic beast)—that, being fond of facts, my interest would flag. No; give me a thorough florist, fond of all flowers. . . . We should never be weary of talking about our favourites; and, you may depend upon it, we should grow *something*.

St James's Hall was engaged at a cost of thirty guineas for the day, as also the services of the Coldstream band—'a mistake, because their admirable music proved to be too loud for indoor enjoyment'. They advertised with gigantic posters all over London and subscriptions came pouring in enabling a schedule of prizes to the value of £156. The great day came.

He describes the early start, arriving at the hall at about 5.30 a.m. from Nottinghamshire to find the carpenters busy erecting stands, and the excitement as vans and 'four-wheelers' deposited their precious boxes from Hertfordshire and Hereford, from Suffolk, Essex and Somerset.

It was an anxious moment when the actual opening of the exhibition was due. They knew that there was already an outstanding amount of £100 to be cleared before any profits could ensue. An admission cost of one shilling meant that a full hall was needed before they could feel easy in their minds. He writes: 'A gentleman, who earnestly asked my pardon for having placed his foot on mine, seemed perplexed to hear how much I liked it . . .' One more shilling, Reynolds Hole was thinking to himself.

The success of the show was recorded in the *Gardening Chronicle* by Professor Lindley: 'No words can describe the infinite variety of form, colour, and odour which belonged to the field of roses spread before the visitor.' The mention of 'odour' in this context is not, of course, surprising but it meant more 120 years ago than it would today and this point was captured cleverly by John Leech in a subsequent issue of *Punch*. This was the connection between the sweet smell of the roses and the stench which invaded London at that time from the Thames.

The following year the second Rose Show was held at the Hanover Square rooms but it was clear that more accommodation was needed and in 1860 the Rose Show took place in the recently erected Crystal Palace. From such grandeur it is interesting to reflect on the first rose show the young curate was asked to judge at Nottingham, organized in the upper room of an inn by working men in their shirt sleeves, for this was the spark which had set him off on his quest for roses.

In the autumn of 1860 he met, reputedly at an archery meeting, Caroline Francklin of Gonalston and it is on her account that he writes in *A Book about Roses* of handing over much of the administrative work for the Rose Show—although it was still 'his show': 'I was very grateful . . . to transfer to abler hands a work which . . . interfered at times unduly with my other engagements. Moreover, to tell you all the truth, in the happy springtide of 1861 I had a correspondence which occupied all my time, upon a subject which occupied all my thought—a subject more precious, more lovely even than Roses—I was going to be married in May'. The following letter shows the state of affairs:

Caunton Manor.   8 Feb., 1861.

My very dear Sara, I am engaged to be married! After prowling about the hen roost for 'many roving years', I have made selection of a beautiful pullet, and intend to carry her off. Wish the old fox success, and a career of happiness! More earnestly, my dearest, I have been for some time oppressed with drear anticipation of that loneliness, which, long distant as I hope and pray, would overshadow Caunton when the good Lord of the Manor should leave it 'as full of grace and years' and had resolved to seek a congenial helpmate, one 'born alike my tears and joys to share'. And I have found, and have wooed, and have won, such a sweet, bright, gentle lady, that I am really astonished at the impudence of my own conjurations, and entirely *spifflicated* by *her* condescension in endorsing them. I can only wonder, and be thankful, and ask to be made more worthy of this crowning happiness of my very happy life. Sometimes I think that our dear Mother and Sister, who loved me with such a deep undeserved love, have asked and obtained this blessing for me.

The lady is Miss Francklin, of Gonalston, in this county, a *lady* in the fullest meaning of the word—a lady by birth and education, a lady in mind and mien. She is rather young, 20 yrs (I have spoken to her seriously concerning this delinquency, and note improvement) tall, 'a daughter of the gods, divinely fair, and most divinely tall' for she is 5 feet 8 inches in height, fair with much roseate glow, her hair the colour of yours. You will form a good idea of your sister from the photograph which I inclose, remembering that this style of portraiture always adds some dreariness to a face, and never improves the expression thereof . . . Next Christmas if Matrimony allows I mean to bring out a Book for Gardeners—now publishing in the Florist and called 'The Six of Spades'. Always believe me my very dear sister your very fondly affectionate brother,

S. REYNOLDS HOLE.

Perhaps the letter needs one or two explanations. First: Sara was his very dear sister who had married the Revd John Raven and who was now living in New Zealand.

Second: towards the end of the first paragraph he writes that he sometimes thinks 'that our dear Mother and Sister, who loved me with such a deep undeserved love, have asked and obtained this blessing for me.' His mother, who had been Mary Cooke, had died in 1852, and his sister Mary Elizabeth, who married John Hilton, died in May 1859.

Third: after giving the lady's name and adorning it with most of the requisite adjectives of a newly affianced bachelor, he goes on to mention the fact of a 'settlement', not large, 'but an Aunt, with a discretion and elegance of mind which command my liveliest sympathy, has since bequeathed to each of them (the sisters) about £7,000 in addition.' Might he be criticized for paying too much attention to the question of a settlement? But this was the attitude of the day to such matters. For instance, in *Emma*, when Mr Elton returned to Highbury after becoming engaged to Miss Hawkins, it was discovered that in addition to all the usual advantages of perfect beauty and merit, she was in possession of an independent fortune, of so many thousands as would always be called ten—'. . . The story told well: he had not thrown himself away—he had gained a woman of £10,000 or thereabouts and he had gained her with rapidity . . .' *Emma* was written only about forty years earlier than his own engagement, and in mentioning the settlement he was merely following the fashion of the times.

But his general idea was to cut down on outside activities and, writing about the Fourth National Rose Show, he mentions his gratitude in being able to hand over much of the work to other recruits.

As Caroline was a Ward in Chancery, her mother having died some years earlier leaving her to take over the care of a young family as well as her father, and then her father's death having left the family with no possessions or home (owing to the necessary paying off of debts), she had been cared for by her grandparents. It was they who now offered to arrange the wedding.

Reynolds writes with warm appreciation of the support of his dear friend John Leech, who was his best man in June 1861. Leech was also a much loved friend of Thackeray, a famous *Punch* artist and member of the Garrick Club.

Leech took as much lively interest in my engagement and marriage as though he had been my brother; insisted on accompanying me when I went on the somewhat anxious mission of discussing settlements with the young lady's guardian, to the door of his house . . . and having requested and received long notice of the wedding-day, 'Because,' he said, 'his coat, waistcoat, trousers, and especially his scarf, must be gradually and carefully developed,' he appeared in due course, a combination of good looks, good temper, and good clothes, as my best man.

A honeymoon letter comes for her grandmother from Caroline, dated 17 June 1861 and written at Thun, relating travels which included Paris, Macon, Geneva, where 'Reynolds gave me such a lovely watch, in a double case, and outside a wreath of roses and forgetmenots on both sides'.

Her next letter to 'dear Granny', dated 1 July, was the first one she wrote from her new home. It describes their arrival at Newark in the afternoon 'on Thursday, about half past three, all safe.' The village had turned out to welcome them.

Letters from John Leech, which came with some frequency, now always ended with a note to include Mrs Hole. 'Give my kindest regards please to Mrs Hole and to your Father. . . .'; 'Please give our very best regards to Mrs Hole and to your Father. . . .'; 'Mrs Leech is out and will write to Mrs Hole. . . .'; 'With my most kinderestestestest regards to everybody. . . .' In a letter with the envelope franked February 15th, 1862, and stamped Garrick Club, there comes something different—another literary plum: 'You have just been elected at the "G" unanimously.' And in a following letter, dated 19 February 1862, this short statement is amplified: 'I am very happy that you are pleased with your election at the "G". It would have gratified you I think to have heard the good word, or rather good words, that Thackeray said for you. . . .'

John Leech goes on, in his letter, to enumerate some of the blessings of becoming a member of the Garrick Club. He is looking forward to showing Mrs Hole over the club on a visiting day, the reading and lecture rooms, and hopes that it will mean they can all pay a visit to the opera together—in fact, he longs to introduce Mrs Hole to this 'box of delights'.

But one of the first of many letters of love and affection from Mr Hole to his wife does not come from the Garrick Club—it is from a rose show in Birmingham:

Queens Hotel,
Birmingham,
July 1, 1862.

Own Darling, how I wish you were here! The loveliest Show of Roses I ever saw, and ours, altho' competing with the best in England, carrying off the *first honours*. They have won the *two best prizes*, namely the first for 48 varieties and the first for 24 varieties (not to mention the second for 18, and the third for 12) and are acknowledged both by nurserymen and amateurs to be unsurpassed by either of them. The immense Town Hall of Birmingham is completely filled with roses, from 14 different counties,—and seen from the galleries above is one of the most charming spectacles I ever looked on. In addition to the flowers, there is a most interesting collection of garden implements and ornaments and of most beautiful articles for the dessert table & I have selected my two best prizes from the latter (to the amount of 7 £ and 5 £) and I think you will allow that you never saw more graceful things of their kind.

I have never had such a complete victory, since I have fought in these Wars of the Roses; and again and again I keep longing for you, to see and share it with me. You would hardly believe how well the roses have travelled, and I was really surprised when I lifted the lid this morning—many of the flowers having expanded and all looking as freshly as in the garden.

I shall travel to Derby and sleep there tonight and meet you at Thurgarton tomorrow, you tweetiest tweet! The train arrives there at 11.22. . . .

—Ever believe me, my own dear love,

Your fondly affectionate husband

The Deserted Village,
Tuesday.

Deliciousest Ownums,
Limp as a balloon without any gas in it, and residing in a mansion, which, ever since you left it, has been about as merry as a mausoleum, I do not feel at all equal to any cheerful correspondence . . . and must sit like Constance (. . . the girl in the song) 'sad silent, and alone', until the happy morrow brings me to my Love. . . .

Give that Tweet [their baby] a few thousand extra ones for me. I shall expect to see him much grown.

. . . believe me, my own darling darling Wife, your most fondly and faithfully loving

S. Reynolds Hole.

Caunton Manor
alias
The Deserted Village.
Dec. 9, 1862.

'Tweet of the tweetiest', it seems already a fortnight since I saw baby, and three weeks since I saw you; and so many events of immense importance have occurred since your departure, that I hardly know how to begin their history. . . . We have a dinner-party this evening, James and Willie, but the house looks awefully dismal without *the Dear Thing*, and no *music* charms the listening ear. [On this occasion Mrs Hole had been staying with her own family—which she did from time to time.]

I hope, own darling, to come & see you by Rail on Thursday, and to find your *beauty self* stronger & better.

Give my very sincere regards to Mrs Storer, the Doctor, & the young ladies, & believe me as ever, nay more than ever, your most fondly loving Husband, S. Reynolds Hole.

ROYAL HORTICULTURAL SOCIETY

MEMORANDUM.   5 o'clock p.m.
                                                    July 1. 1863.
From Revd. Reynolds Hole   To His Wife Caroline.

Dearest Darling, This is the only bit of available paper I can find in the superintendent's office, and I have about five minutes in which to fill it.

The southern roses, fully in bloom, have beaten mine, as I thought they would, but I am *quite as good* in quality tho' not in quantity.

The Queen of Prussia and the two Princesses, Helena and Louise, came, while we were judging the roses, *and I was presented to them*! So if I am rather high, when I return, you will know the reason. Perhaps it would be better if you were to call me 'Sir' for a few days at all events. . . . Hay fever entirely gone, since I took the camphor this morning, and this under a morning sun!

I shall . . . return by the train that leaves *between five and six tomorrow* afternoon. Please look it out in Bradshaw, and send the Brougham to meet us.

Kiss the tweet a million and rather less to my Father. . . . believe me always and in my very heart
        Your loving husband
              Reynolds.

Letters of a loving husband to his dearly loved wife, of small parish events, of his loneliness without her, of the excitement of a rose show. So began—and continued—the great happiness of his marriage.

Although he was now a member of the Garrick Club and enjoyed very much his meetings there with good friends who included men such as John Leech and Thackeray, it appears that even more hospitality than before was now dispensed from Caunton Manor—now that there was an enchanting young hostess as head of the household. She was a lover of country things; social life for itself alone meant little to her. She was known, in fact, to have put the kitchen staff into a turmoil on more than one occasion when guests arrived, apparently uninvited, and food had to be prepared hurriedly while the mistress of the house came in from perhaps riding or a walk, having completely forgotten about any engagements made. However, her youth and charm meant that such a lapse was soon overlooked and forgiven, and numerous visitors came happily to Caunton Manor, some of them for a meal or for the day, while others came to stay. (A visit to the country in those days often meant either a long weekend, or a week at least, and John Leech writes on one occasion: 'Seriously, my dear Hole, I am cordially obliged both to Mrs Hole and yourself for your great kindness in offering us a fortnight at Caunton. . . .')

In 1876 the National Rose Society was formed and this now publishes a Rose Annual, which gives a list of Presidents and Awards, the Dean Hole Medal among them. (For those who love roses there can be no better investment than to become a member of this Society.)

A Book About Roses, having established the Rose Show, gives instructions on how to grow roses and is illustrated with lively anecdotes, indicating a genial sense of humour in the author. Commenting on the fact that he had won two prizes at a rose show which he had helped to organize, he relates that the process of presentation was '"gratifying, but embarrassing," as Mrs Nickleby remarked when her eccentric lover would carve her name on his pew, and suggesting to a suspicious mind the trustee described by Mr Wilkie Collins, in whose accounts occurred the frequent entry, "self-presented testimonial, £10."'

Reynolds Hole, with all his store of knowledge, is refreshing about botanical names and classifications: 'As to any scientific arrangement, ethnological, genealogical, or physiological classification, I am helplessly, hopelessly incapable. . . . "I am no botanist," as the young chap pleaded to the farmer who reproved him for riding over a field of wheat.' This approach is encouraging—especially to those who may tend their gardens with affection but cannot remember, or pronounce if they did, many of the Latin names by which familiar flowers are sometimes known.

In the matter of practical advice the book stands on firm ground. One chapter, 'Position', deals, for instance, with the best place in the garden to select for rose beds. It is just as bad for roses to have too much wind—draughts or gusts—as it is for them to be suffocated by other trees or large shrubs. He writes:

> Some, having heard that a free circulation of air and abundance of sunshine are essential elements of success, select a spot which would be excellent for a windmill, observatory, beacon or Martello Tower. . . . Others, who have been told that the rose loves shelter, peace, etc., have found 'such a dear snug little spot', not only surrounded by dense evergreen shrubs, but overshadowed by giant trees. A rose under trees . . . can no more flourish than a deer can get a good 'head' who never leaves the forest for the moor.

Then come direct instructions:

> . . . expose to the morning's sunshine, protect from cutting wind. Give the best place in your garden to the flower which deserves it most. In the smallest plot you may make, if you do not find, such a site as I have described. You *will* make it if you are in earnest. I have seen old boards, old staves, old sacking, torn old tarpaulins—yes, once an old black serge petticoat—set up by the poor to protect the rose.

He always expresses most fervent admiration for those gardeners who may not be blessed with the most propitious growing conditions, but who are yet undismayed by whatever difficulties befall them. In connection with ideal situations for rose-growing which might include clean country air, a sunny aspect and some shelter, among other things, he quotes the case of his friend, Mr Shirley Hibberd: '. . . if he could grow good roses within four miles of the General Post Office (London)—and I have seen the London rose-shows, to my high surprise and delectation—it is quite certain that he would have been nulli secundus with the full advantage of situation and soil.'

'Soil' is the heading of the next chapter and the same principles apply here as were mentioned in connection with the position of the rose beds. Not everyone has perfect soil for rose-growing. Some people have to contend with heavy clay where the first step to be taken must be some form of drainage—roses do not care to stand with their feet in a pool of water throughout the winter any more than most other plants. Drainage of soil must be followed by lightening with every possible means, even if it involves using old feather cushions, worn-out mats or carpets, spent hops, tea leaves, or soaked cardboard broken up into small pieces. Others have to deal with too sandy a soil, where the roots may have difficulty in finding an anchorage. But there is always some means of balancing these extremes and much of the ordinary garden soil does not fit into either category.

To complement the case of Mr Hibberd's growing first-class roses under difficult town conditions, Mr Hole here quotes that of a railway worker who applied for and obtained a tenement adjoining the line to which was 'attached the meanest apology for a garden which I ever saw in my life. . . . it seemed to me a gravel-bed and nothing more.' He knew this man and knew also that he was fond of flowers, and so offered him his condolences on such a gravel patch. However, he had reckoned without the man's persistence or his ingenuity. On seeing this same 'garden' about a year later, full of flowers, fruit bushes, vegetables and fruit trees all in vigorous health', he expressed his amazement. 'Why, Will, what have you done to the gravel-bed?' 'Lor' bless yer,' Will replied, grinning, 'I hadn't been here a fortnight afore I swopped it for a pond.' This determined gardener had removed from his own patch of land a stratum to the depth of three feet and carted it to the edge of an old pond, which had become filled with silt and leaves over the years. It was this mixture that he had brought home a distance of about 200 yards in wheelbarrow loads. He had worked hard for his garden and at the next show he meant to be 'stirring up them cottagers with roses. . . .'

'Manure' is the next chapter-heading and on this debatable subject Mr Hole collects together the opinions of about ten of the leading rosarians of that time. The answer, although there may be a few variations, is always the same—farmyard or stable manure. Mr Keynes of Salisbury adds to his recipe of a 'good wheelbarrow-ful of compost, two thirds of good turfy loam and one third well-decomposed animal manure', the following reminder: 'It is difficult to give the rose too good a soil.'

There is little variation on the timetable for applying manure. It should be given liberally to rose-trees in November when the ground is dry, leaving it 'as a protection as well as a fertiliser through the winter months' and dug in during March. This application should be supplemented in late May or early June by a strong liquid stimulant. If our neighbours expostulate over the extravagance of such a procedure, Mr Hole suggests that we remind them of Victor Hugo in *Les Misérables*: 'the beautiful is as useful as the useful, perhaps more so.'

Describing his own efforts of applying the later dose of a liquid stimulant, he writes:

> I wait for the indications of rain, that the fertilising matter may be at once washed down to the roots. . . . During the extradinary drought of the summer in 1868 I watched day after day . . . and at last, feeling sure of my shower, wheeled barrow after barrow . . . and distributed it. . . . Soon the big rain came dancing to the earth and when it had passed, and I smoked my evening weed among the rose-trees, I fancied that already the tonic had told.

(It was this year that he won 'fourteen first prizes out of sixteen collections shown, including that which was then considered the champion prize of all, the first awarded to amateurs at the Grand National Show of the Royal Horticultural Society.')

A convenient summing up of important points to remember about roses, in connection especially with these three chapters on position, soil and manure, comes as follows:

> Let them be planted in the best place and in the best soil available, avoiding drip and roots. Let them be manured in the winter and mulched in the spring. In the summer months let them be well watered below and well syringed above, two or three times a week. Let grubs and aphides be removed, and sulphur, or soot, or soap-and-water be applied as soon as mildew shows itself.

In *A Book About Roses* there is a most valuable appendix for the amateur entitled 'Memoranda for the Months'; these are some notes from it.

> *October:* I begin with this month because both he who desires to form, and he who desires to maintain, or extend, a rose-garden, must now make his arrangements for planting in November. . . . The ground intended for rose-trees or stocks must be thoroughly drained and trenched to receive them.
> *November:* is the best month for transplanting. Ah, how it cheers the Rosarian's heart amid those dreary days, to welcome the package from the nurseries, long and heavy, so cleanly swathed in the new Russian mat, so closely sewn with the thick white cord! . . . Let him plant his rose-trees as soon as may be after their arrival; but if they

reach him, unhappily, during frost or heavy rains, let him 'lay them in' as it is termed, covering their roots well with soil and their heads with matting, and so wait the good time coming. When planted they must not be set too deeply in the soil—about 4 or 5 ins. will suffice—but must be secured to stakes, firmly fixed in the ground beside them. Established rose-trees should, if the ground be dry and the weather fine, have a good dressing of farmyard manure. And in

December: you should take advantage of the first hard frost to wheel in a similar supply for the new-comers. In both cases the manure must remain upon the ground to protect and to strengthen too, and need not be dug in until March.

January: . . . We must make up our minds to some losses among the old and young . . . but, with our ground well drained, and our rose-trees well secured and mulched, we need not fear for the hale and strong. . . .

March: is the month for our final planting of all save Noisettes and Teas. . . . Different varieties will, of course, require different treatment. . . . Some roses of very vigorous growth, such as Blairii No. 2 . . . will not flower at all if they are closely pruned. . . . See to your stakes when the stormy winds do blow, and towards the end of the month dig in the manure left about the newly planted rose-trees and briars.

April: Prune tea-scented, noisette, and Bourbon roses, observe the previous rule—that is, cutting very abstemiously, when the growth is vigorous, as with . . . Gloire de Dijon. . . .

May: . . . Of all the months, this to the rosarian brings most anxiety. Nothing so adverse to his roses as late vernal frosts, cold starving nights in May . . . The trees, which were growing luxuriantly, suddenly cease to make further progress. . . . Wisely did our forefathers fix their Rogation Days at this most perilous time. . . . A surface application of manure, as previously recommended, should now be laid on the surface of the soil.

June: . . . If May has been genial, June will be glorious. . . . If situation, soil, and supervision be such as I have suggested nothing but weather of unusual severity will bring aphis or harm to the rose. Once a Rosarian asked me 'what I did for green-fly?' I told him truthfully that they never troubled me, and I suppose I spoke too conceitedly; for soon afterwards they attacked me in force for the first time since I understood the art of rose-growing. But in that year, the bitterness of May was extraordinary, as the farmer, the fruitist, and the florist know to their cost; and it was evident, in the full look of the leaf, that the trees were frostbitten, and that the usual consequences must come.

July: . . . Should mildew make its appearance, remove the leaves most affected, and cover the rest with flower of sulphur when the tree is wet from shower or syringe, giving them another good washing next day. Mr Rivers recommends soot as a remedy, and kindly sent me a letter some years ago, the result of a successful experiment. Have you mildew? he asks—*try soot.* . . . That yellow-bellied abomination, the grub which produces the saw-fly, in this month attacks the rose, sucking the sap from under the leaf, and changing the colour of the part on which he has fed from bright green to dirty brown. The process of 'scrunching' is disagreeable, but it *must* be done. . . . During the continuous droughts which frequently occur in July, it is desirable, of course, to water every evening. . . . Everywhere, I would advise that the surface of the beds be loosened from time to time with the hoe . . . but there is nothing like a mulching of farmyard manure. Fading roses should be removed from the tree. . . .

August: . . . if the weather is hot and ground parched, it will be desirable to give the beds a good drenching with water 'when the evening sun is low'.

September: brings us little to do, except to remove suckers and weeds, and to enjoy our second harvest of roses. . . . When at the end of this month the chill evenings come, and curtains are drawn and bright fires glow, who is so happy as the rose-grower, with the new catalogue before him?

Afterwards comes a list of exhibition roses.

A Book About Roses, which went into many editions, is a classic and represents Reynolds Hole's great contribution to rose literature.

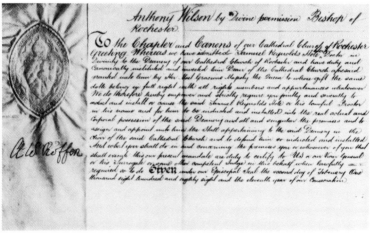

5 *The authority appointing Reynolds Hole as Dean of Rochester in 1888*

In 1893, by then Dean of Rochester and in his seventy-fifth year, he undertook an exhausting trip to the States. In the preface to *A Little Tour in America* he discusses the numerous reasons for his tour:

I had other inducements, personal, to visit the States—genial invitations from ecclesiastics and florists promising fraternal receptions and financial successes if I would give public lectures. This pecuniary incitement was decisive. Our funds for the restoration of Rochester Cathedral were exhausted, and if I could bring home a substantial sum, I might invoke new generosities, energies and hopes, and should feel that, while I was enjoying my excursion, I was not neglecting my work and duty.

'And he wrote with a quill pen.' Dame Sybil Thorndike was remembering the Dean of Rochester, in the library, writing letters, writing books. How did he find time for his ever-growing correspondence, over which he took so much trouble? There was no dashing off of a letter without care and thought—he would sometimes be so engrossed that he would forget engagements. Dame Sybil recalls the time that he was writing in his library. Whittaker, over seventy, Dean Hole's father's nurse, appeared. 'The fly's at the door, Sir.' He went on writing: 'Fly . . . fly . . . what should I want with a fly?' 'Don't you remember that you're preaching at St Paul's and spending the night at the Deanery?' 'God bless my soul—so I am.' He rushed out, picked up his hat in the hall and off he went.

A man of extensive interests, of unending energy in his work for the Church, for anyone he could help, and for the promotion of the development of the rose, his life was brimming over with love for his fellow men, with good humour and with deep feeling for those in unhappy circumstances. The hybrid perpetual rose grown by George Paul at their Cheshunt nurseries as his namesake was, at his own request, named simply 'Reynolds Hole', 'without any prefix, because by that name I am best known to my friends'.

Canon H. N. Ellacombe

1822–1916

I often regret that George Herbert did not add
another chapter to his *Country Parson*, and tell us
his views of the parson in his garden. With his high
views of the importance of the parson's character
showing itself in the minutest details of daily life—
'he leaveth not his ministry behind him, but is
himself wherever he is'—it would have been
pleasant to have been taught by him.

CANON ELLACOMBE
In a Gloucestershire Garden

Henry Nicholson Ellacombe was born at Bitton vicarage, near
Bath, on 18 February 1822. His father, H. T. Ellicombe (as the
name was then spelt), was the vicar of Bitton parish and known
especially for his love of music, for his garden and for his interest in
bell-ringing. He was the author of *Practical Remarks on Belfries
and Bell-ringing* and had invented a method whereby several bells
could be rung by one person. Astonished visitors to his church
record a young boy chiming the whole set of bells without any
undue exertion.

In writing of Canon Ellacombe it will be seen, I think, as
essential to write first of his father. (The Canon did not take over
the garden at Bitton until two years before he married, in 1852, at
which time his father removed to a parish in Devonshire where he
started again to make a garden, after handing over to his son a fine
collection of plants which had come from far and wide.) This
remarkable man had followed a variety of pursuits other than bell-
ringing. For instance, before adopting the clerical life he had
shown serious leanings towards engineering and part of a letter
written to him as a young man by Brunel, under whom he was
working at Chatham, indicates his change of direction: 'The share
I had assigned to you, left me at leisure to ponder upon what came
next; but now no one have I at the helm—none through whom I
can convey my directions and ideas—and by the co-operation of
whom I can proceed with confidence. If you still continue in your
determination of returning to the Church, may you, my good
friend, prove as great an ornament to it as you would have been in

44

that most arduous career in which you leave your very sincere friend, with one of his lights out.'

Ellicombe, after taking his degree at Oxford, was ordained by the Bishop of Exeter in 1816. While at Chatham he had met and become engaged to a beautiful young woman, a Miss Nicholson, whose father was a Government Contractor (responsible incidentally for putting up many of the Martello towers in readiness for the expected Napoleonic invasion). Of this marriage there were five daughters and one son. Elizabeth was an ardent church and social worker as well as a keen botanist and gardener, a great walker over the Swiss mountains, and a close friend of Mrs Ewing and the Gattys. Jane became a member of Dr Pusey's first sisterhood, and the only one who married became Mrs Welland of Tollerton. Their son, Henry Nicholson, was born in February 1822. His mother died at a relatively early age. His father married again, twice, and having been deeply involved with the Oxford movement and with his friendship with Newman, devoted a large store of his energy to rebuilding or altering parts of Bitton parish church, casting out the old double pews and introducing the chanting of certain parts of the services at an early date.

Of course he was reforming the belfry and in 1848 drew up a set of rules for the ringers, one of which went: 'The use of the bells is to be strictly confined to ecclesiastical purposes; they are not to be rung for any political matters such as elections; nor law suits, trials, and such like; nor for prizes; nor for any unusual purpose.' It is thought that his interest in bell-ringing was stimulated as much by his love of music as by his engineering abilities. In his will he left his collection of bells to the South Kensington Museum.

In 1850 he became the rector of Clyst St George in Devonshire and he left all the plants at Bitton as a precious legacy to his son. A list of the trees and shrubs to be found in the Bitton garden, taken from a manuscript dated 1831, was given in *The Garden* of 31 July 1880, followed by a list of herbaceous and bulbous plants. The vicar wrote in a footnote: 'I am indebted to the filial courtesy of my son for this list of plants.' It is a very long catalogue. In addition, at Kew, there is a collection of letters to H. T. Ellicombe from some of the leading horticulturists and botanists of that time. These were handed over by his son. There are letters from the head of Kew, the Chelsea Physic Garden, the Oxford Botanic Garden, Trinity College Garden, Dublin, and others.

Henry Nicholson Ellacombe—the spelling of the surname which he used—had been educated first at home, was then sent to Bath Grammar School, subsequently going to his father's college (Oriel) at Oxford, and in 1848 took his MA degree. He succeeded his father as vicar of Bitton at the age of twenty-eight and two years later he married Emily Aprilla Wemyss whose father, General Wemyss, served under Wellington through the Peninsular War. They had a large family, of which two sons and three daughters survived. His home life meant a great deal to him and he usually contrived, however busily occupied, to fit in a daily ride with his wife. He developed a keen appreciation of good cooking and specially prepared dishes. A person of many accomplishments and interests, his knowledge of pottery and porcelain, architecture and archeology was extensive. He loved walking, riding and fishing and was a keen sportsman generally, in addition to which he was a classical scholar and made a close study of Shakespeare. But, before all these interests, came his love for his church and his parish and, close behind, his love of his garden.

He had inherited an especially fine collection of roses from his father. In the early catalogue of its trees and shrubs, already mentioned, there are about 250 under the genus *Rosa*. This was a heritage indeed, and one which he cherished and improved on in his own lifetime.

The garden is still in existence, lying close to the churchyard with a fine view to the Lansdowne hills from the rectory windows. It is not large—about an acre and a half in all—and is approached by a country lane lined with lime trees. Perhaps its chief characteristic is that it is sheltered and yet is open to the sun, having shade and protection without any feeling of being enclosed or shut away.

In William Robinson's *The English Flower Garden* there is a plan of the Ellacombe garden, which Robinson described as being 'one of the oldest and most richly stored with good hardy flowers of all English gardens . . . an example of a small garden of the highest interest, and withal of simple and sensible plan.'

About it Canon Ellacombe writes: 'It lies on the west side of the Cotswolds . . . and about fifteen miles to the South are the Mendips. These two ranges of hills do much to shelter us from the winds, both from the cold north and easterly winds, and from the south-west winds. . . .' He goes on to talk about this particular point: 'I attach great importance to the kindly shelter from the great strength of the winds, for plants are like ourselves in many respects, and certainly in this, that they can bear a very great amount of frost if only the air is still, far better than they can bear less cold if accompanied by a high wind.'

Here is a gardening truth emphasized by a great gardener and in his attitude to his garden he exemplified another. It was said that 'he was more concerned about the well-being of its inhabitants than with the aesthetic appearance of the place itself'. Another reference to him read: 'Each little flower meant much to him. It was not merely a pretty bit of colour; he would tell you something interesting of its native haunts, its likes and dislikes. . . .'

His writings *In a Gloucestershire Garden* and *In My Vicarage Garden and Elsewhere* give many indications of the kind of man that he was—his taste, the type of garden he loved and the plants that he liked to have in it.

6 *The catalpa tree in Bitton Vicarage garden. An illustration from Canon Ellacombe's* In a Gloucestershire Garden

For instance, in the first of these two publications, he votes against a bed consisting only of tulips (an ugly object) but writes with affection of his Banksia rose 'that is certainly seventy years old and may be older' and suggests that a favourite 'Souvenir de Malmaison' 'is never so beautiful in summer as in autumn'. He remarks of the winter cherry *(Physalis alkekengi)* 'that it is of no great beauty in flower but very handsome in fruit'; of the *Nandina domestica* (the Chinese so-called sacred bamboo) 'Its great beauty is in the foliage, the leaves being very various both in colour and shape and very graceful'; and of the white Japanese anemones 'Indeed I think there is no more beautiful hardy flower . . . and when cut will retain its beauty in water.'

He describes 'great pleasure in watching the ways in which different plants come through the ground' and mentions especially the tenacity of a clump of white crocus pushing their tender new leaves each spring through a gravel path recently laid across a flower-bed. He had a place in his affection even for weeds:

I am sorry to say that the April record of the garden would be very incomplete without some mention of the weeds; for it is in April they first show themselves, and some of them only in April. In new gardens it is possible, and not very difficult, to keep the weeds under; but in old gardens it is almost impossible. It is an old and very true gardening proverb, that one year's seed is many years' weed; or as Hamlet laments, 'An unweeded garden grows to seed' and so 'things rank and gross in nature possess it merely'. In the history of an old garden there must have often been a one year's seed; and there must be in it from time to time many an unweeded corner. But I have almost an affection for weeds . . . and I have not much sympathy with those who say that a garden is not worth looking at unless it is as clean as a newly-swept floor; it is a counsel of perfection which I have no great wish to reach. . . . Daisies are not perhaps in their right place in lawns, but I should be sorry to see my lawn quite free from them, and so I am sure would the children. Buttercups have a shining beauty that is not surpassed by any other flower and I do not think that Jean Ingelow's comparison, to the great advantage of the buttercups, is much exaggerated; but they must be kept out of the garden. . . . But some weeds are so beautiful that I should certainly grow them in the garden if only they could be kept in place, and if they were not already too abundant. I should be sorry to banish from my walls the creeping toadflax and the yellow fumitory, and as long as they keep to the walls they do no harm. But there are two plants that are sad weeds, but which, if lost, would be sorely missed. The dandelion is one—surely no other flower can surpass it for beauty of foliage, beauty of shape, and rich beauty of colouring. The second that I often wish to transplant into my garden, but dare not, is the goosegrass, or silver weed, *Potentilla anserina* . . . it is better kept outside the garden and it grows everywhere. It is found in the Arctic regions and it is found in New Zealand and so has as wide a range as almost any known plant, except perhaps, the little fern

Cystopteris fragilis, which not only grows as far north as lat. 76 deg., and as far south as New Zealand, but was also found by Whymper in the Equatorial Andes.

But it is not only for their beauty that I have an affection for some of the weeds, but, speaking as a gardener, I am sure that they are often very useful. . . . One of the most interesting gardens and the most untidy I ever saw was Professor Syme's in Fifeshire. It was a mass of weeds, and rampant weeds; but among the weeds, and apparently rejoicing in them, was a collection of some of the rarest plants, growing in greater luxuriance than I had ever seen elsewhere. The weeds keep the earth moist, and prevent the radiation of heat. . . .

He also writes: 'The more I study flowers the more I feel how little I know about them', and of scent:

It is a well-known fact that nothing recalls the past like scents, and this is so especially true of the scent of flowers that I suppose most of us can name instances in our own experience. I never gather a leaf of the fine-leaved form of the oak-leaf geranium without at once going back in memory to a pleasant home in the Midlands, where the genial host was so fond of the leaf that it always formed a part of the 'button-hole' of his guests. . . . Of all the associations which flowers keep for us, none can equal those connected with persons or places. . . . My beech-fern recalls Cader Idris to me, and my oak-fern Snowdonia, though it is many years since I collected them; and my Osmunda recalls North Donegal and Slieve League, not because my plants come from there, but because I never saw them elsewhere so beautiful . . . and as to other gardens, both public and private, they are recalled to me most pleasantly in almost every yard of my garden. And these associations have what I may call a reflex character that doubles the pleasure. . . .

Tennyson records the same double pleasure brought to him in connection with one small flower:

> We took our last adieu,
> And up the snowy Splugen drew,
> But ere we reached the highest summit,
> I plucked a daisy, I gave it you;
> It told of England then to me,
> And now it tells of Italy.

And these memories and associations that our flowers give us are independent of seasons or of age. They come to us as well in autumn and winter, in spring and summer; and as to age, the older we get the more, from the very nature of things, do these memories increase and multiply. . . . There are trees on my lawn which were planted when children were born; there are hundreds of plants which tell me of the liberal help given by such gardens as Kew, Edinburgh, Dublin and many other public gardens, both British and foreign.

Canon Ellacombe's love for his garden built up something of lasting value. It produced a garden unique in its way in its own period. It also produced a garden which generally supplied other gardens with treasures from its store, and encouraged other gardeners in the enjoyment and excitement of collecting special plants or in seeing how simple plants could look best in the right setting.

In 1871 when sending off a basket of plants for Kew (it is emphasized by A. W. Hill that it should be noted how many plants went from Bitton to Kew over the years) he wrote to Dr Hooker: 'Most of them are good healthy plants, but some will require a little nursing. Such as they are I hope you will be pleased with them. If you find any wrongly named let me know of it. I try to be as accurate as I can but perfect accuracy in plant naming is not granted to man.'

The process of encouraging gardeners 'in the enjoyment and excitement of collecting' meant that the Canon made many friends, some of whom he knew only through writing letters to them. Here is a note to Arthur W. Hill:

Dear Mr Hill—   27.9.1912
Your note received this morning reminded me that I have never had the pleasure of making your acquaintance. I should be very pleased if you could pay me a visit. I am always at home (not quite accurate) and have lots of spare rooms so you cannot propose a day that would be inconvenient to me.
    The sooner the better.

But there were others that he had known over a long period of years, and many visits were paid between these friends with great regularity. One of the most important was known in this friendship circle as EAB.

Mr E. A. Bowles, of Myddleton House, near Enfield, Middlesex, always said that his first enthusiasm for gardening derived from Canon Ellacombe and that the Bitton garden was the most interesting he had ever seen. He writes:

Canon Ellacombe gave me this snowdrop [*Galanthus Imperati*] and quite half of his garden treasures besides . . . [referring to *G. ikariae*] I have never seen more than one variety of it, that is an early flowering seedling with deeper coloured leaves that appeared under the celebrated south wall at Bitton. A bulb, kindly given to me by Canon Ellacombe, has retained its character here. . . . A silver cowslip of palest yellow Canon Ellacombe gave me. . . . [Of *Sempervivum*

Comollei]: Canon Ellacombe noticed this fine thing in the Jardin des Plantes in Paris, received a rosette from there, and after a few seasons was able to distribute it, and so it came back with me after one of my visits to Bitton.

Other friends included Gertrude Jekyll, who mentions a visit to 'Canon Ellacombe's most interesting garden at Bitton' where she first became acquainted with the earlier mentioned *Nandina domestica*. The Canon stayed with Dean Hole at Rochester and also crossed over to Dublin to visit Glasnevin—'the prettiest Botanic garden I have seen'. Mr Wolley Dod was a friend and introduced Ellen Willmott (both subjects of later chapters) to the Bitton garden. It was her garden at Tresserve in France which Canon Ellacombe visited in 1904 when he was on one of his many travels abroad.

In *Henry Nicholson Ellacombe: A Memoir*, there is this reference to them: 'During the last forty years of his life the Canon took his holidays very frequently on the Continent, usually in company with relations or friends, but sometimes alone. Of many of these journeys he wrote up a detailed record, which he preserved. Visitors to Bitton Vicarage will remember a long row of these black notebooks on one of the library shelves.' Let us see what the appropriate entry for this particular visit has to tell us:

> *Saturday, May 21, 1904.* Spent the day at Tresserve. The place is a delightful one; the house on the top of a low hill and the garden reaching down to the pretty lake Bourget, which, with the fine hills behind, that separate the lake from the Rhone, makes an ideal setting for the garden. . . .
> After seeing the Les Barres and Tresserve collections of roses I have come to the conclusion that, as I have long suspected, I know very little about roses; and I really think there is no one who is a complete master of them.

> *September 22.* [of the same year] Gave up the day to a trip to Padua and was delighted with it. From the station I drove at once to the Botanic Gardens which are the oldest Botanic Gardens in Europe.

Some of his comments and diary entries are here selected from *In My Vicarage Garden and Elsewhere*. (In the preface he writes: 'This little volume may be considered a sequel to my former book, *In a Gloucestershire Garden.*')

> Another shrub or small tree that much interests me is the *Parottia Persica*, from the Eastern Caucasus, and apparently as hardy as an elm.

It is one of the most beautiful shrubs for autumnal foliage, but it is interesting also for its flowers. . . . The tree does not flower till it is of some age, but then it seems to flower freely, and the flowers are curious and pretty. They are little balls about the size of a nut, composed entirely of bright crimson anthers. On my own tree there are only these male flowers; the female flowers I have not seen and know nothing about them.

In 1900 he writes: '. . . in my own garden, the *Parottia Persica*, often a marvel of many colours, showed none this year', and of a rock garden:

I once saw near Chester a noted rock garden of really good design and one on which much money and labour had been spent, but which was completely spoiled by too great neatness and trimness. Not only was every shrub carefully clipped, but every stone was twice a year thoroughly scrubbed, so that though it was more than twenty years old when I saw it it looked as if made yesterday . . .

Again:

This is the secret of the success of the rock garden at Kew. The surface of Kew Gardens is almost a dead level but when the time came to make a large rock garden, it was wisely determined not to place on the level a huge mountain of stones, but the happy thought was acted on to imitate the dried-up bed of a stream through a rocky soil, of which the banks would form the rock garden.

Further notes on Kew Gardens:

And in all the best gardens the value of shade and protection is now fully recognised. At Kew there are many very attractive beds composed of one shrub, and with lilies and other plants coming up in their midst. Mr Wilson's celebrated garden at Wisley owes, I think, the greater part of its success to the abundance of shade which he is able to get in his wood. In Miss Jekyll's equally celebrated garden at Munstead the most interesting parts are those in which she so cleverly cultivates her plants in a thin wood. It has come to be recognised that a garden without trees and shrubs is not only ugly in itself, but it loses the great help in the cultivation of plants which trees and shrubs will give.

A very busy Londoner once told me that he thought it the duty of every Londoner to go once a week to Kew, not merely to please his eyes, but as the readiest and nearest place of refreshment to his body. . . . Such an exodus from London would overtax even the resources of Kew. . . .

The beginning and progress of Kew as a public and national garden have an interesting history. A little more than a hundred and fifty years ago the whole property was in private hands, but even then the gardens were reckoned among the best in the country. After being leased to the Prince of Wales, they were bought by George III and under the able advice of the Earl of Bute . . . the gardens were maintained. . . .

It is worth mentioning that gardening is carried on at Kew under great difficulties. The soil is a wretched one—in some places little better than a seashore—

. . . to all my brother-gardeners I should say, go to Kew as often as you can . . . but go to learn, go to enjoy yourself with the sight of many treasures that you can see nowhere else, and you will come away with the boast that England can show a national garden which has no equal anywhere.

On scent:

It is well known how strong is the scent of the sweetbriar after rain; this is supposed to arise from the breaking of the scent-glands by the rain, which is also the explanation of the strong scent of mint, thyme, and other low-growing herbs when trodden on. How large a part in the structure of some plants is filled by these scent-glands may easily be seen by holding up a myrtle leaf to the light; the transparent dots are the glands containing the scent.

On railway gardens:

In a cutting on the North Kent line, near Gravesend, the sides of the cutting for nearly two miles are completely covered with wild Valerian. When they are in flower it is a most beautiful sight, and almost worth a special journey to see it. The flowers are of all shades of red, from the palest pink to deep crimson; white specimens have been reported to have been found among them, but I have not seen them. [Seen on the walls of Bodiam Castle by the author.]

Canon Ellacombe was made Rural Dean of Bitton and an Honorary Canon of Bristol. He died during the First World War in 1916, a few days before his ninety-fourth birthday, in the rectory where he was born. The lych-gate leading into the church was put up in his memory by his friends in 1931. A. C. Bartholomew (who accompanied him on many of his travels abroad) wrote in the 1919 *Memoir*: 'Recalling many happy hours with Canon Ellacombe at Bitton I feel that the dominant characteristic of the man was his loving kindness. His knowledge, classical, antiquarian, literary, and botanical, was wide and varied, yet in one's memories of him it is that that stands out before all.' D. C. Lathbury (of the *Manchester Guardian*) in the same *Memoir*: 'His favourite doctrine was that a true gardener is known by the pleasure he takes in giving plants to his friends. And certainly, judged by this standard, he was a prince among gardeners.'

Shirley Hibberd

1825–1890

The late Mr B. N. Ward, an eminent surgeon . . .
not only added to the embellishments of the English
home and the recreations of English domestic life,
but his invention [the Wardian case] has been of
incalculable service in the introduction of valuable
exotic plants to this country, for if shut up close in
Wardian cases they travel over sea far more safely
than by any other system of protection.

SHIRLEY HIBBERD
The Fern Garden

Shirley Hibberd, known best perhaps for his classic entitled *The Fern Garden or Fern Culture Made Easy*, first published in 1869, was born in the parish of St Dunstan, Stepney, in 1825. He was the son of a retired sea captain and it was intended that he should enter the medical profession. This was unusual in itself as this was a period when a boy was not often consulted about his career—it was generally taken for granted that he would follow his father, and so in this case would have been sent to sea. However, it turned out that medicine was out of the question. His father died young and this meant the boy's following a trade. He was apprenticed to a Stepney bookseller.

The young man settled well into his work and soon became interested in writing himself. In a short time he was doing a certain amount of journalism, much of it devoted to various branches of horticulture. He had other enthusiasms—he was a vegetarian and a temperance advocate—but his interest in growing fruit, vegetables and flowers soon superseded everything else. He moved farther out into the suburbs of London so that he could have greater opportunities for research and experience, most of which provided the material for his many books later on in life. Like Miss Gertrude Jekyll, William Robinson, Canon Ellacombe and others, he wrote from personal trial and error. In the preface to *The Amateur's Kitchen Garden*, first published in 1877, he wrote: 'The book in the reader's hands has its defects no doubt—at all events, no pretensions are made to infallibility, or any near approach thereto—but it is no compilation: it is original

54

in the fullest sense of the word, so far as it can be applied to such a
work: and it embodies the results, in a comparatively small
compass, of the work of a quarter of a century in gardens largely
devoted to fruit and vegetable culture.'

7 *Shirley Hibberd, a prolific writer on many gardening topics*

It would be difficult to decide which were his special subjects in
the fruit and vegetable world. He carried out various experiments
on the potato and was consulted by the Government concerning
the potato disease in Ireland in the 'eighties. On the other hand,
shortly before he died he sent to *The Times* a letter entitled 'Fruit
Culture', which was later described as being written on his
favourite subject.

As to the cultivation of fruit, every conceivable kind is fully discussed in *The Amateur's Kitchen Garden*. In the section on apricots it is interesting to note that the variety 'Moorpark' heads his list of the best for 'a small place' and that this is the variety which is obtained for the restocking of trees at Aynho, Northants, famous for its apricots, where earlier plantings 'were the same or a very similar variety'. In *Garden Glory*, Ted Humphris, former head gardener at Aynho, describes 'Moorpark' as 'a hardy and vigorous variety—its fruit is very juicy and exceptionally large, particularly when the fruit has been properly thinned'. Mrs Norris in *Mansfield Park* remonstrates with Dr Grant that his apricot tree in the Parsonage garden must be good-tasting: 'Sir, it is a Moor Park, we bought it as a Moor Park . . . and I know it cost seven shillings and was charged as Moor Park;' they had put it in against the stable wall, and one feels that that indefatigable lady's verdict must also count for something.

Back in *The Amateur's Kitchen Garden*, Mr Hibberd has a cheerful piece of philosophy about the 'enemies' of the kitchen garden: after instructions as to 'deep digging and liberal manuring' being the 'surest preventitives' and exposing them (caterpillars, slugs, snails, etc.) to the 'keen eyes of the thrushes, and robins and nightingales', he settles for an optimistic disregard:

> We must confess we do not trouble ourselves much about vermin, for life seems to be too short for such small things to interfere with our happiness. We mentally ignore their existence, and they probably sicken through loss of importance, for we so rarely suffer by their depredations, that we know of no better way than to persuade oneself that such things exist only in morbid imaginations.

In the pages after the index there are descriptions of some of his other books, including one on *The Ivy*. Among many appreciative recommendations from contemporary journals there is the following from the *Scotsman*:

> Mr Shirley Hibberd's 'Monograph of the Ivy' is a fine work and forms an enduring monument of his literary research, original industry, breadth of generalization, and patient and successful cultural skill; should the work become as popular as it deserves to be, ivy-hunting will become as favourite a pastime as fern-gathering.

As well as the book on ivy and the one on the popular subject of ferns, he also wrote another on roses and yet another on field flowers. Dean Hole, expounding on the desirability of pure air for rose-growing, mentions him (as quoted earlier) as an example of what can be done in London:

> I have seen good roses, it is true, which were grown within three miles and a half of St Paul's Cathedral, and were exhibited at the first Crystal Palace Rose Show by the grower, my friend Mr Shirley Hibberd.

This was at Stoke Newington and in *The Rose Book* Shirley Hibberd mentions this problem of impure air and how to overcome it with intensive culture and, sometimes, by the use of a glasshouse. Like Dean Hole, he particularly praises the 'Gloire de Dijon', in these words: 'The most prized of all roses, the Teas, are continuous and abundant bloomers. But with the exception of Gloire de Dijon, which is the most useful rose in existence, they are too tender to be generally used. . . .' and again, 'The finest yellow Tea rose for outdoor growth is Gloire de Dijon, yellow-shaded salmon, good as a standard, a wall rose, a pot rose, or for a pillar under glass. It does best on brier or its own roots.' And

> The yellow roses of this family (tea-scented) are certainly its gems and of those there are full particulars in the chapter on yellow roses. The most superb of the whole series is Gloire de Dijon, which is so hardy that it thrives at Aberdeen; and at the Temple Gardens, in the city of London. . . .

We all have our favourites—and he writes in glowing terms of three of mine:

> *Blairii No. 2* a superb rosy-blush, with magnificent foliage. . . . The finest of all delicately-coloured roses is *Souvenir de la Malmaison*, which when happily circumstanced will produce nearly as many flowers as leaves, and it has tremendous vigour of growth when encouraged; . . . All the true *Banksian* roses are sub-evergreen climbing shrubs of very rambling and disorderly habit, vigorous in growth, with small glossy leaves and producing a profusion of clusters of small, pretty flowers. . . .

This shows Mr Hibberd's keen interest in roses and after growing them for nearly twenty years he had learnt enough to write a book devoted to them.

But the book which may have had most to offer in the way of new material, based to some extent no doubt on the work of Sir Joseph Paxton, was *The Amateur's Greenhouse*, which is full of practical details of the construction and costs of the actual buildings. In his introduction he writes:

Considering the treacherous nature of our climate and the length of the winter season, it cannot be said we have as yet attained to a full knowledge of the value of glass in horticulture. Nevertheless immense progress has been made since glass and bricks and timber were rendered free of duty. . . .

Before he embarked on so much literary output he had become the first editor of the newly established *Floral World*. He managed this paper until 1875—a matter of nearly twenty years—with success. It is not surprising that one of his first articles in the *Floral World* was entitled 'About Ivy':

. . . Among all the beauties of autumn, I know of none to beat a fine sheet of ivy in full bloom . . . The question arises: 'Does ivy destroy the wall to which it clings?' No, it does not; it neither destroys it nor renders it damp, but is an actual preservative . . . [a long paragraph follows emphasizing this]. If I thought it necessary to *say* anything further with a view to the utter explosion of the absurd notion, that ivy causes damp when attached to buildings, I could heap up evidence from noted architects, experienced builders, and horticulturists innumerable, but there is no such need; it is a protector, not a destroyer, and, for many other reasons besides its beauty, is worthy of the universal admiration accorded it.

8 *Shirley Hibberd walking away from his fern house. This he had converted from a greenhouse after a neighbour's building activities had shut out the afternoon sun*

He had also, during this time, become connected with Loudon's *Gardener's Magazine*, of which he was editor at the time of his death.

Shirley Hibberd's first interest in ferns began when he was a boy bird's-nesting in Epping Forest. There he came across tufts of the common polypody fern which he found useful for lining his basket to hold the birds' eggs.

In *The Fern Garden*, there is a charming wood engraving showing the one built against his own house, which only became a fern garden because a near-by construction blotted out the afternoon sun. It had begun life as a house for half-hardy plants, but when the objectionable building put up by Hibberd's neighbour cut out the sunlight, instead of complaining bitterly, he re-arranged his ideas and converted his small greenhouse into an ideal fern house. This became Mrs Hibberd's care and delight, about which her husband writes with understandable pride.

This seemingly small event of the lean-to greenhouse for flowering plants being converted into a shady fern house gives as good an indication as any of his philosophy and for this reason it seems worth while to give the description of it in his own words.

> In the course of time, some building and planting took place a little way off towards the west, and the nice gleam of sunlight that enlivened the house from 2 p.m. till sunset was effectually blocked out, and the house became unfit for flowering plants. Instead of bringing an action against the neighbour who devoured my sunshine, I brought an action against myself, and the verdict was, that the shady house should be forthwith converted into a fernery.

This approach to a problem which so often arises between neighbours, sometimes 'out of the blue' in one form or another, spells out good sense and tolerance as well as determination to turn what might have become a source of bitterness into a source of benefit and even pleasure, giving an important clue to Hibberd's character. It is difficult to think of Shirley Hibberd without also calling to mind the benefits of the Wardian Case (a small glass case in which plants are grown indoors). He relates the history of its development, 'being the invention of the late Mr B. N. Ward, an eminent surgeon, many years resident in Finsbury Circus, who died at a ripe age in 1868'. Mr Hibberd reminds us of the importance of this case, not only for the decoration of the home or the conservatory, but for its even greater value in making possible the transport of plants, shrubs and cuttings sent or brought from abroad by collectors at a time when sea travel was not only slow but also unreliable. In the *Floral World and Garden Guide* of January 1858, there is an article on the 'Planting of a Fern Case' by Shirley Hibberd. He writes:

9 The Wardian case, an invention much admired by Shirley Hibberd. It was used decoratively for growing plants indoors, and for transporting plants from abroad

I planted this case last May, with a few select exotic ferns, and their rapid growth and present (December) healthy appearance, surpass any example I have ever had on the *close* method of treating Wardian cases. . . . In planting, a layer of small cinders was first laid over the perforated bottom of the soilpan, and upon these, two inches of small crocks and rough charcoal of the size of hazelnuts. Upon this was placed a thin layer of rough turfy peat, to prevent the finer compost from getting down among the drainage; and then the compost for the ferns was worked in. . . .

He was the product of an age which provided unbelievable opportunities for industrious and detailed work—which encouraged it and expected it—and perhaps the book which is most typical and indicative of his period is his *Rustic Adornments for Homes of Taste*, published in 1856. 'Who would live contentedly, or consider a sitting-room furnished without either a Ward's Case or an Aquarium?' he asks. There are suggestions for ferns for the Wardian Case and fish for the aquarium. Rustic seats for garden furniture, a 'dark cave for the growth of mosses and ferns', sundials, arbours and beehives, all come to his notice. He describes the furnishings for a grotto like this:

A rustic table, a rustic bench, and a locker would be useful, if ideas of picknicking came into one's head; and to enhance my own solitary and selfish enjoyment, I would have an inner chamber luxuriously furnished with a couch, a locker for whatever I might choose to put into it, such as a bottle of Burgundy and a box of cigars, and a few of the choicest books, quaintly bound, and arranged neatly in a recess. . . .

Among other valuable information, this book gives a clear picture of the arrangement of flowers for indoor decoration in the mid-Victorian era. There is an illustration, for instance, of what he likes to describe as 'a simple fireplace decoration'. In the centre of the mantelpiece a large pedestal bowl supports a heavy-leafed plant. Four others all contain flowers, and below are three large vases, one full of foliage, one of flowers and one of grasses, flowers and leaves. This is not only an indication of the taste of the time: it is an example of the close link between the gardener and the arranger of flowers. No wonder Miss Jekyll wrote in *Home and Garden*, about forty years later, 'There comes a point where the room becomes overloaded with flowers and greenery. During the last few years I have seen many a drawing room where it appeared to be less a room than a thicket.'

And so we have, from Shirley Hibberd, one indication after another of the taste of the time. As a social historian of his period he stands almost unchallenged. He tells us of furnishings, flower arrangements, indoor plants, garden ornaments, the conservatory, the growing of vegetables and fruit. The art of picnicking is described in such detail as would make the disastrous Box Hill picnic in *Emma* seem elementary in its planning. He is alleged to have written an account of the Crimean War and known to have been consulted about the potato famine in Ireland. He makes clear the popularity and usefulness of a certain shrub or flower, for example, the fuschia, of which in 1859 he names and recommends no less than fifty varieties. But perhaps one of his most interesting and almost startling historical assessments is that of the herb garden. He does not mince matters. 'The Herb Garden, as an institution,' he writes, 'has ceased to be, and, although it "lives in history", its claims on our attention as a matter of business are few and small. . . .'

He compares the nineteenth-century herb garden with that of one or two hundred years earlier: 'Nay, if we go back only a century we shall find the herb garden and the still-room, and the still-room maid in happy association, but they have all become memories embalmed for us in a peculiar odour of sanctity. The Herb Garden, therefore, in the historic sense, we are bound to ignore. . . .

But he does not, after all, ignore the *growing* of herbs, as the passage from his herb chapter shows. (Happily we are in a position to know that during this century there is great interest in herbs and that although we may not be able to produce a still-room maid, we have herb gardens of which to be proud, and writers of herbs whose work we enjoy. Eleanour Sinclair Rohde was only a child when Shirley Hibberd died and could have shown little sign of her years of study and practical work in this subject that were to come, although we do see her in an early photograph as a little girl with a border of lavender in the garden at Nymans.)

The working title of Mr Hibberd's notes in *The Amateur's Kitchen Garden* is 'Formation of Herb Garden' and he writes:

The month of September is the best time in all the year for the formation of a herb-garden. For all the woody, aromatic plants required for flavouring soups and meats, such as thyme, sage, etc. a dry, sunny, sandy bank is the best situation possible. The fragrance and flavour of these plants are much enhanced by a dry, rather calcareous soil, and full exposure to air and sunshine. . . . It must be remembered, however, that all aromatic herbs in common use will not thrive alike on a dry, sunny, sandy bank. Some require a deep, moist, rich soil, and of this class parsley and mint are notable examples. Places for such as these should be found independent of the supplies the gardener may be able to furnish, for they may be wanted when there is no one at hand to obtain them, and the kitchen garden may be too far away for a journey in wet weather. It is impossible to predicate the wants of every household; but, having found it greatly to conduce to domestic comfort to have herbs of all kinds scattered about the pleasure garden, though we have a complete and rather large collection of them all in their proper place, we propose these plants for the good of others and have only to beg of each reader to accept, modify, or reject, as a consideration of individual circumstances may render advisable.

Then follows a list of twenty-seven herbs with detailed instructions about conditions for planting, suitability for flavouring and/or general attractions of the plant itself as an asset in the garden. These are, in alphabetical order (where the modern botanical name varies from that quoted, it is given in square brackets):

angelica, *Archangelica officinalis*: anise, *Traqium anisum* [*Pimpinella anisum*]; balm, *Melissa officinalis*; sweet basil, *Ocymym basilicum* [*Ocimum basilicum*]; borage, *Borago officinalis*; bugloss, *Anchusa officinalis* [now known as alkanet]; burnet, *Poterium sanguisorba* [*Sanguisorba minor*]; chervil, *Choerophyllum*; chives, *Allium schoenoprasum*; clary, *Salvia sclarea*; dill, *Anethum graveolens*; fennel, *Anethum* [*Foeniculum vulgare*]; horehound, *Marrubium vulgare*; hyssop, *Hyssopus officinalis*; lavender, *Lavendula spica*; marigold, *Calendula officinalis*; marjorum, *Origanum majorama, O. hereacleoticum, O. onites*; spear mint, *Mentha viridia* [*Mentha spicata*]; woolly mint, *Mentha rotundifolia* [also known as apple mint]; purslane, *Portulacca oleracea, P. sativa*; rosemary, *Rosemarinus officinalis*; rue, *Ruta graveolens*; sage, *Salvia officinalis*; tarragon, *Artemisia dracunculus*; thyme, *Thymus vulgaris, T. serpyllum, T. corsicus, T. vulgaris variegatus, T. azureus*; wormwood, *Artemisia vulgaris* [*Artemisia absinthium*].

Some detailed advice follows:

Angelica. A coarse-looking plant of the Umbelliferous order. It grows five or six feet high, and requires a deep loamy soil and a damp situation. It is suitable, in fact, to plant out beside a lake or river. The stalks have a warm aromatic flavour; when candied with sugar, it is considered scarcely inferior to ginger as a carminative and stomachic stimulant . . . In the north of Europe it is much used, and is believed to have the property of prolonging life. Angelica should be raised from seed, but it should be sown as soon as ripe. . . .

Balm. This is a general favourite in the country, for its grateful lemon-like odour, and the refreshing drink which is prepared from it for the sick. It is a coarse-looking plant, growing two or three feet high. It will grow in any soil, but is best in poor clayey stuff. Seed may be sown in April or May, but a quicker method is to obtain plants and part them. . . .

Sweet Basil. . . . If there are no conveniences for raising plants under glass, sow the first week in May on a sunny bank and the plants will appear in the early part of June. Basil is used in soups and salads, and some prefer it to flavour peas instead of mint. If strong plants are put out at the end of May, seed may be obtained in September, but seed imported from Italy is far better than can be ripened in England.

Borage. A rough-leaved rustic annual, producing the most lovely blue flowers. Sow in March, April, May, June and September, to have a succession. The young tops have the flavour of cucumber and are used in the preparation of a 'cool tankard'. . . . Bees are very fond of the flowers, and a rough piece of ground, not wanted for any particular purpose, might be sown all over with borage, both for the bees and to give a cheerful air to what might otherwise be quite a waste.

Burnet. A pretty plant, requiring a very sunny, poor dry soil. . . . Sow the seed in March, April and May. . . . Sometimes the seed will remain in the ground a year before germinating. It is used in cool tankards, soups and salads.

Chervil. (Also known as Sweet Cicely). A hardy annual, requiring a dry, sandy or chalky soil fully exposed to the sun. Sow in March, April, May and August, the last sowing being left to stand the winter. It is used for soups, salads and for garnishing.

Chives. This is a valuable salad herb, as it gives to a salad the piquancy and pungency of the onion, in a subdued form. . . . wherever salads are in request chives should be handy. Plant a few small tufts and leave them alone one whole season, after which cut the tops as required, but do not injure the roots. Any soil will suit them but a sunny position is essential. If used for soups divide the patches in March, and plant them a foot apart every way, in good soil. . . .

Clary. An annual plant, the seed of which may be sown in April and May on a dry, sunny, sandy bank. . . . It is used in soups, sauces. . . .

Dill. This is grown in quantities in some gardens, for the preparation of 'dill water'; in others it is kept merely for flavouring soups and sauces and for pickling. A dry, poor sand suits it. . . .

Fennel. Sow in April and May; better still, as soon as the seed is ripe in the autumn . . . It may be propagated by pieces of the root. If allowed to ripen seed, it does not last more than three or four years; therefore, where only a few plants are grown for occasional use, it is advisable to cut out the flower-stalks as soon as they begin to rise in spring. As in some families this is much used to flavour sauces for fish, it is worth making a bed expressly for it. This should consist of two or three loads of bricklayers' rubbish, in the form of a low mound, with a thin skin of any kind of loam on the top. It will however, grow in any soil or situation and is especially fond of chalk.

Lavender. This well-known garden favourite thrives best in a sunny open spot on a sandy soil, but will live almost anywhere, even in a sooty garden in the midst of houses. Cuttings of ripe wood planted firm in October will flower freely the next spring. . . . At the end of the season, transplant them, or thin them, leaving part to remain. Gather lavender when the flowers are beginning to expand; it is then most rich in its aromatic fragrance.

Spear Mint. This invaluable herb loves a damp, rich soil and should always be propagated by dividing the old plants, or by pieces of the roots. In every garden a plantation, however small, should be made every year, either in spring or autumn, and should be allowed to become strong before being gathered from. It is a good rule to grow a row on the same ground with the peas, to be handy to put into the basket with them. . . .

Woolly Mint. Is one of the most useful herbs of its class, and the very best kind of mint for the making of sauce to eat with lamb. The plant is coarse in growth, the leaves large, roundish, of a soft woolly texture, and very bright and grateful in flavour. The young tops should be pinched out and used quite fresh, and without washing. Mint sauce made quite thick with this mint will make even house-lamb at Christmas eatable, and such tame meats need some flavouring to justify the absurdity of eating them.

Rosemary. . . . The soil cannot be too poor and dry for this useful shrub, which, when growing on a wall from self-sown seeds, is longer lived than when growing in a garden border. The hot sandy bank will, at all events, be a good place for it. . . . Most of the preparations for promoting the growth of the hair consist chiefly of infusions of rosemary.

Rue. The 'Herb of Grace' thrives well on the top of a wall, or on a heap of brick rubbish, or on a bank of chalky or sandy soil. The variegated-leaved rue is a beautiful shrub for a rockery or wall. The only uses for rue are as a stomachic and to provoke appetite, and also to destroy worms in the intestines. For both of these purposes it is steeped in gin, and the gin is taken as a medicine. It is certainly effectual.

Shirley Hibberd was taken ill at 74 The Hermitage, near Muswell Hill, on Sunday morning 16 November 1890, and died within a few hours. On the previous Thursday he had attended the Chrysanthemum Society's Dinner. He was a Fellow of the Royal Horticultural Society, a judge at the Guildhall Flower Show, and was considered to be one of the best authorities of his time on the cultivation of fruit, vegetables and flowers. Prolific in his literary output he was also a practical gardener, trying out things for himself, and with a great love for the natural countryside.

A few years after his death he is quoted at the heading of a chapter entitled 'Topiary' in *The Book of Topiary* by Charles H.

Curtis and W. Gibson (he did not care for topiary but was incapable of aggressive disagreement):

> If I do not defend the taste through thick and thin, I am prepared to admit that much may be said in its favour, and it is far from my intention to denounce it as either extravagant or foolish. It may be true, as I believe it is, that the natural form of a tree is the most beautiful possible for that particular tree, but it may happen . . . that we want one of our designing and expressive of our ingenuity.

Being fair and just in his comment he could make the point of his belief that the 'natural form of a tree is the most beautiful possible for that particular tree . . .'

But perhaps one of his most attractive characteristics was his quiet sense of humour. For example, in his Introduction to his book *Field Flowers*:

> A little knowledge is a dangerous thing. A keen razor is also a dangerous thing; ditto a lucifer match, a boiling kettle, petroleum oil, and any so-called 'royal road' to knowledge. Ignorance is a dangerous thing, and a little knowledge of something or other may be as equally safe and useful; . . . everyone who has been questioned by an inquisitive youngster when strolling through fields and lanes will admit that a little knowledge is better than none at all. . . . But undoubtedly the more complete our knowledge the better.

And again, this time going back to *The Fern Garden*:

> We want a fern house—oh dear! how our wants increase with increase of knowledge and advance of taste. Any man could live contented on just double the amount of income he has already, and the fern grower at any time could promise to be satisfied if he could be sure of advancing from a frame to a house . . . or from a house to another and a larger house.

The Revd C. Wolley Dod

1826–1904

But of all these friendly gardeners, the one whom I felt to be the most valuable was the Revd C. Wolley Dod, scholar, botanist, and great English gentleman; an enthusiast for plant life, an experienced gardener, and the kindest of instructors.

G. JEKYLL
A Gardener's Testament

'Propagate, propagate, propagate'—this was the watchword of the Revd Charles Wolley Dod. He came to gardening relatively late in life but made up for any lost time in the amount of energy he expended on his plants. Apart from his appeal for propagation— 'Mr Dod finds that in the second year the plants are better than in the first year, but that they degenerate in the third year, hence his advice to divide and multiply'—he was also a maker of rockeries. This article in the *Gardeners' Chronicle* goes on: 'Mr Dod says one ought to demolish an old and construct a new rockery every year' (7 October 1882).

Although some of his ideas differed widely in this matter of rockeries he forged a link both with E. A. Bowles and later with Reginald Farrer. In *My Garden in Spring*, the former writes:

> I suppose it is inevitable that I write of my moraines . . . No one would read a gardening book nowadays that did not deal with this latest fashion in gardening. The name and popularity and prattle of the thing are new, but many good cultivators had their porous, gritty, raised or sunk beds for alpines, whatever they called them, long ago. Mr Wolley-Dod laughingly called his narrow raised mounds 'potato-ridges'. But they proved the ideal home for many difficult plants that would not exist domiciled otherwise on the cold, sticky clay of Edge Hall.

The Revd Charles Wolley Dod was born in 1826, and came from an old Cheshire family, dating from the time of Henry II. His father, the Revd J. F. Hurt of Derbyshire, married Miss Mary Wolley and assumed by Royal Sign-manual the surname and arms of Wolley. Charles Wolley was educated at Eton as a Scholar, and eventually became a Fellow of King's College, Cambridge. In 1850 he married Frances, granddaughter of Mr T. C. Dod of Edge Hall, Malpas, Cheshire, and in 1861 his son was born and christened Anthony Hurt. Seven years later, Charles Wolley took on his wife's surname by Royal Licence. But he also retained his own name.

10 The Revd Charles Wolley Dod whose garden was at Edge Hall, Cheshire

He was an assistant master at Eton for many years, and during that time was ordained Deacon by the Bishop of Lincoln. It was not until after his retirement that he was able to devote the whole of his time and attention to the garden at Edge Hall.

In chapter three of *The English Flower Garden* (5th edn, 1897), William Robinson describes the Edge Hall garden under the heading: 'Various Flower Gardens: mainly chosen for their beauty. . . .' These include Wilton and Powis Castle, Compton Wynyates and Penshurst Place, examples of Mr Robinson's favourite cottage gardens and Gilbert White's garden at Selborne. Edge Hall was large in comparison with, for instance, Canon Ellacombe's garden at Bitton (about two acres) or Miss Jekyll's stretch of wooded heathland at Munstead, and there was ample room for propagating and rebuilding of rockeries.

A tribute is paid here, in a *Gardeners' Chronicle* article on Edge Hall, to the owner's skill and industry:

> Personal observation will do much, friendly hints of fellow workers will assist, but nothing but actual subjective work will lead on to success. Not only is experience shown in the selection of appropriate plants, but, perhaps even more strikingly so, in the subtle way in which the special requirements of individual plants are provided for.

Plants were everywhere. 'They clothe the slopes, they are dotted on the lawn, they edge their way in up to the very hall door. . . .' But there were also stretches of parkland at the foot of which ran 'a small brook full of trout', and woods which

> in spring are carpeted first with primroses and wood anemones, then with wild hyacinths and pink campion; while later there is a tall growth of *Campanula latifolia* and large breadths of *Polygonum cuspidatum*, which has been planted to supersede nettles, while overhead is abundance of hawthorn, crab and wild cherry.

In this article a long paragraph is devoted to

> British wild plants here cultivated. . . . Foxgloves and *Lytherum salicaria* are [also] not unexpected inhabitants; but in addition to these more common plants Mr Dod has succeeded in collecting from their native haunts some of the rarer British species. . . .

Certainly this was the kind of garden to appeal to the taste of William Robinson, in spite of so much activity in an overabundance of flower beds. There was an important point which may have especially won Mr Robinson's heart as he writes in *The English Flower Garden*: '. . . the hardy flowers of the northern world are grown in numbers for the owner's delight and the good of his friends. . . .' So much of Wolley Dod's gardening was done for the benefit of his friends. 'Make a note of what you want' he would say to his guests as he took them round his garden. He was a ready gardening friend and adviser to anyone who was genuinely interested and wanted his help.

Miss Gertrude Jekyll mentions her debt to him in the introduction of her first book, *Wood and Garden*, published in 1899, and years later in *Gardening Illustrated* (27 August 1927) she records her gratitude to her many gardening friends in these words: 'But of all these friendly gardeners, the one whom I felt to be the most valuable was the Rev. C. Wolley Dod, scholar, botanist and great English gentleman; an enthusiast for plant life, an experienced gardener, and the kindest of instructors.'

11 Pulsatilla at Edge Hall

Miss Ellen Willmott, too, was a friend who stayed at Edge Hall and asked for advice.

Mr Dod grew many narcissi and daffodils and was quoted by Mr Robinson as an authority on a certain form of disease, known as 'basal rot', which affects these bulbs. He also grew quantities of *Fuchsia*, especially *F. fraseri* and the hardy *F. riccartonii*. It is reported that he confined himself exclusively to hardy plants.

Notes on a visit to Edge Hall garden in the month of September include mention of *Salvia patens* (perhaps one of the least hardy of the plants he grew), hybrid *Lobelia*, *Michauxia campanuloides*, a lemon-coloured form of the common sunflowers, some of the toadflaxes, including *Linaria reticulata*, and the handsome *Senecio pulcher*.

Then there were all the plants for his rock gardens. The rocks for some of these gardens were formed from great slabs of limestone similar to those which are found at the Great Orme's Head, North Wales. The following quotations from Reginald Farrer's *My Rock Garden* help to show his respect for Wolley Dod's achievements in the study and collecting of alpines: Writing of limestone:

> No other formation has the same romantic quality as mountain limestone; both granite and sandstone are apt to be too square, to offer monotonous slab-like faces, and altogether, not to present those many varied surfaces that make a rock so much more attractive. Of course culturally the sandstone is rather more porous, moist and adhesive than the limestone, but the slight superiority it has in this way is so slight as to outweigh the far greater picturesqueness of the other. Mr Wolley Dod took all the trouble to import mountain limestone to Edge, and though that marvellous garden of his made little claim to artistic construction . . . yet the beauty of the stone employed completed the attraction of those splendid plants of his.

Of *Omphalodes Luciliae*:

> . . . there is far greater chance of establishing Lucilla's Omphalodes (whoever she may have been. Mr Wolley-Dod told me once, but I have forgotten . . .) in light, warm poor stuff than in any heavy loam or peat.

Of *Gentiana verna*:

> . . . you put it anywhere in the open garden, and away it romps. But even Mr Wolley-Dod at Edge (Hall) could only keep it barely alive, with barrels, and granite, and all manner of contraptions.

Of *Primula capitata*:

> Perhaps our cool mountain air may have something to do with it, but, all I can say is, not only do I find *P. capitata* one of the easiest of all my primulas, but I also find it a most trustworthy and hearty perennial. How well I remember astonishing Mr Wolley-Dod with the news that I then had a four-year-old clump of *capitata* that went on improving from year to year.

Of various saxifrages he says:

> *S. Wolley-Dod* has only just been given to me. To be worthy of its name (as I suppose it is) the plant ought to be very beautiful. . . .

Of alpines:

> But it will always, I fancy, be vain to expect of them any great longevity. In fact, my idea is that we ask too much of all our alpines in

that way. Mr Wolley-Dod once said to me that he believed the average life of an Alpine plant, such as the high mountain Androsaces, would hardly exceed five, seven, or perhaps ten years. Now when the collector sallies forth to work, if he be very inexperienced, the plants he brings home are middle-aged, if he is wiser they are younger, but few collectors are fortunate enough to be able to get seedlings . . . So that, by the time a plant is well established in a rock-garden, it is certainly more than three years old, possibly more than five.

There is an interesting note in Bunyard's *Old Garden Roses* which refers to 'Janet's Pride', one of the sweet briar roses (*R. rubiginosa*). He writes that 'This was found in a Cheshire lane away from other roses, on the authority of the Rev. C. Wolley Dod.' In *The Development of Garden Flowers* Richard Gorer comments on 'Janet's Pride' that it 'is slightly double with cerise petals and a white eye'. The suggestion it was this rose which gave Lord Penzance the idea of his now famous Sweet Briar Hybrids is attributed to Miss Ellen Willmott. Other *rubiginosa* hybrid sweet briars raised by Lord Penzance include 'Meg Merrilees' (1894), crimson, and 'Julia Mannering' (1895) a clear light pink.

Charles Wolley Dod was a frequent contributor to gardening journals, especially the *Gardeners' Chronicle*, and as early as January 1879 he had an article in *The Garden* entitled 'A Substitute for Nettles', written from experience in his own woodlands. He writes of them:

> . . . they flourish so luxuriantly in the woods here, away from all cultivation, that we have sometimes made walking sticks out of them. Nettles were certainly well known to the ancient Greeks and Romans. Pliny, who was well up in all the plant-lore of ancient Italy, and gives a long account of their medicinal qualities . . . begins his description by saying: 'What can be more odious than the nettle' and as many will agree with him, I advise them to try to supersede Nettles in their grounds, as I am doing, by substituting for them Polygonum Sieboldi.

There is a doubt in his mind about *exactly* which polygonum and with his usual care for accuracy (he was a purist in the matter of plant nomenclature) he mentions this, having bought it years earlier as *P. japonica*. 'However', he writes, 'I think this is the right name as I have compared the different species which are named at Kew. . . .' He then goes on to describe his success with a certain pride, although admitting: 'It does not spread fast in the middle of the Nettles, though it quite holds its own, and gradually beats them.'

However, fascinating as the vanquishing of nettles must be as a subject for the good gardener, it is to Mr Dod's devotion to his detailed work, his accuracy, his love of the individual plant and its special requirements that we are asked to turn our attention. The result is undoubtedly summed up in one word—perfection. The final paragraph in the *Gardeners' Chronicle* reads:

> The space at Mr Dod's command is so large, and the richness of his collection so great, that he can well afford to try the same plant in all sorts of different situations, with a view to determine which is best. His collection, moreover, is so thoroughly representative, and care taken in securing correct nomenclature so great, that we can hardly imagine a more useful and instructive task as a guide for other cultivators than the formation of a monthly, or in the height of the season of a fortnightly, list of the plants as they come into bloom, with occasional notes on their cultivation, structure, and relative value as plants for different purposes and positions. . . .

He won the Jubilee Gold Medal of the Royal Horticultural Society, and after his death in 1904 it was said that 'in later times horticulture has not sustained a more severe loss. . . .' His name lives on in 'Wolley Dod's rose', *Rosa pomifera duplex*, a double form of the apple rose, with soft-pink flowers and luxuriant grey-green foliage.

Mrs Maria Theresa Earle
1836–1935

The Dean of Rochester (Dean Hole) wrote me a
most kind letter reproaching me for saying I could
not grow roses, and implying that the fault is mine.
This I know to be true, but the fact is I am so fond
of variety in flowers, as in all else, that I grudge too
much room in the garden being given to Roses.

MRS C. W. EARLE
More Pot-Pourri from a Surrey Garden

Mrs Earle is probably best remembered as the author of *Pot-Pourri from a Surrey Garden*, published in 1897, which she followed shortly afterwards by *More Pot-Pourri from a Surrey Garden*.

She was born Maria Theresa Villiers, in 1836, into an aristocratic family background providing an atmosphere of financial security and well-being, among a group of intelligent, educated friends. Her parents were devotedly in love throughout a short married life lasting only seven years. Maria Theresa was born a year after their marriage; then came the birth of twin girls. Their father died of tuberculosis at Nice in October 1843 and Mrs Earle's own memories of him are few, but they were kept and translated into hero-worship by her mother. Years later, she wrote about the atmosphere of a home with a widowed mother to whom death had brought such irreparable loss, describing it as 'peculiar and unlike other homes'.

The garden of her childhood home in Hertfordshire was 'beautiful, wild, old-fashioned' and was surrounded by a mill-stream which she remembered and loved all her life, with hedges of China roses, sweet briar, honeysuckle and white hawthorn forming the boundary. She recalls her interest in the flowers growing in this garden—the tall, white, double rockets, the oriental poppies, the feathery *Spiraea aruncus*—but confesses to little knowledge of them.

Her education was handed over to the care of governesses. She had eight different ones before the age of fifteen, only one of whom she liked. In spite of this lack of continuity she was intelligent and recalls the impression made on her mind when 'as quite a girl' she was taken to pay her first visit to William Morris's shop in Queen Square, Bloomsbury. 'It had the effect of a sudden opening of a window in a dark room', she writes in *Pot-Pourri from a Surrey Garden*, recalling her immediate appreciation of the light, clear colours and the simplicity of the furnishings. Throughout her life she was greatly influenced by Morris and especially by his 'Lectures on Art'.

Perhaps experiences with the string of governesses gave her mother the idea that foreign travel might be more educationally successful than lessons in the schoolroom. She took her contingent of young children travelling abroad, often on visits to friends. One of these later visits Maria Theresa always remembered with nostalgia—a long stay in Florence when she was twenty, and how she used to 'dance half the night through at balls'.

In her *Memoirs and Memories* she recalls:

I must go back now to the family history of the six years that my future husband was in India. In 1859 my sisters were seventeen, and came out, and for two or three years, until one of them married, I went out very little, and devoted myself more and more to my drawing, working at the School of Art in South Kensington, a queer building with tin roofing, which used then to be called the Boilers [where Miss Gertrude Jekyll also studied]. . . . In the autumn of the same year we again went abroad for my mother's health. We hated going, and liked our winters with our cousins. . . . I think it was that year we got to know Henry Loch. He came to see Lord Clarendon about his going to China on Lord Elgin's second embassy. . . . he later on married my sister Elizabeth, one of the precious twins. They were so alike at that time and long after, hardly anyone knew them apart. 'Daughter of the gods, divinely tall and most divinely fair,' my mother and I were both equally proud of them . . . The winter was an eventful one for me, as I was very near marrying some one who was introduced to us in Paris, and who travelled with us to Nice. I was not very gracious, as I was absorbed in one of the most remarkable books of my time, 'Jane Eyre'. I had not been allowed to read it before. . . . I consider it one of the strengthening and powerful novels in the English language. Seeing more of this man during the early part of the winter, I felt I never could care enough for him to marry him . . . and so I refused him, greatly to his indignation.
  In July 1863 Captain Earle returned, handsome and improved in every way, from his work in India, and in a month we were engaged. . . . He did not leave the army to please me, though I think I should never have married him had he not wished to leave the army. I knew I was quite unfit to be a soldier's wife.

Miss Villiers married Captain C. W. Earle in 1864 and they
rented a house in London in August. 'We stayed about in different
houses in London and when the winter came we moved into my
mother's house at Rutland Gate, where my eldest son was born.
. . . In July 1865 Charley got another small directorship. . . .'

12 *Captain C. W. Earle, after whose tragic death in a bicycle accident
Mrs Theresa Earle turned to gardening*

He was frequently ill, at one time very seriously. Eventually
they took a 'small house at Watford' where their youngest son
was born, but 'In the summer of 1867 my husband was very ill
again'. Illness, moving house, building up a home for a short space
of time, these were everyday conditions. She writes: 'This all
sounds very miserable, but we were not at all miserable, and
probably happier than we should have been in ordinary life. . . .'
They now had three sons, and at last their father's health began to
improve. Financially they were more secure. Things became more
cheerful.

Some years later, in May 1878, Charley's youngest brother
George died in India and the next year his brother Ralph, of whom

he was extremely fond, died in Germany. The latter, to their great surprise had left everything to them in his will, 'much more than we knew he had'. 'The complete recovery of my husband's health and the accession of wealth . . . took from me what I had always considered my two vocations in life, namely to nurse my husband and to be a good poor man's wife', writes Theresa Earle. She continues:

> Two years afterwards we inherited our settlement money; all this made a very great difference in our means. Everybody naturally congratulated us very much,—and William H—sent me a lovely little cream jug, in recollection of an old family joke, because at the time of his engagement to my cousin, in a discussion about household expenses, I had said, 'Really, Willie's ideas about cream make my hair stand on end.' With the cream jug came a note, saying how delighted he was to hear that I should now be able to afford some cream.

For a time they lived in Bryanston Square with their three sons and there they entertained a large circle of artistic and intellectual friends. At their house one would meet Burne-Jones, William Morris and Rossetti. Gardening held little or no attraction for Theresa Earle at this period of her life. She had many other interests and there is special mention of a visit to Dante Gabriel Rossetti's while he was working at the small replica of his *Dante's Dream*, now at Liverpool, and of a receipt for varnishing plaster cases given to her by Sir Edward Burne-Jones. She was herself an amateur painter, some of her work receiving high praise from no less an artist than Millais.

They later moved from London to a house called 'Woodlands' in Cobham, Surrey, with what she describes as 'a small piece of flat ground surrounding an ordinary suburban house. Kitchen-garden, flower-garden, house and drive can scarcely cover more than two acres.' The present owners of Woodlands are glad to be able to keep the 'whole five acres' going with the help of only one gardener. (Mrs Earle may have underestimated, or perhaps some adjoining land may have been added since her time.) However, the important thing is that hers was a garden of a reasonable size both from expense and upkeep, and not beyond the possibilities of present-day gardening. It is pleasant to know that, unlike the gardens of some other famous gardeners, it is still being looked after and cared for.

It was Whitsunday, 1897, and they were at Woodlands. She received a letter from Smith, Elder & Co. to say that a first copy of her book was in the post to her. She told her husband, and asked her son Sydney if he would bicycle over to Cobham Post Office to collect it for her. 'Of course, Mother,' he replied. And so Mr Earle spent most of the day reading it, and obviously enjoying it, which gave his wife much pleasure.

On Whit Monday some of the children had decided to go into the Surrey hills on bicycles, and to have lunch with a friend. They especially wanted Mr Earle to accompany them. He said quietly to her: 'Shall I go? Shall I not spoil their ride?' 'Oh, do go,' she said. 'They will love to have you.' They set off, on that June day, and soon came to a rough piece of road, with deep ruts on a steep slope. He lost his pedal, was thrown off the bicycle on to his head. . . . He breathed for over an hour, but never again opened his eyes or regained consciousness. That was the end—after that, everything was different.

It was not until after the death of her husband that Mrs Earle became keenly interested in her garden. 'I took up gardening later in life,' she writes, and the book to which she often refers for information and to which she chiefly gives the credit for her finally acquired knowledge, is William Robinson's *English Flower Garden*. She also expresses gratitude to Miss Gertrude Jekyll, especially on the appearance of *Wood and Garden*, writing that 'one must read and re-read it', and that it is 'a never-ending lesson of how to lay out a piece of ground by using its natural advantages instead of hopelessly destroying them by clearing the ground to make a garden.'

Like Miss Jekyll, Mrs Earle also came to gardening with a background of many interests and they had certain other things in common. Both talented women, educated and artistic, they were interested in and delighted in foreign travel, and numbered intellectuals amongst their friends. Mrs Earle eventually visited Miss Jekyll's home at Munstead.

They both enjoyed cooking and in their writings both included a chapter of cooking receipts. Although they may not have known it at the time, they felt alike about what Mrs Earle describes as 'wholesale present-giving at fixed anniversaries, whether birthdays, Christmas or New Year', and Miss Jekyll wrote: 'Forgive us our Christmasses as we forgive them that Christmas against us.' Mrs Earle goes on: 'It is almost laughable, the way that people who are apparently the greatest supporters of this custom of present-giving at stated times groan over the trouble and expense it entails, and congratulate themselves and each other when the terrible Christmas fortnight is at an end.' Miss Jekyll was supremely irritated by the sending of numerous cards to people 'for whom she felt no affection and hardly knew' and vice versa.

Some of their youthful memories must have been similar, especially in the way that they were both involved in painting and were connected with artists. Mrs Earle writes of paying visits to Rossetti's studio, while Miss Jekyll was noting 'a visit to William Morris, in March 1869', and writing of meeting Ruskin in Venice, and of his attack on the 'assassination of St Mark's'. William Morris and Burne-Jones organized in England the protest against the style of restoration. Mrs Earle records the death of Sir Edward Burne-Jones in her diary when staying in Florence: '. . . the sad news has come from England today. . . . what a loss'.

She writes in *Memoirs and Memories*:

> Among other remarkable people I remember the Countess Guiccioli, of Byronic fame. . . . G. F. Watts, the painter, who was a life-long intimate acquaintance to us all, was then living with Lord and Lady Holland at Florence, painting all those pictures which are still to be seen at Holland House, and which are so different in their hard dry style from the Venetian methods he afterwards adopted. I heard in later years that he went out thinking he was to pay the Hollands a short visit and he remained over three years.

They tackled their difficulties and problems—Mrs Earle that of facing up to the loneliness of widowhood and Miss Jekyll the disaster of extreme myopia—with similar weapons: hard work, many interests and a complete lack of self-pity. Mrs Earle had to learn to live alone and to fill her days so that she did not miss too much having someone at hand 'to whom one can go with those numberless little things which are often big things in life's routine, and that one hides away from the outside world as guests, be they ever so near and dear'.

Mrs Earle's childhood had not done a great deal to equip her with gardening knowledge, but she describes how, in a strange way, memories of the Hertfordshire garden became a comfort to her. She remembered how she would 'rush out after lessons and ask the gardener what the weather was going to be. He would stop his digging, look up at the sky, and say: "Well, miss, it may be fine and it may be wet, and if the sun comes out it will be warmer,"' she recalls in *Pot-Pourri From A Surrey Garden*. She became greatly attached to her garden, so much so that to go away from it for short periods was usually an anxiety.

It was only for one of her travels abroad that she would leave it willingly. But a foreign journey was always one of her greatest delights. Perhaps the seeds of this love were sown by her mother on those early visits to various friends with villas in Italy or Germany or Switzerland. She would snatch at any opportunity. In 1897 she was invited to Germany for a short visit. At that time travel was not as quick or comfortable as it is now. Her friends were astonished that she should consider undertaking such a journey at all, when even a holiday in Torquay might have been thought unsuitable for a period of only ten days. It was a mark of her independence that she not only went, but that she undertook it so lightly, leaving her now precious garden with hardly any feeling of guilt at all.

In 1898 she decided to make a journey to Florence and towards the end of May, when she arrived, drove through the town with friends to the village of Arcetri, where she had rooms in a *pensione*. Mrs Earle had previously read some of the obvious books by well-known writers—George Eliot, Henry James, Mr Hare, Edmond de Goncourt and a collection of short essays by John Richard Green, author of *The Short History of England*. She was especially impressed by the writings of Bernard Berenson:

> For serious modern criticism of Italian painters and their work I have found nothing that has interested me so much and which seems to me so new as Mr Bernard Berenson's three little volumes—'The Venetian Painters of the Renaissance', 'The Florentine Painters of the Renaissance', and 'The Central Italian Painters of the Renaissance'.

She describes the pattern of her stay there.

> My first fortnight at Florence was spent in driving about seeing villas, wandering through the poderes, resting and drawing. For the amateur sketcher, what a mental struggle it is!—whether to give the time to drawing, or to see all one can. . . . The villas of the rich that I saw round Florence—and of course there are a great many which I did not see—are to be recognised by the fact that the vine and olive, lemon and pomegranate, fig and mulberry, are turned out for the planting of

laurels, deodars, and other conifers, rhododendrons and coarse-growing, unpruned shrubs. The beautiful old walls are often levelled to the ground, to make a slope of coarse-growing grass; or the wall formerly used for the trained and well-pruned vine is smothered with a mass of untended creepers. The newly planted Crimson Rambler is doing very well and making excessive growth. . . . My time was half over in Florence before I went to the picture galleries at all—not because I did not wish to go, but there was so much else. . . . Of course I re-read Romola; everyone does and ought as being in the atmosphere extraordinarily increases the enjoyment. . . . We went inside the large, bare Duomo, beautiful to me from its size, its majesty, its cool shades. . . . Just before I left I went to see the Riccardi Palace in the Via Cavour. The chapel I thought, as everyone does I suppose, one of the most interesting gems in Florence. . . .

Her books deal with a variety of subjects and her writing is almost of the quality of Mrs Jane Loudon's letters to a young wife entitled *The Lady's Country Companion*. She writes entertainingly of Berenson's art criticism, of dew-ponds and railway travel, of wild gardening and Michelangelo, of how to pack cut flowers and make good coffee, as well as how to grow echevarias and hepaticas, and how to be a good daughter.

Fascinating as all these subjects are it seems to me that there are one or two more important ones which stand out and for which we should be especially grateful.

Mrs Earle writes with sincerity and feeling but also with a high degree of understanding of many of the problems of girls growing up and how they can best deal with them. She writes quite superbly, without a trace of affectation or sentimentality, about love—either to those who are eagerly expecting it, or having experienced it need sometimes confidence, sometimes reassurance—but always she presents the value of real love as opposed to infatuation, and some of the profound difficulties that may be encountered. In other words, she gives us many pages of reflections and thoughts, sometimes illustrated by poetry from Mrs Browning and George Eliot, which tell us that love may come and, if so, should be welcomed, but that to keep it may mean more hard work than one would expect. For instance, about marrying for money she is unusually broad-minded:

I hear many people condemn the girl who 'marries for money'. . . . This seems to me unfair. Marriage and even love do not alter a nature; and if a girl knows herself, and is quite well aware that she cares most for the things that money alone can give her. . . .'

it is better to take money into account than try to struggle
through in poverty. She goes on: 'What is supremely idiotic . . . is
to imagine that when you marry a man for his money. . . . you are
to have as well all the joys of life which no money can buy.'

Mrs Earle was obviously not in favour of the 'roses round the
door' or 'Mr Right will come along' schools of thought. She was
much more likely to agree with Lucas Malet, whom she quotes:
'Do two human beings, especially of the opposite sex, ever fully
understand one another? Have any two ever done so, since the
world began?' She writes herself:

> Every girl after marriage should expect to be not understood, and to
> remember this part of the mysterious scheme of life which probably on
> the whole tends to good; at any rate it sharpens the interest of life. . . .

Her philosophy in these matters appealed to the young people
she knew well and resulted in a relationship with most of the girls
whereby she wrote of them as 'all my dear nieces, real and
adopted'. It will be remembered that Mrs Earle herself had three
sons; and this brings us to another subject which she emphasizes
throughout her writing—the fact that she came to gardening 'so
late in life'. Unlike Miss Jekyll or Eleanour Sinclair Rohde, Miss
Willmott or the Viscountess Wolseley, Mrs Earle was married,
with three sons who rightly claimed most of her attention for a
good many years. And so she does not take for granted the fact
that her readers know the preliminaries of gardening, or the Latin
names of the plants, or the conditions they will like in which to
flourish best. Instead she gives practical suggestions about
tackling these questions and one immediately feels that she is on
the side of the beginner. She writes:

> For those who have not got very good memories for the names of
> plants, I strongly recommend them, if they can draw, to make a little
> coloured sketch, however small, on the page of a gardening book next
> the name of the plant. This will be found a great help to the memory; I
> began gardening so late in life that I had to get all the help I could.

She describes particularly one method available today. 'I have
lately been visiting what I call intelligent gardens. . . .' With all
the wealth of selection provided by the National Trust and many
other gardens throughout the British Isles almost every existing
gardening query must be answered in one garden or another. 'Not
the least delightful part, in my opinion, of the growing knowledge

of gardening is the appreciative visiting of the gardens of others,' she writes:

> On first going into a garden one knows by instinct, as a hound scents the fox, if it is going to be interesting or not. One's eyes are sharp and a joyful glow of satisfaction comes over one on seeing something not by any means necessarily new, but unknown to oneself.

Still writing for those who are just beginning, she says: 'A notebook is a most important companion on gardening expeditions. . . . I write the date and name of the place, then jot down the names of plants and general observations' (probably the kind of soil, aspect of the garden, whether subject to draughts, overhanging trees, availability of water). This suggestion one might almost feel is too simple even to be mentioned, but such a notebook can be invaluable when thinking back over various garden visits. Without one, many small points may easily be forgotten over a period of time.

It seems to me that many of Mrs Earle's practical ideas may be used as stepping-stones leading from the difficult thoughts of future retirement to the satisfying and always changing situation of learning how to care for a garden. She was, after all, over sixty when she wrote her first book. One is not assailed by too much knowledge all at once, but led gently from one point of interest to another—from the pleasure to be attained from seeing the results of planning a flower border or growing the vegetables which appear on the dining table to the fruit enjoyed when ready for eating.

Other subjects studied by Mrs Earle, related closely to gardening, include the cooking of vegetables and the cutting of flowers for arrangement in the house. There are many useful receipts for the former in the text of *Pot-Pourri from a Surrey Garden* and various others in *More Pot-Pourri*.

The eighth edition of the former book has an appendix which contains one of the first articles on Japanese flower arrangement to be published in this country, which includes notes taken from Sir Josiah Conder's remarkable book, *The Flowers of Japan and the Art of Floral Arrangement*. From the point of view of flower arrangement this is a stepping-stone indeed. The appendix was written by Lady Constance Lytton, Mrs Earle's niece, whose approach was evidently in sympathy with the Japanese style and she must be regarded as a pioneer of the art in this country. She writes:

> Roughly speaking, the Japanese art of cut-flower decorations may be classified into three fundamental principles:
> 1. Not alone the flowers and leaves, but also the stems or branches should be considered as part of the design—in fact, it is the most important part.
> 2. The branches are not allowed to lean against the edge of the vase, as in the English manner, but must be firmly supported either by a wooden fixer fitted into the neck of the vase, or by coils of iron if open basin-shaped or flat-bottomed vessels are used, this giving to the stems the appearance of growth and self-support.
> 3. Only such flowers and trees as are easily obtainable should be used. Rarity is not considered a merit, and foreign or out-of-the-way plants are only permitted to be used by those who have a thorough knowledge of the nature of their growth, characteristics, etc. The flowers used should be in season, and the design of the decoration suited to its position in the room—i.e., if under a picture, on a shelf, in the centre of an alcove, etc.—as well as adapted to the vase which holds it.

Lady Constance Lytton concludes her appendix with these few lines:

> To the Japanese every flower has its meaning and associations, as well as every combination of flowers. . . . Without learning the grammar of their complicated flower-language, might we not nevertheless increase our artistic pleasures in flower arrangements by trying to give them a suitableness and a meaning which they have hitherto lacked? The old, long-established English fashion of massing together in a vase may still hold its own for certain kinds of flowers; but, so strong is the fascination of the Japanese principle, that, once it is adopted, it will probably assert its authority even amongst a bunch of primroses or violets.

In a footnote she states:

> Mr Conder's articles are beautifully illustrated with numerous plates of Japanese designs, reproduced from photographs; and in the text he sums up many of the most interesting points contained in his book. He does not suggest that the art of which he writes could be applied to the arrangement of flowers in England, but it is to be hoped that these articles may be republished in book form . . . as the great beauty of the illustrations would do more to spread the practice of the art amongst English people than any written theory about it.

Mrs Earle's scholarship must not be overlooked or under-estimated in the liveliness and fun of much of her writing and this emerges in some of her quotations and in the detailed descriptions of books on gardening. Among many others, she quotes from Henry James, George Eliot, Froude, Ruskin, Goethe, Balzac, Berenson and Elizabeth Barrett Browning. But these are only a few taken at random, which may perhaps give an indication of her literary taste. In the lists of gardening books it is evident that in many cases she is describing examples from her own bookshelves and her range of interests in this subject, especially in herbs, is unusually extensive and far-reaching. In *Pot-Pourri from a Surrey Garden* nearly the whole of the chapters for March and November are devoted to her garden-book lists and will be found on pages 49–69 and 207–48. It is, of course, much more than a booklist of publications giving a few dates and now and again a line or two from favourable reviews. Mrs Earle knows these books intimately, unless she states otherwise. For instance, when mentioning *The Gardener's Magazine*, edited by J. C. Loudon, she not only discusses it generally but gives us the fascinating life stories of the Loudons—how they met and married, and their work together.

There are many references to gardeners of her own time, especially to William Robinson, Canon Ellacombe, Joseph Paxton and Shirley Hibberd. Mr Robinson is, without doubt, the friend to whom she turns most frequently, but she also writes warmly and with appreciation of Gertrude Jekyll and Mr Wolley Dod. Dean Hole was also a good but critical friend: 'The Dean of Rochester wrote me a most kind letter reproaching me for saying I could not grow roses, and implying that the fault is mine. This I know to be true, but the fact is I am so fond of variety in flowers, as in all else, that I grudge too much room in the garden being given to roses. . . .' However, in a review for *Nineteenth Century* the kind rosarian from Rochester seems to like the 'sweet, spicy "Pot-Pourri"' and ends with advice to the reader (in italics) *'Buy it.'*

A friend of mine recalls learning to ride a bicycle on Mrs Earle's lawn and helping her to water the agapanthus growing in tubs on the terrace. She connects her, also, with making the most delicious salads and knowing the right use of herbs, particularly using chervil and tarragon.

Indoors there was the lightness everywhere of white paint, and she has never since seen books look more attractive in their different colours of binding as they did against Mrs Earle's white-painted bookshelves. In the hall there were majolica plates and flat porcelain dishes in wire supports against the white-painted wall.

The influence of William Morris was everywhere in this light, homely house and in the garden could be seen the result of studying the two foremost leaders who were breaking away from the formal garden—the natural gardening, in fact, of William Robinson and Gertrude Jekyll.

13 Mrs Theresa Earle with her grandson and dog

My friend also remembers a great profusion of alpine strawberries and especially the enjoyment of eating them. Mrs Earle has written at some length in both *Pot-Pourri from a Surrey Garden* and its successor about growing strawberries and much of what she has to say is written with so much enthusiasm and obvious pleasure that we who read it may well feel inclined to try out some of the ideas without delay. There are also the connections both with homeopathic medicine, the Linnaean cure for gout, and the especial beauty of the alpine varieties and their cultivation. Mrs Earle writes in explanation in June:

> For many years this fruit was poison to me; now it gives me pleasure to think that I live almost entirely upon it for some weeks in the summer, eating it three times a day, and very little else, according to the practice of Linnaeus, as quoted in March.

In March, she wrote of Linnaeus:

> He was born in 1707, was the son of a Swedish minister, and the grandson of a peasant . . . He married at twenty-seven, and his father-in-law seems to have put small faith in his botany, and advised him to apply himself more exclusively to the theoretical and practical side of physic. After his marriage he made money as a doctor in Stockholm, and it is not otherwise than interesting to know that when attacked with very severe gout at forty-three, and the doctors who attended him began to despair of his recovery, he cured himself by eating nothing but strawberries for a time. Afterwards he kept the gout entirely in check by taking a strawberry cure every summer.

It is only a short step from here to homeopathic treatment:

> I was considered a very delicate child, and was certainly a victim to the ordinary medical treatment of the day, curing by drugs. The relief came between the ages of twelve and fourteen, when I was put under a homeopath, and the same benefit occurred with me as with many others, from the stopping of all strong medicines; whether the infinitesimal doses did any good or not, I am unable to say, but I am inclined to believe that the benefit of homeopathy, like the water cure, was from allowing nature to have full play and do her best for herself; rest, fresh air, and a healthy life, above all no tonic nor alcohol nor stimulants of any kind. . . .

She was well known among her friends for her devotion to vegetarianism, and in the chapter intitled 'March', page 216 onward, of *More Pot-Pourri*, she gives detailed instructions, quantities required, receipts and general knowledge on the subject. She describes her own method of keeping fit as she gets older. 'But', she writes, 'if I am asked to account for this improvement, in one word, it is—Diet.'

Added to all this good taste and knowledge, there was also the courageous way of life of a woman alone: '. . . but to meet life with courage, both for oneself and others, that must be the real aim'. Then she adds realistically, though perhaps a little sadly: 'But courage is rather strength than happiness.'

William Robinson

1838–1935

> Those who look at sea or sky or wood see beauty that no art can show; but among the things made by man nothing is prettier than an English cottage garden.

WILLIAM ROBINSON
The English Flower Garden

William Robinson is known as the originator of the herbaceous border, a champion of the wild garden, the vanquisher of the Victorian formal garden, the enemy of bedding-out (especially as practised at the Royal Botanic Gardens, Kew, under Sir Joseph Hooker), and the author of *The English Flower Garden*.

When he was born in Ireland in July 1838, the formal garden in England was well on its way to success; when he died, at the age of ninety-seven, the picture was a very different one. 'But', wrote Mr Ralph Dutton in *'The English Garden'*, 'long before the close of Queen Victoria's reign better influences were at work under the leadership of William Robinson, who in the course of his long life, brought an overwhelming improvement in the standard of gardening, and, as the virtual introducer of the herbaceous border, may be said to have created a greater change in the English garden than any of his contemporaries.'

Little is known of Robinson's boyhood except that he started his gardening career on the estate of an Irish baronet, Sir Hunt Johnson-Walsh, at Ballykilcannan. He must have acquitted himself well because at twenty-one he was in charge of the large range of greenhouses. Then comes the story of his bitter quarrel, either with his employer or the head gardener—there seems to be some doubt about the exact details. The fact emerges that on a cold winter night the fires for heating the greenhouses were either drawn out or allowed to die out, and some accounts say that the windows were opened wide. Meanwhile Robinson was on his way on foot to Dublin, where he arrived early the next morning.

These greenhouses were full of tender plants, most of them raised from seeds and cuttings, representing months of loving care and attention and much hard work. If, as he was striding along by the banks of the Liffey, he had suddenly thought of the unstoked fires and the resulting drop in temperature, it would have been too late to turn round and go back again to repair the damage. It does not seem credible that a man who loved plants as Robinson loved them would have killed—in fact, murdered—them at a stroke, however hot his temper, any more than a mother would kill her child in anger.

However, whatever the truth of the matter, on his arrival in Dublin he went at once to see Dr David Moore, head of the Botanical Garden at Glasnevin, who was an old family friend, and poured out his story and asked for advice. Dr Moore must have felt that there was some justice on Robinson's side as he gave him an introduction to the Curator of the Royal Botanic Garden Society in London. He was given work and soon became a foreman again, but for obvious reasons he was not put in charge of the glasshouses. Instead he was given the hardy herbaceous plants to care for, which included wild flowers found in England.

This beginning to his career obviously influenced his later work considerably. For ever afterwards he disliked greenhouses—he abolished all the greenhouses from his home at Gravetye—and one of his most valuable books was called *The Wild Garden*.

Writing years later in the Introduction to *The English Flower Garden* of this period in his life, he says:

I came to London just when the Royal Horticultural Society's garden at Kensington was being laid out, a series of elaborate patterns set at different levels, and the Crystal Palace, in its glory, was described by the Press of the day to be the most wonderful instance of modern gardening—water-temples, water-paths, vast stone basins and all the theatrical gardening of Versailles reproduced in Surrey.

The flower garden planting was made up of a few kinds of flowers which people were proud to put out in thousands and tens of thousands, and with these patterns, more or less elaborate, were carried out in every garden save the very poorest cottage garden. It was not easy to get away from all this false and hideous 'art', but I was then in the Botanic Gardens, Regent's Park, where there was at that time a small garden of British plants, which had to be kept up, and this led me into the varied country round London, from the orchid-flecked meadows of Bucks to the tumbled down undercliffs of the Essex coast, untroubled by plough, and so began to get an idea (which should be taught to every boy at school) that there was (for gardens even) much beauty in our native flowers and trees. . . . And so I began to see clearly that the common way was a great error and the greatest obstacle to true gardening or artistic effects of any kind in the flower-garden or home landscape and then made up my mind to fight the thing out in any way open to me, and with this view began writing in *The Field* and other rural papers, and then came my own books. . . .

Meanwhile the hard-working young Irishman was being noticed by more experienced members of the gardening world. He was selected to represent the nursery-garden firm of Veitch at the 1867 Paris Exhibition and also became horticultural correspondent for *The Times*.

In 1868 Robinson published his first book, *Gleanings from French Gardens*, a signed copy of which he presented to Dean Hole, inscribed 'May 18th'. As he explains in the Preface: 'Some of the matters treated of in this book have lately been the subjects of much discussion in *The Times*. . . . I went to France in January, 1867, with a view to study the horticulture of the country so far as possible while continuing my connection with the horticultural press. . . .' The book is full of appreciation for various methods of French gardening (even, in the parks, in some cases for bedding-out) and also for fruit-growing, with special reference to pears. For the Parc Monceau he had a particular comment to make relating to an old friend: 'Dr Moore, of Glasnevin, once told me that he considered this in its full dress the most successful example of flower-gardening he had ever seen, and therefore it may be well if we look at it in that state.'

The garden was laid out in 1778 supposedly as an 'English garden', but has since been taken over and developed by the Municipality of Paris who 'have converted it into a charming garden'. Robinson then goes on in his blunt manner: 'The system of planting adopted here as well as in other gardens of the city is often striking, often beautiful, and not unfrequently bad.'

After further visits to Paris, whence he travelled to other gardens in France, and a journey into Italy via the Swiss Alps, Robinson paid his first visit to the United States in the autumn of 1870.

His interest in America was not entirely focused on seeing gardens, as it had been in France and Italy, but rather concentrated on an energetic hunting for new trees and shrubs and for meeting the American people. Certain American gardens he visited and commented on—George Washington's old home at Mount Vernon being one of them—but it was the noble trees and flowering shrubs found on mountain slopes which meant most to him and he even asserted that days spent one autumn in the forest lands of America were 'among the happiest one could desire'.

14 *A variety of plants in the Parc Monceau, Paris, the layout of which was praised by William Robinson*

It was in this same year—1870—that *The Wild Garden* was published, following on *Alpine Flowers for English Gardens.* The first edition of the former of these two books contains in Part IV an enchanting essay entitled 'The Garden of British Wild Flowers'. For some reason this was not included in later editions, which deprives those not fortunate enough to possess or have access to the first edition of some of his best writing. With the aid of a quotation from Byron he emphasises in almost lyrical writing the importance of planting the white water-lily in small groups:

> The queenly white Water-lily, not thickly planted, but a single specimen or group here and there. It is most effective when one or a few good plants are seen alone on the water; then the flowers and leaves have full room to develop and float right regally; but when a dense crowd of water-lilies are seen together, they are usually poorly developed, and crowd each other out. The effect is never half so beautiful as when—
>
> > 'Some scatter'd water-lily sails
> > Down where the shallower wave still tells its bubbling tales.'
>
> See how the author of 'Childe Harold' chances inadvertently to note the beauty of the Water-lily when isolated, compared to what it is when choked together in a river bed or garden water.

Again, depending here on his own direct style, he discusses another water plant:

> Not rare—growing, in fact, in nearly all districts of Britain—but exquisitely beautiful and singular is the Buckbean or Marsh Trefoil, with its flowers elegantly and singularly fringed on the inside with white filaments, and the round unopened buds, polished on the top with a rosy red like that of an apple blossom. In early summer when seen trailing on the soft ground near the margin of a stream, this plant is very beautiful, and should be grown in abundance in every piece of ornamental water. It will grow in a bog or any moist place, or by the margin of any water.

So far the aggressive and rather feverish approach of some of his later writing is not apparent. It is his genuine love of naturally growing plants, shrubs and trees which shines through the written word. In 1871 he founded his own gardening journal and the Revd Reynolds Hole describes helping him to choose a title for it:

> . . . I sat with my friend, William Robinson, under a tree in the Regent's Park, and suggested *The Garden* as a title for the newspaper which he proposed to publish, and which has been so powerful in its advocacy of pure horticulture of the natural, or English, school, free from rigid formalities, meretricious ornaments, gypsum, powdered bricks, cockle-shells and bottle-ends.

This description by Dean Hole enumerates the gardening aims of William Robinson as clearly as one could wish. He even here attributes the 'natural' type of garden to the 'English' school and describes it as being 'free from rigid formalities' and so on. It is a measured declaration of a way of gardening under the leadership of the author of *The Wild Garden*.

15 William Robinson, who travelled widely to look at other gardens, and founded the journal, The Garden

The first issue of *The Garden* was published in November and soon the contributors included many well-known gardening names: Dean Hole was among these as also Canon Ellacombe, James Britten (later to become Keeper of the Department of Botany at the British Museum), Oliver Wendell Holmes and Ruskin. There is little doubt that Robinson had read a good deal of Ruskin's work and indeed his own writing shows its influence from time to time. The Ruskin lectures which were received with such a storm of protest when published in the *Cornhill Magazine* under Mr Thackeray's editorship were later put together and known as *Unto This Last*. Sir Oliver Lodge, in his Introduction to a later edition of these essays, writes:

In all our manufactures and commercial activity at present we are blindly seeking, what? It is a question somewhat hard to answer. We seem to expend energy by instinct, rather than by reason, and to be satisfied with much exertion without great regard being paid to the direction in which it is being expended. Upon all this blind and ant-like activity Mr Ruskin flashes the light of his analysis and shows that the true wealth of a nation may depend in the long run upon quite other activities. . . . The artificial ugliness of portions of England, after visions of Switzerland and Italy, the strange ambition of English leaders to convert their own garden in a manufacturing desert, the clear and strong perception of the truth that after all the supply of food and necessities must come out of the land, lead him to speak thus: 'All England may, if it so chooses, become one manufacturing town; and Englishmen sacrificing themselves to the good of general humanity, may live diminished lives in the midst of noise . . .' but fortunately the world cannot support its population by manufacture alone. Wherefore he rejoices to think . . . 'So long as men live by bread the faraway valleys must laugh as they are covered with the gold of God, and the shouts of His happy multitudes ring round the wine-press and the well.'

It was the heart-felt cry of an evangelist against the horrors of the industrial revolution and the ravages of the countryside, and when William Robinson later quotes Ruskin in *The English Flower Garden* he does so to support his own argument that as men have to grow accustomed to life in cities, architecture should restrain itself wherever possible to the confines of necessity and not 'carry the dead lines of the builder into the garden'.

The Garden was not a great financial success but it did help to establish Robinson more firmly in the world of journalism and provided a useful platform from which he could expound his ideas unhindered. His selection of authors and articles was often of general interest. For instance, an article by Ruskin in the issue dated 3 February 1872 entitled 'North and South' gave the physical characteristics of countries, birds and animals and in 1879 he had an article by William Morris on 'The Art of the Future'. This also meant that his circle of friends was enlarged and included Edward Woodall of Scarborough, Mr Wolley Dod, and Miss Gertrude Jekyll. In 1879 he launched another journal *Gardening Illustrated* written largely for the wealthy dwellers of suburbia. This was so successful that he was able to invest money in London house property.

His next, and perhaps most important, publication came in November 1883—*The English Flower Garden, Design and*

Arrangement shown by existing examples of Gardens in Great Britain and Ireland followed by a Description of the best Plants for the Open-air Garden and their Culture. In the introduction he writes:

> *The English Flower Garden* consists of two parts: the first dealing with the question of design—the aim being to make each place at various seasons an epitome of the great garden of the world itself. I hope to prove that the true way to happiest design is not to have any stereotyped style for all flower gardens, but that the best kind of garden grows out of the situation, as the primrose grows out of a cool bank.
>
> The second part includes most of the plants, hardy and half-hardy, for our flower gardens, and it is illustrated with a view to show the beauty of many of the plants, as few know the many flowers worth a place in our open-air gardens, and it is useless to discuss arrangement if the beauty of the flowers is hidden from us. . . . At present, too often there is no art, no good grouping, no garden pictures, no variety—little but repetitions of ugly patterns. The choke-muddle shrubbery, in which the shrubs kill each other, shows betimes a few ill-grown plants, and has wide patches of bare earth in summer, over which pretty green things might crowd. Yet the smallest garden may be a picture, and not only may we have much more variety in any one garden, but, if we give up imitating each other, may enjoy charming contrasts between gardens.

For this second half of the book he acknowledges the use of articles taken from *The Garden* and also the help of many contributors who have written on specialist subjects. Among these contributors are the Revd C. Wolley Dod, the Revd H. D'Ombrain, Canon Ellacombe and the Dean of Rochester (Canon Hole), four clerical gardeners of the time, representatives of many other dignitaries of the Church with good rectory or vicarage gardens behind them. Another contributor was, of course, Miss Jekyll, and except for the first few paragraphs the chapter on 'Colour in the Flower Garden' is all her work. Others include her friends, Miss Ellen Willmott, Mr Edward Woodall and Mr G. F. Wilson, a representative of France, M. Maurice de Vilmorin, and a painter of flowers much admired by William Robinson (he had a collection of his flower pictures at Gravetye), Mr H. G. Moon.

Miles Hadfield, in *Pioneers in Gardening*, describes it as 'a great work . . . the true successor to the world by Miller and Loudon'. It went into many editions and even today, when most sizeable bookshops now devote a complete stand to gardening literature, it emerges from among so much contemporary material as one of the most valuable of all garden textbooks.

Much has been said and written about the worth of this book—the standard of writing, the comprehensive knowledge of shrubs, plants, and other matters, but one of the aspects which seems to me of special interest is William Robinson's opinion of the value of the cottage garden. He is connected frequently with 'wild' gardening, with breaking down the barriers of formal planned gardens and the military lines of bedding-out, with planting for wide herbaceous borders, with half-hardy plants for the open flower bed, with annuals and biennials, with shrubs, trees, alpines, roses, water gardens, bog gardens and many others, but his love of a cottage garden sometimes goes unnoticed. Perhaps anyone who writes so fully of a garden like Shrublands, near Ipswich in Suffolk, where there was plenty of work for forty gardeners, might not be expected to have much use for the roadside strip of mixed flowers sometimes interplanted with vegetables. Built in 1740 with English classical gardens laid out by Sir Charles Barry and additions by William Robinson, Shrublands is now a well-known health clinic.

In *The English Flower Garden* he has written of his love for such gardens and of his appreciation for their planting. The text is well illustrated by cottages from Somerset, Kent, Surrey and elsewhere. Like Miss Jekyll, who also designed big gardens but ackowledged her great debt to the cottage garden, Robinson points out many useful lessons to be learnt, some of them equally applicable to the large estate of many acres. 'One lesson of these little gardens, that are so pretty, is that one can get good effects from simple materials.'

Although William Robinson was now at a stage in his life when financial reward was no longer something remote, something to be dreamt about and hoped for, but a firm reality, his head was not turned. He could still appreciate the true values in his work. One success led to another—his money brought him greater financial security—and in 1884 he was in a position to be able to buy the Elizabethan manor of Gravetye near East Grinstead in Sussex, together with about two hundred acres of rich pasture and woodland.

This was the beginning of a new phase in William Robinson's life. He was forty-six years of age and had come a long way since his all-night walk from Stradbally to Dublin when he was a young, hot-headed gardening apprentice of twenty-one. In a letter to his wife, dated 12 September 1889, Dean Hole wrote describing a visit to the house:

> Dearest Own
> Delightful day with Robinson at Gravetye Manor yesterday, and you must take Isa to see it, before the beauty of the garden is gone. The only drawback is the tedious tardy journey by rail, and you must not arrange to give only one day to the visit: in fact, it would not be practicable. You must go from London and return for the night. Victoria is the station and the Hotel Windsor might be your place for sleep.
> Think of Robinson, the working gardener, Lord of the manor of Gravetye and 700 acres of land!
> The house is Elizabethan, of grey stone, as pretty and comfortable a home as man could desire, surrounded by woods, green fields, hills, slopes, and distant views, with 7 acres of lake. The stables cost £2000. I asked him if he had any horses and his reply was '30'. He does not live in the Manor House, at present unfurnished, but in a smaller house adjoining. The plan is of course in process of formation and will ultimately be, on a small scale, one of the most attractive in the land.
> I brought back a huge bouquet of tea roses. . . .

This letter gives us some interesting points of information about Gravetye Manor and bears out the descriptions of rebuilding of fireplaces, and other major alterations which necessitated Robinson's living in a smaller house on the estate while all these were going on. It gives us some idea of the lay-out of the grounds, the beauty of the garden and, coming from Dean Hole, one might expect mention of the roses.

Gravetye Manor is well known as an Elizabethan manor house, and a member of the Culpeper family must have married one of the first owners, according to a record entitled 'The Sussex Colepepers', in vol. 48 of the *Sussex Archeological Collections*, dated 1905:

> Catherine (Culpeper), baptized at Ardingly 3rd July, 1597; married there 24th February, 1619, Richard Infield, of Gravety, Westhothly. She died without issue in 1623 and was buried at Westhothly. Her husband died the following year, when Gravetye came to his brother James, who also died without issue in 1633.

The rebuilding of the fireplaces, to Robinson's own design, took place on account of his fanatical resistance to the use of coal. He wrote two books on the subject of wood fires. He only burnt wood, even for cooking, and so the use of the fireplace must have reverted to the days when they were first built—when the Culpepers and the Infields were domiciled there. He was ardently supported in this passion for burning wood by Miss Jekyll, who wrote a chapter in her book *Old English Household Life* on 'The Evolution of the Fireplace' in which she discussed the type of fireplace originally built to burn wood, peat or turf, according to its locality.

There seems to be some disparity with regard to the number of acres of woodland which went with the purchase of Gravetye, but whatever their acreage it is, without any doubt, to these woods and fields that William Robinson gave his heart.

His diary of planting is full of valuable information. It is published under the title *Gravetye Manor or Twenty Years of the Work Round an Old Manor House*. It makes fascinating reading as the following few excerpts show:

1885 All the Wellingtonias were cut down as being at once ugly and unsuited to the climate . . . also many spruce, which rarely ever does well in this part of England.

1888 Our friend, Mr Marnock, the landscape gardener, thought the best thing to do was to make most of the fields into a park.

1891 Planted on July 3 some of my favourite Apennine Anemone (windflower) at the bases of the oaktrees in the grove of these between the house and the moat.

1892 Five years ago planted a moist slope in new drive in Warren's Wood with the Cardinal Willow and ever since it has been a pleasure to see the young trees.

1892 This beautiful plant (winter jasmine) is so well known that it occurs in many cottage gardens, facing our winter with its delicate buds and flowers. We have not enough of it, and it is not placed in sufficient variety of situation so that we might secure successive bloom. If we put it around the house it ought to be in different aspects and in some quantity so that if it catches the sun after a sharp frost on the one side of the house it would escape on the other.

1894 Planted many almonds. . . .

1897–8 Resolved to do away with the gravel walks here (west garden) and pave walk round the garden with stone, using old London York stone used for paving. . . . Laid by John Fell in sand. Formed also a paved bed here on which to place plants in tubs out for summer, if we can get a good set of fragrant plants for this purpose (plants that cannot be grown out of doors in the district). In the crevices of the stone-paving planted very dwarf rock plants: thymes, the fairy mint, creeping speedwell, tufted harebell and like plants. Stone pathways in this and the little front garden completed last week in July . . .

1899 Plants (rhododendrons on own roots) from Dickson's Nurseries at Chester, very good ones, and from a loamy (not peaty) soil.

1900–1 Summerhouse in SW corner of west garden—built this from design by Mr Ernest George: all in oak.

1904–5 Planted over 50,000 narcissus, of various sorts in the pasture, woods and orchard, the last planted late in March.

These excerpts, taken at random, illustrate not only the vast range of interest associated with the purchase of Gravetye Manor but Robinson's love of simple plants and wild gardening, of the effect in woodland of young willows furnishing 'a moist slope' or of banks of pure white narcissus—some of them planted 'along the margin of the Lower Lake', and others in 'the pasture, woods and orchard'. His diary is not littered with entries of rare and unobtainable plants and he cut down the wellingtonias because they were 'unsuited to the climate'. The emphasis is on plants and trees which do 'well in this part of England' and one of the most decorative winter effects round the house is to be achieved by plantings 'in some quantity' of the cottage garden climber, winter jasmine.

A further entry gives yet another line of interest—his love of painting. In the year 1895 there appears: 'Four different landscape painters painted our water-lily pond in the summer and autumn of 1895, viz. Mark Fisher, Alfred Parsons, H. A. Olivier and H. G. Moon.' There is further confirmation of paintings being commissioned in the notice of an exhibition given in *The Times* of 14 November 1892:

At the Stephen Gooden's gallery, 57, Pall Mall, there is on view for a short time a very charming little collection of cabinet pictures by two artists, Mr W. E. Norton and Mr H. G. Moon, who were settled for the summer of 1891 at Gravetye Manor, Sussex, and have painted the house, the garden, and the neighbouring woods and fields in every aspect and under every condition of sun and shade. Mr Norton is an American trained in Paris, Mr Moon is English, but there is enough likeness between their methods and points of view to make the Collection pleasantly harmonious. . . .

His great friend from among these various artists was, perhaps, Mr H. G. Moon and it is his collection of paintings which is chiefly remembered today among those who can recall the house in the last years of Robinson's life. But his own mention in his writings of Corot indicates his admiration for this painter and he is reputed to have possessed at least two of his pictures. In *The Garden Beautiful*, published in the same year as Miss Jekyll's *Colour in the Flower Garden*, he writes:

Great landscape painters like Crome, Corot and Turner seek not things only because natural, but also because beautiful; selecting views and waiting for the light that suits the chosen subject best, they give us pictures, working always from faithful study of nature and from stores of knowledge gathered from her; that also is the only true path for the gardener, all true art being based on her eternal laws.

Again, writing of the term 'artistic', he gives the following illustration:

> As I use the word 'artistic' in a book on the flower garden, it may be well to say that it is used to mean right and true in relation to all the conditions of the case, and the necessary limitations of all human arts. A lovely Greek coin, a bit of canvas painted by Corot with the morning light on it, a block of stone hewn into the shape of a dying gladiator, the white mountain rocks built into a Parthenon—these are all examples of human art, every one of which can only be fairly judged with due regard to what is possible in the material of each— . . . if we are happy enough to find a garden so true and right in its results as to form a picture that an artist would be charmed to study, we may call it an artistic garden, as a short way of saying that it is about as good as it may be, taking everything into account.

The mention of Turner may have stemmed from his appreciation of Ruskin, but it must be admitted that his gardening ideas, in many ways like those of Miss Jekyll—there is, for instance, frequent reference to making 'a garden picture' which is a phrase she constantly uses—were influenced to no small extent by his feeling for painting and his knowledge of art.

There is little difficulty in understanding his affinity with Ruskin. Robinson bought, as soon as he could afford it, an old manor house set among fields and woodland at some distance from means of communication with the outside world. He could not possibly have heard any passing traffic from his house and there was no railway line within miles of the drive gates. He ensured that the air was unpolluted by chimney smoke from coke or coal by his enthusiasm for long fires and his burning of wood under all circumstances.

When Ruskin writes in *Praeterita* of 'the grotesque conditions of variously typhoid or smoke-dried London life' and one compares this life with his description of a visit to Cumberland:

> The inn at Coniston was then actually at the upper end of the lake, the road from Ambleside to the village passing just between it and the water: and the view of the long reach of lake, with its softly wooded lateral hills. . . . Lowood Inn also was then little more than a country

cottage—and Ambleside a rural village; and the absolute peace and bliss which any one who cared for grassy hills and for sweet waters might find at every footstep. . . .

his reaction stands out exactly as does that of Robinson. Again, Ruskin writes of his regret in relation to Carlyle's Chelsea home:

I have felt bitter remorse that I did not make Carlyle free of the garden, and his horse of the stables, whether we were at home or not; for the fresh air, and bright view of the Norwood hills were entirely grateful and healing to him, when the little back garden at Cheyne Row was too hot, or the neighbourhood of it too noisy, for his comfort.

Before we follow Robinson's diary of planting at Gravetye farther into the twentieth century, mention must be made of the battle of the printed word which took place when *The Formal Garden* by Reginald Blomfield was published, and the reply which came smartly back from William Robinson in *Garden Design*, published 1892. In *Garden Design* and in the first two chapters of *The Garden Beautiful* (published 1907) there are probably the most intense examples of Robinson's invective against the formal garden and of bedding-out. Unfortunately this period of his work seems to be one that catches the eye of posterity and is not always alleviated by the many other books that he wrote, full of valuable knowledge and experience, often untouched by bitterness.

The battle was between formal and informal gardening, between bedding-out plants and hardy perennials, between the architect and the landscape painter. But in so much of their writing and in so many of their ideas the two authors were (unwillingly) in agreement.

Published from *The Garden* office (37 Southampton Street, Covent Garden) in 1882 was a different venture entitled *God's Acre Beautiful or The Cemeteries of the Future*. Like Baroness Burdett-Coutts with her interest in open spaces and especially in children's playgrounds, William Robinson was concerned about the state of urban churchyards, overcrowded, without dignity or beauty, lacking often in even rudimentary hygiene. This is a tastefully designed publication, with delightful illustrations in sepia, many of them showing early Greek and Roman urns. One full page consists of 'marble, porphyry and terra-cotta cinerary urns and chests' drawn from specimens in the British Museum.

In his anxiety to win over an unwilling populace to the idea of cremation, Robinson did not hesitate to give unsavoury details of various happenings in connection with certain graveyeards in crowded cities. He pointed out that perhaps two generations might be allowed to rest peacefully and then, when there were few relations left who would visit or remember their family graves, the site might be sold to a contractor. One specific example was when the remains from a disused cemetery in the west-central district of London were spread over a couple of acres of Kensington Gardens.

The answer was a 'Permanent and Beautiful Cemetery' made possible with urn-burial.

> In graveyards of the size of the present overcrowded London ones, urn-burial could be carried on for hundreds of years without the slightest offence to the living. By the common consent of mankind 'God's Acre' is most fittingly arranged as a garden. . . . The Cemetery of the future must not only be a garden in the best sense of the word, but the most beautiful and best cared-for of all gardens.

The illustrations show some of the urns of early Greek and Roman design. Something of the same kind could be incorporated into what would be, in effect, a natural garden, with stretches of grass and planting of trees. The whole design would ensure an atmosphere of peace and restfulness which would also be economical in upkeep. A vista of grass, the dignity of well-chosen trees—these would take the place of headstones, toppling or sloping as the years go by, of untidy grass verges which, almost impossible to cut owing to protruding stonework, or the sadness of floral tributes perished and dishevelled.

Like Dean Hole, he had always been an advocate of grass and the Dean quotes him in *Our Gardens*: '"The Lawn," writes Mr Robinson, "is the heart of the garden, and the happiest thing that is in it."' The Dean goes on: 'Flowers may come and leaves may go, the lawn goes on for ever. It refreshes the spirit through the eye, which never tires.' When William Robinson looked at the depressing sights of some of the London cemeteries of the period, his imagination must have conjured up the smooth and dignified effect of a stretch of grass.

When his own obituary notice was inserted in *The Times*, William Robinson was one of only three among a long list whose funeral service was announced as being followed by cremation.

The Garden Beautiful, in spite of its title, deals chiefly with trees. In some ways it might be regarded as a lightweight successor to Loudon's *Arboretum*, and as a forerunner of Selby's

British Forest Trees, except that Robinson deals with many other than British trees—Swiss pines, Norway spruce, summer-leafing trees of the American woods, and so on. He has a store of information to impart, not only in the knowledge of trees, but in methods of planting, cultivation and planting the various types of tree suitable for different locations—the seaside, mountain slopes, waterside planting, national and public parks. The bitterness and aggressiveness of the first two chapters melt almost imperceptibly as he becomes engrossed in his subject. He was, like William Morris, Ruskin, Madame Bodichon and Miss Jekyll, ahead of his time, and he felt for the English countryside and for its gardens with the fervour of an Old Testament prophet. His chapter on national and public parks could have come direct from the Department of the Environment of today:

> One of the greatest gains from national parks would be in the opportunity they might afford for planting our native trees in bold masses and forests. . . . In all the more fertile parts and by streams and in valleys these trees would serve the two purposes of showing their natural form and values and of giving a home to woodland creatures.

The prevalent craze in trees at the turn of the century was for the *Wellingtonia gigantea* and the *Araucaria imbricata* (the monkey puzzle tree). They were solid status symbols, as videotapes and freezers are today. That Robinson had all the wellingtonias at Gravetye down in 1885 says much for his complete independence of any social network. He had indeed become Lord of the Manor of Gravetye but did not, on this account, become subservient to any contemporary craze or fashion.

He does not, however, hold his fire in the chapter headed 'English Names for Trees'. The unnecessary use of Latin names is a constant irritant throughout his life and here he writes with vigour on the subject with regard to trees:

> A good English name should have precedence of all others for general use. . . . An Englishman speaking to English people should be able to find in his own tongue names for all things to which he needs to refer. There is no forest tree of Europe, Asia or America for which a good English name might not be used, and, once generally adopted, we should not then care so much what each succeeding botanist might do towards inventing new Latin names or hunting up old ones.

Most people, except perhaps botanists, would agree with this attitude. As Miss Mitford wrote: 'One is never thoroughly sociable with flowers till they are naturalised, as it were, christened, provided with decent, homely, well-wearing English names.'

It has been suggested that this dislike of Latin plant names was stimulated by Ruskin's ideas on the subject, and it would be difficult to decide how much Robinson was influenced by him. He is known to have had great admiration for *Proserpina*, and it was here that Ruskin gave his explanation of interpreting Latin and Greek flower names for the benefit of his 'young English readers'.

Whatever Robinson's feelings for Ruskin's doctrine, they must have depended on the reading of his lectures or essays and not on personal contact, according to a mention of him in the book on clematis planted at Gravetye (entitled *The Virgin's Bower, Clematis, Climbing Kinds and Their Culture at Gravetye Manor*):

> The idea that we injure a tree by placing on it a more fragile one is wrong and against all Nature's ways. . . . I have many strong vines put on apple trees, and people say to me 'What about the Apple?' That always reminds me of a saying of John Ruskin, the only time I had the pleasure of talking to him, when it was a question of the beauty of the orchard in spring or fall, and he said, 'Give me the flower and save me the stomach ache.'

The Virgin's Bower is one of the most delightful of all Robinson's publications. His opening sentence in the Preface gives some indication of the general tone:

> I have had so much pleasure from the cultivation of these lovely plants that I venture to print a little book on the subject, as one sees even large gardens desolate so far as they are concerned. . . . A garden is of all things in the world the place to select. In botany all plants are of equal value; but in gardens we must choose or suffer. If we go in for all kinds, good or bad, we end in a museum or a botanical garden; but that rarely gives us beauty. Therefore I omit all graceless kinds and those that do not climb.

The descriptions of the various types of clematis are sketched in with a delicate touch and some are of special interest on account of the mention of gardening friends, who have grown them, or of conditions where the plants flourish. For instance:

> *The Harebell Virgin's Bower*. Clematis Campaniflora. I love this fragile kind (pale purple), which grows freely here. A blue form I have failed hitherto to get and have seen it only in Mr Wilson's garden at Weybridge.
> *The Noble Virgin's Bower*. C. lanuginosa. It was sent to us by Robert Fortune. It flourishes in the North of China on the Chekiang

Mountains, near Ningpo, on the hillside, in light and rocky soil. . . .
Siebold's Virgin's Bower. C. florida. Its first introduction was in 1829
. . . to the Botanic garden at Ghent. . . . I have only seen this kind well
grown in Miss Willmott's garden at Warley, who writes: 'One
pecularity of C. Sieboldi is that about a third of the flowers are
absolutely quite double. There is the outer circle of bracts filled in with
a coronalike centre. I believe my plant is the only one in cultivation in
England. I counted 500 flowers and seemed only to have some way in
reckoning up the total.'

Robinson, with his love of simple flowers, here expounds his
views on the question of having double or single flowering plants.
The heading is 'Double Varieties':

I never plant one if I know it. The wondrous grace of buds and flowers
are lost by doubling. And as to colour, by turning the flower into a
mop we lose the divinest colour of all the flowers happy in our
northern air.

It is not surprising, having read *The Virgin's Bower*, to discover
that in *The English Flower Garden* William Robinson devotes the
best part of nine pages to clematis. His affection for this flower was
almost in the same class as the love of Dean Hole for the rose.

Shortly after this small, charming book on clematis, came a
magnificent production, *Home Landscapes*, published by John
Murray, 1914. The rapidity with which one large chunk of work
followed another is even more difficult to comprehend when it is
remembered that for the last thirty years of his life he was a cripple
confined almost all of the time to a wheelchair. When one
consideres the hard facts which went into his books and the
research and checking this must all have meant, it is astonishing to
realize his achievements.

Certainly *Home Landscapes* is largely composed of splendid
photographic reproductions, but these are accompanied by text,
and the whole work must have meant a great deal of patient
application. Whereas the earlier book on Gravetye gave detailed
day-by-day plantings, this volume presents a broader canvas.

By way of comparison he quotes from an article by Miss March-
Phillips on Italian gardens, in which she says that an Italian
garden-maker's last consideration would be to prepare space for
growing flowers and fruit. This would have seemed like choosing
his curtains and carpets before anything else if he was constructing
a house. 'The garden was to be *built*; first, and before all, a
framework was to be made. . . .'

This mention of 'framework' sends Robinson's thoughts off into
the realms of painting and he compares this idea with producing
'the frame before the picture! We have examples of this in our own
Academy already', he goes on, 'But that was not the way of
Rembrandt or Hobbema, or our own Constable! . . . It is the very
opposite way we must follow to win their grace and charm, as we
see in our day. Take the rock garden at Warley Place (Miss
Wilmott's garden), the Vale garden at Wakehurst. . . .' And
then, perhaps feeling that he may have been over-enthusiastic to
the exclusion of everyone else, he admits that these examples are
not the only kind of good garden, but allowing for that, maintains
that they are 'by far the most beautiful, and in the best sense
artistic. . . .'

Bearing out his theme of trying to establish 'the value and the
meaning of landscape gardening', many of the illustrations show
vistas rather than flower beds, geological features rather than
borders, tree plantings rather than rock gardens. An instance of
this is shown in plate xxix, 'The Rise of the Medway'. The caption
reads: 'Several streams arising in pools and woods near meet in
Mill Place Farm and, united near the bridge shown, start on their
way to the Medway. Such streams are a gain in the landscape and
often graced by oak and ash. . . .'

I think it would be fair to say that William Robinson shows in
his writings an almost unequalled concern and love for the English
countryside. He was a Preservationist of the first order and would,
one feels sure, have been actively on the doorstep of the
Department of the Environment, or leading the way for National
Parks to ensure the wild life preserves, if he had been alive today.
Where others might be satisfied by expressing their views, he
would have taken action.

Of his personal life it is not so easy to determine a complete
picture. He never married, although he had women friends. He
knew Ellen Willmott socially as well as through gardening
interests and not only met her at lunch as a visitor to the
Wolseleys but sometimes visited a flower show with her. 'I had no
idea of seeing the Chelsea Show, but Miss Willmott has begged of
me to go and I am going tomorrow', he writes in May 1931 to
Lady Moore. He was first taken to Miss Jekyll's Munstead
garden by Dean Hole, but although visits were frequent for the
first fifteen years or so of their friendship, they were intermittent

after that for a long period of time. Whether this was because of disagreement or something deeper one may only conjecture. It was partly due to Mr Herbert Cowley, the well-known plant collector, that they came together again and although Robinson at the age of ninety-four was terribly crippled, he travelled thirty miles by road in the month of December to be present at her funeral.

Perhaps his housekeeper had the answer when she showed Frances Wolseley (chapter eleven) and her mother round the house after their first visit to the Gravetye garden. After seeing so many lovely things in such a setting as this old manor house—'we looked with admiration at the flower paintings by Fantin Latour that hung upon the panelled walls. There were also Corots . . . and the flower paintings by Moon. . . .' Lady Wolseley asked rather hesitantly if there was a Mrs William Robinson. The housekeeper sternly replied: 'Mr William Robinson is not married. If he did so, the lady would have to be as lovely as a flower.'

There were many visitors to Gravetye, among them Robert Marnock who had been Curator of the Royal Botanic Society's garden, where Robinson had his first job in England. Their friendship lasted until Marnock's death, in 1889, and it was Marnock who advised Robinson in the early days of the developments at Gravetye. (There is a mention of his advice on making some of the fields into a park in 1888.) E. A. Bowles was another visitor (although the two men did not always see eye to eye) and Dean Hole wrote of his appreciation of the Gravetye Manor garden in almost lyrical terms. He had been a staunch friend for many years, as also were the Moores of Glasnevin.

As Robinson grew older he is reported to have become full of inconsistencies. When he rode round his estate the workmen never knew whether they would get a rise or be dismissed. He had been a heavy smoker and enjoyed good wine and suddenly one night took all the drink out into the garden and threw the bottles down a well—and burnt his pipes. It is also said that after this he rather unkindly served wine for his visitors and offered them cigarettes, even provided them with ashtrays, but that if any-one should be foolish enough to accept this part of his hospitality they would receive a notice on their breakfast tray the next morning giving them the time of the next convenient train to London.

However this may be, he still had many friends to visit him, some of them lifelong, and the three people who were closest to him on account of his physical disability all stayed with him over a long period of time. Annie, the parlourmaid, who was described as slightly 'fey' and a 'dear old thing', was with him for many years. There was a poltergeist at Gravetye, but when Robinson died Annie left the house and went into an old people's home, and the poltergeist ceased. Nurse Gilpin, Robinson's resident nurse, was with him for twenty years, and Ernest Markham of clematis repute (and who had one of the most complete collections of clematis at that time), his head gardener, was at Gravetye for over twenty years.

Another affection, coming close to that of clematis, was for pears, and the walls of the kitchen garden were clothed with pear trees. Like H. G. Wells and his fetish for a correctly boiled egg— his wife used to boil one after another for breakfast until he came downstairs, so that there would be one ready for him at whatever moment he decided to appear—Robinson used to be equally fussy about eating a pear. 'There is only ten minutes in the life of a pear when it is fit to be eaten' he would say, and Markham was sent to fetch the pears from the fruit room when they were needed for dessert, just ten minutes before the meal was served.

Perhaps it is the variety of his knowledge which is most impressive as one looks back over his life and work. Not only in the realms of hardy plants, the herbaceous border and wild gardening, the planting of trees and the skill in landscape gardening, but his writing on alpines and rock gardens often coincided exactly with what Reginald Farrer had to say and his under-planting of house windows with sweet-smelling flowers might have been described by Jane Loudon. His ideas for the planting and layout of cemeteries were similar to those of Baroness Burdett-Coutts and his appreciation and knowledge of cottage garden plantings was shared by Gertrude Jekyll.

His genius is probably best summed up by Miss Jekyll in an article, 'The Idea of a Garden', in 1896.

About five-and-twenty years ago, when English gardening was mostly represented by the innate futilities of the 'bedding' system, with its wearisome repetitions and garish colouring, Mr William Robinson chose as his work in life to make better known the treasures that were lying neglected, and at the same time to overthrow the feeble follies of the 'bedding' system. It is mainly owing to his unremitting labours that a clear knowledge of the world of hardy-plant beauty is now placed within easy reach of all who care to acquire it, and that the 'bedding' mania is virtually dead. Now, by easy reference to his practical books as an aid to personal industry, we may see how best to use and enjoy the thousands of beautiful plants that have been brought to us by the men who have given fortune, health and often life in perilous travel that our gardens may be enriched and botanical knowledge extended.

Miss Gertrude Jekyll
1843–1932

Her capacity for entering into the world of a child was one of her greatest accomplishments. There are constant references throughout the book to humour, adventure and magic. . . . There is also a nice comment on a tortoise which unaccountably appeared one day on her lawn. 'How it got there I cannot think,' she wrote, 'for there are only three houses within a near walk and none of their owners had a tortoise. It has always remained a mystery. But I like mysteries and I hope you do too.'

GERTRUDE JEKYLL
Children and Gardens

In *The Education of a Gardener* Russell Page writes: 'I can think of few English gardens made in the last fifty years which do not bear the mark of her teaching, whether in the arrangement of a flower border, the almost habitual association of certain plants or the planting of that difficult passage where garden merges into wild.'

Born on 29 November 1843, Gertrude Jekyll had an elder sister and four brothers. Her family can be traced back to the sixteenth century, but one of her most distinguished forebears was her grandfather, Joseph Jekyll (1753–1837). A politician, well known for his ready wit, he was also a barrister and a founder of the Athenaeum Club and was elected a Fellow of the Royal Society of Arts.

Two of her earliest recollections were a preference for almond sweets, and making daisy chains in the garden of Berkeley Square. The key for the garden was kept at the recently opened Gunter's teashop and the commissionaire who gave the children the key also gave them the sweets. When it was not hot enough to sit in the Berkeley Square garden they went for walks in Green Park, where the main attraction was the dandelions. And so, although a London child until she was nearly five years old, Gertrude Jekyll's first memories were country ones.

In 1848 her family moved from their Grafton Street home to Bramley House, about three miles south-west of Guildford. There were few restrictions and her true contact with nature and with country people began.

At about this time her governess gave her a copy of *Flowers of the Field*, by the Revd C. A. Johns. She wore one copy out completely and later on possessed two more, always keeping one close at hand for reference. Her background at home was intellectual and artistic. She was greatly interested in Greek art, drawing, painting and music.

16 Gertrude Jekyll, from a portrait painted by William Nicholson in 1920

Her mother was a pupil of Mendelssohn and musical evenings were an important part of the family life. Engrossed by the country, by music and painting, outside events hardly entered into her life at this time. When she was only just in her teens the Crimean War may not have seemed very close at hand; she would probably have heard her parents mentioning the name of Florence Nightingale, but the general lack of speedy communications would mean that news penetrated slowly into this corner of West Surrey.

111

The year 1861 was an important one for Gertrude Jekyll.

She now took a characteristically intrepid step for a young lady at this time by enrolling as a student at the Kensington School of Art, where she studied for two years.

Although fashions and ideas were changing in the 1860s the world of painting, especially for young women, was still regarded with some suspicion. In 1853 Queen Victoria had been shown studies in the nude by Mulready and surprised everyone by wanting to buy one. She was expected to be shocked.

Now there came the next event of importance in Gertrude Jekyll's life: 'When I was just grown up, though still in my late teens, I had the great advantage of going with friends (the Newtons) to the near East—the Greek islands, Constantinople, Smyrna, and Athens with several weeks in Rhodes.'

Charles Newton, the distinguished orientalist and excavator of Halicarnassus, was Keeper of the Greek and Roman Antiquities at the British Museum. His wife, Mary Newton, herself an artist, was the daughter of Joseph Severn, the painter, friend and companion of Keats, and was closely linked with Ruskin. Her brother, Arthur Severn, was Ruskin's lifelong friend, and her husband was his contemporary at Oxford. Gertrude, who had been a fervent follower of Ruskin through the schoolroom, was now moving into his circle and was to become a close friend of the Newtons. Every connection seemed at this time to lead towards painting, and this journey with the Newtons was a most important influence on the whole of Gertrude Jekyll's life and work.

At twenty-three, with a picture hung at Burlington House to her credit, Miss Jekyll spent much of her time in the National Gallery making copies of paintings by Turner and Watts, and she saw a great deal of the Newtons, going with them to the Royal Academy, museums and art exhibitions. They were her dearest friends and must have influenced her considerably. It was a great personal loss when Mary Newton fell ill with a severe attack of measles and died in 1866.

In April 1868 she found herself faced with a move of the family home from Bramley to Wargrave, in Berkshire, but at least the journey to London was no more difficult than before, and so her art studies could continue. There were still stimulating meetings with Ruskin (discussing housing conditions with Octavia Hill), G. F. Watts and William Morris in 1869.

Gertrude Jekyll was fortunate in her friends. First there had been the Newtons, who had introduced her to the Ruskin circle. Then there were the Blumenthals; they frequently held musical evenings and it was at one of these occasions that she met Brabazon, the water-colourist. Having become a friend of Brabazon, she met through him Barbara Leigh Smith (Barbara Bodichon), one of the founders of Girton.

Brabazon was the most important of these new friends, owing to his influence as a painter. It was from him that Miss Jekyll learnt her lessons in colour. He 'carried on the tradition of Turner's later and more abstract water-colours . . . Light and colour became the essence, the reason of his pictures. . . .'

The Duke of Westminster, a fellow guest at the Blumenthals' musical parties, called in Gertrude Jekyll for advice on the furnishings at Eaton Hall after the extensive alterations carried out there in 1870. These were on a grand scale. The work of craftsmen and artists from various parts of the Continent and from this country was brought together: 'the drawing room is elaborately decorated and has silk embroidered panels, designed by Miss Jekyll, and executed by the Royal School of Art Needlework at South Kensington', he wrote. The work for Eaton Hall went on throughout the winter and in 1875 the Duke was writing to ask her to undertake the responsibility for the whole of the furnishing and to give her advice generally.

Soon there was to be another move of the family home—this time from Berkshire back to Miss Jekyll's beloved West Surrey. The move, occasioned by the death of her father in 1876, took place within a year.

They soon settled into Munstead House, near Godalming, which was reasonably near to Bramley House, their old home, and also accessible to London from Godalming station.

Miss Jekyll's friendship with William Robinson was developing, perhaps because of the articles she had written for his journal *The Garden*. In 1880 Robinson visited the Munstead Garden, taking with him Dean Hole, who had organized the first Rose Show eleven years before. Her near neighbour was now G. F. Wilson, whose property, Wisley, close to Cobham has since become well known as the Royal Horticultural Society's gardens.

In 1881 Miss Jekyll was asked to judge at the Botanic Show—precursor of the now famous Chelsea Flower Show.

Mrs Jekyll, who was now well over seventy, began to find the constant stream of visitors to the house rather tiring. It was decided that separate establishments should be occupied by mother and daughter, to allow for greater freedom for the one and greater quiet for the other. A strip of land, about fifteen acres adjoining Munstead on the northern side, was purchased and the foundations of Miss Jekyll's own garden were laid, although the house was not yet built.

In 1885 Getrude Jekyll took up a new interest, the art of photography, then in its infancy. As with all her other interests this was done thoroughly, sinks and dark rooms being fitted up for experiments, and farm buildings, lanes and trees tried out as suitable subjects. Her enthusiasm led her to get up at four o'clock in the morning so that certain shots might be photographed with success.

One afternoon in 1889 Miss Jekyll visited her friend and neighbour, Mr Harry Mangles of Littleworth, who was one of the pioneers of rhododendron growing. On that occasion there was another guest who was to prove of special interest, a young man, aged twenty, working near by on his first architectural commission. Edwin Lutyens describes the meeting over the teacups, 'the silver kettle and the conversation reflecting rhododendrons'.

Miss Jekyll must have liked him instantly as she invited him to go to tea with her at Munstead on the following Saturday.

This meeting and the friendship that followed were to shape her life in the crisis which was coming very close. The summer months were still taken up with painting and working in the new garden, visits to friends—Madame Bodichon, Hercules Brabazon, the Blumenthals—the winter months with dark-room work, silver work and wood carving.

In December of that year she wrote the following letter to Brabazon, which mentions and in a way sums up most of her activities at this time:

Dec. 13th/89.   Munstead, Godalming.

Dear Mr Brabazon, We are very glad to have news of you after a rather long interval. . . . We are all very well; my mother, as usual younger than anybody. I have been doing some vigorous landscape gardening for home and friends—doing living pictures with land and trees and flowers!

I suppose you know the Blumenthals are at Hyde Park Gate—a month earlier than usual. I hope to be with them for a few days early in January.

Yours very truly,
Gertrude Jekyll

To all appearances the same life was going on in much the same pattern, and there was little sign of the approaching disaster round the corner.

For many years Miss Jekyll's eyes had troubled her. She must have been physically strong, as well as mentally alert, to fit in so much work during these years, but some of the finer details, especially the embroidery and the painting, were proving a strain on her eyes.

It is believed that she suffered a good deal of pain as well as inconvenience. In the summer of 1891 she was prevailed upon to consult the famous eye specialist Pagenstecher of Wiesbaden. Nearly all her work was discouraged, if not forbidden, and in particular the two subjects she loved most, embroidery and painting. The oculist professed to be able only to arrest the condition but held out no hope of a cure.

In an article written many years later she refers to the incident: 'When I was young I was hoping to be a painter, but to my lifelong regret, I was obliged to abandon all hope of this, after a certain amount of art school work, on account of extreme and always progressive myopia.'

She was nearly fifty years of age. We know from her religious belief, which shines through her writing, that she would not be defeated by her failing eyesight and to combat it she had trained herself to be discriminating in what she observed.

Gardening did not require the very close scrutiny necessary for painting and embroidery, and it was to the circle of William Robinson, Reynolds Hole, Harry Mangles of Littleworth, G. F. Wilson of Wisley, Charles Wolley Dod, Canon Ellacombe and Edward Woodall of Scarborough that she was now able to turn. She came with a background of knowledge, interest and love for this subject which had developed beside her other activities.

Perhaps the greatest compensation of all was to come through her friendship with the young Ned Lutyens. This was a new partnership, beginning at a crucial moment for both, which was to last for over forty years.

In 1894 beginnings were made for Miss Jekyll's permanent home. First, 'the hut' was designed and built and of course discussed with Lutyens. This was to provide a temporary roof until he could have the main house ready for her and then it was to act as an overflow for the workshop and gardening paraphernalia. 'The hut' was ready for occupation in November 1894, although in July of the next year Mrs Jekyll died, after a week's illness, at the age of eighty-two.

There was probably never before or since a happier collaboration between owner and architect than while the building of Munstead Wood was going forward. They both had the same feeling for the use of the right materials and they both felt the importance of an honest solidity and the inclusion of regional characteristics.

17 *A drawing of Gertrude Jekyll, made about 1896 by Lutyens, with whom she worked closely in garden design*

In October 1897 Miss Jekyll moved from 'the hut' into Munstead Wood. The day before the move she received the award of the Victoria Medal of Honour from the Royal Horticultural Society. Her garden, already of some years' standing, was well known in the horticultural world and visited by gardening enthusiasts from many parts of the country. Her relationship with Lutyens was expanding and it is interesting to reflect on how much they were each responsible for the success of a collaboration which produced such a contribution to the English way of life as 'a Lutyens house with a Jekyll garden'.

By now Lutyens was a name in the architectural world. The addition to Crooksbury for the Chapmans (1899), Orchards, near Godalming, for Lady Chance (1898–9), Deanery Garden, Sonning, for E. H. Hudson (1899), Marsh Court, Stockbridge, Hampshire (1901)—all these were enlarging his reputation, and the basis and foundation of it all was the house built for Gertrude Jekyll at Munstead.

In 1904 Marsh Court and Thakeham were finished or nearing completion. Country Life offices were commissioned and the renovation at Lindisfarne was on its way. New Place, Shedfield, was undertaken in 1905 and before New Place was finished Lutyens started work on Hestercombe at Taunton in Somerset.

Of the Hestercombe gardens, Christopher Hussey of *Country Life*, wrote that they 'represent the peak of the collaboration with Miss Jekyll, and his first application of her genius to classical garden design on a grand scale'.

In her book *Garden Ornament*, which she wrote years later with Christopher Hussey, she describes the terrace and the steps leading down to the parterre where she had designed flower beds bordered with bergenia.

Her writings were now becoming known. In addition to her contributions to *The Garden*, the *National Review* published a short article on house decoration, and the *Edinburgh Review* a longer one on garden craft from ancient times until the nineteenth century. She was also writing periodical notes for the *Manchester Guardian* at irregular intervals as a guide for amateurs. These notes were collected together and in April 1898 an agreement with Longmans was reached for their publication in book form. The illustrations were to be taken from her own store of photographs. *Wood and Garden*, the Longmans publication, came out in 1899—'notes and thoughts, practical and critical, of a working amateur, with 71 illustrations from photographs by the author'. It ran into at least six editions in the first year and was so successful that the publishers urged her to follow it up with further notes on the garden and also on the house. These were published in 1900 under the title *Home and Garden*.

There followed years of large literary output—almost a book a year—and of successful collaboration with Lutyens.

In 1901 *Lilies for English Gardens*, published by Country Life, made its appearance with the subtitle 'A Guide for Amateurs'. It was the result of a series of queries sent out to thirty known lily growers by the editors of *The Garden*. At the time, Miss Jekyll was co-editor with E. T. Cook. In the preface she remarks that many less-known lilies have been omitted. 'They concern the botanist, whose business it is to know and to classify everything; they scarcely concern the gardener whose interest it is to know what lilies will best grace his garden.'

Then came *Wall and Water Gardens*, also published in 1901. This is one of the most attractive of all her books, being written from the point of view that—as she explains to children—'nothing is so delightful as playing with water'. A great deal of her philosophy is in this book, and there is poetry in the writing of it, too. After the first publication there were at least thirteen editions. Under the chapter heading 'When to let well alone' she describes a certain wild forest pool:

> Here is a glimpse of quiet natural beauty; pure nature untouched. Being in itself beautiful and speaking direct to our minds of the poetry of the woodland, it would be an ill deed to mar its perfection by any meddlesome gardening. The most one could do in such a place, where deer may come down to drink and the dragonfly flashes in the broken midsummer light, would be to plant in the upper ground some native wild flower that would be in harmony with the place but that may happen to be absent, such as wood sorrel or wood anemone.

There is the beauty of restraint in her treatment of this pond; just as there is beauty in the words she uses to describe it. The suggestion of wood sorrel or wood anemone would be in tune with the woodland scene. One can imagine dreadful things which might be done by someone with eager, but inartistic ideas—perhaps a kerbstone of cement—to such a simple pool set among wild flowers, grasses, ferns and trees.

Miss Jekyll devotes a whole chapter to the importance of 'Water margins'. She emphasizes the value of a natural margin wherever possible. 'For a beautiful old bank or water edge is a precious thing and difficult to imitate.' She writes of the construction of 'any hard edge of walling, cement . . .' as making natural planting an impossibility. 'A pond-head sometimes must be rather straight and in some cases may have to be walled, but when the wall is not needful and the pond edge is to be planted for beauty, its natural shore should be treasured and retained, no matter how boggy or unsound it may be in places.'

This all falls into place with her ideas on 'natural' gardening, with which we are familiar, but quite half of the book has other things to say. These are based on the appreciation, when most suitable, of the formal garden, illustrating clearly the truth of her statement: 'I try always to be co-operative.' She writes:

> For the formal garden of the best type I can picture to myself endless possibilities both of beauty and delight—for though my own limited means have in a way obliged me to practise only the free and less costly ways of gardening, such as give the greatest happiness for the least expenditure . . . yet I also have much pleasure in formal gardens of the best kinds. But it must be nothing less than the very best; and it is necessarily extremely costly. . . .

Miss Jekyll had a great admiration for the Italian type of garden of the Renaissance period and in this book she writes of the opportunities for planting such gardens with the recently collected plants available from abroad, and continues:

> When one thinks of the very few plants known for garden use to the ancients and to those who built and planted the noble gardens of the Italian Renaissance and when one compares this limited number with the vast range of beautiful shrubs and plants we now have to choose from, one cannot help seeing how much wider is the scope for keen and critical discrimination.

And so, in *Wall and Water Gardens* we have her own suggestion for the planting and design of such a formal garden, including a double-page plan of part of it.

This brings us to the question of her garden plans and the revelations to be found among them. (The plans went to the University of California, Berkeley, through the generosity of Beatrix Farrand who, it is said, bought them from the British Red Cross during World War II and left them to the University in her will.) There are plans of more than two hundred gardens, some of them giving details of borders, rock gardens, water gardens, herb gardens, orchard planting, wall planting, wild gardens and above all rose gardens. There was of course much natural design but there was also an appreciation for formality which emerges from these plans. They show, among many other things, her regard for what is right in a certain situation or position, whether formal or informal is required. There are formal water gardens in contrast with roses climbing up into fruit trees, there are vistas giving on to the local countryside of fields and barns and farms seen from a formal paved water tank with urns of flowers and statuary.

A friend who first made his appearance at Munstead Wood about 1900, and visited Miss Jekyll regularly once a month until she died, was Mr Harold Falkner. He worked, among other projects, for the Society for the Protection of Ancient Buildings. He was apprenticed in the office of Sir Reginald Bloomfield (author of *The Formal Garden*) and so was trained from his early days in the ideas of the formal garden. These ideas were then in complete opposition to the naturalistic gardening of William Robinson and, of course, to Miss Jekyll. But when Mr Falkner went round the garden of Munstead Wood he was completely won over. He says that 'it was partly formal, partly controlled wild'. He also recalled Miss Jekyll's attitude to this battle between the formal and the informal garden designers. 'She used to relate with great glee the fact that Robinson designed himself a garden all squares, and Reggy a garden on a cliff with not a straight line in it.' (Robinson's garden at Gravetye had a paved garden close to the house, so that he could easily reach his favourite plants from his wheel chair—most of the paving is still there, as are the ramps, to take the place of steps.)

As already mentioned in 1899 Lutyens had added another wing to Crooksbury, and completed Deanery Garden for Edward Hudson. Of the latter Christopher Hussey wrote:

> Deanery Garden, at once formal and irregular, virtually settled that controversy of which Sir Reginald Bloomfield and William Robinson were the protagonists, between formal and naturalistic garden design. Miss Jekyll's naturalistic planting wedded Lutyens's geometry in a balanced union of both principles.

Mr Falkner contended that Miss Jekyll's own garden was 'partly formal'. He went further and said:

In her first books she seemed to harp on naturalism in gardens in direct opposition [to Sir Reginald Blomfield's *The Formal Garden*], but gradually she and E.L. came to our way of thinking and from the second addition of Crooksbury on to Great Maytham had become *Formal* in garden and classic in houses.

Perhaps Sir Reginald and Harold Falkner had become slightly less formal?

This is the picture, then, at the turn of the century. Miss Jekyll, writing in the *Edinburgh Review*, July, 1896, says:

> Within the last few years . . . another war of controversy has raged between the exponents of formal and the free styles of gardening, and again it is to be regretted that it has taken a somewhat bitter and almost personal tone. . . . Both are right and both are wrong. The formal army are architects to a man; they are undoubtedly right in upholding the simple dignity and sweetness and quiet beauty of the old formal garden but . . . they ignore the immense resources that are the precious possession of modern gardeners, and therefore offer no sort of encouragement to their utilisation. . . . We cannot now, with all this treasure at our feet, neglect it and refuse it the gratefully appreciative use it deserves. We cannot go back a century or two and stop short at the art of the formal gardener any more than we can go back to the speech of our forefathers, beautiful though it was. There is change and growth in all wholesome art, and gardening at its best is a fine art.

It is easy to understand from this paragraph how it was that Miss Jekyll was influenced by Ruskin—by her close friend Barbara Bodichon, and most of all by the water colourist Hercules Brabazon.

Her plans make all these points clear in detail, usually being accompanied by copious designs and drawings. They became more and more indispensable as she grew older and more blind. For instance, during the last fifteen to twenty years of her life she always made it clear that she was unable to travel to visit prospective gardens, however much she was tempted by the owner's promises of having easy transport arranged for her. 'It will only take you an hour to drive over, Miss Jekyll, and we will have you home before sunset' was the kind of persuasive argument produced on more than one occasion. However, she had to be firm in her refusal, but always asked for three guides to help in her designs. One of these was a surveyor's plan. She explained that this was essential at all times, even in the earlier days when she had been able to travel and see the garden herself. Then she always wanted to know if the owner had any favourite ideas or flowers or shrubs or tree planting, or perhaps a water garden, a rock garden, a wild garden, an orchard or a rose garden.

She herself especially loved designing and planting a rose garden, and gives in these plans many various collections of roses which she recommends from her own personal experience for planting. One of her favourites among the climbing roses was always 'Madame Alfred Carrière', and another was the deeply-flushed pink 'Blairii No. 2'. She loved the 'Garland' rose, and trained it into a suitable tree such as a catalpa, and among most lists appears the thornless bright pink of 'Zephirine Drouhin'.

One other point emerges from *Wall and Water Gardening* and that is the importance of close co-operation between the garden designer and the architect. This was emphasized in her second book *Home and Garden* at the time of the building of Munstead Wood with Lutyens, but is gone into here in different detail. She writes:

> The whole question of the relation of vegetation to architecture is a very large one, and to know what to place where, and when to stop, and when to abstain altogether requires much knowledge on both sides . . . The truth appears to be that for the best building and planting, where both these crafts must meet and overlap and work together, the architect and the gardener must have some knowledge of each other's business, and each must regard with feelings of kindly reverence the unknown domains of the other's higher knowledge.

The plans show how these 'feelings of kindly reverence' were shown, especially on Miss Jekyll's side, as there are many instances of her working most successfully with various architects who particularly desired to co-operate with her.

Her partnership for over thirty years with Lutyens is well known, but it is to the plans that we owe the knowledge of many other working relationships. They show not only the interesting pattern of her work and how it developed along certain lines as she grew older and more blind, but also that her ideas were much sought after throughout this country and sometimes in America. Often this involved working with other architects or firms of surveyors. Among these were Oliver Hill, Forbes and Tate, Percy Adams, H. Baillie-Scott. Ernest Willmott and Sir Robert Lorimer. But these are only some of the names which appear on certain of the plans during the years from about 1905 until just before she died in 1932. One of the last plans which she drew for a client was done in December 1931, when she had just passed her eighty-eighth birthday, and on this occasion she was working with the surveyors Usher and Anthony of Bedford.

To return to her books: *Roses for English Gardens* was published in 1902. It was written in conjunction with Mr Edward Mawley and divided into two parts, one part written by each author. The next literary venture in 1904 was something of a rather different character. Away, this time, from roses, lilies, Munstead Wood, rock gardens and water gardens, and back to the memories of her childhood, the book is called *Old West Surrey*. This was enlarged and republished in 1925 under the title of *Old English Household Life*.

18 *The spring garden of Miss Jekyll's home, Munstead Wood, Surrey, designed for her by Lutyens*

The knowledge that Gertrude Jekyll had acquired from going in and out of cottages and cottage gardens, from driving down the lanes in her pony-cart, and from her knowledge of the cottagers themselves, was quite prodigious. She knew about their customs and their means of living, and it is clear from her writing that she was an authority on all kinds of paving (ripple-marked stone and ironstone pitching), wells, bacon-lofts, gates, kitchen fireplaces, clocks, granaries, dairies, straw-plaiting, samplers, patchwork, candlesticks, thatching, inn signs, churchyards and tombstones, and the speech, manners and customs of the village people. She was also particularly interested in bridges.

Another excitement at this time was when Edward Hudson acquired the ruins of Lindisfarne and asked Lutyens to restore the castle. This work went on during 1903/4, and was one of his best restorations. The atmosphere is welcoming, with a feeling of solidity but also of comfort. The wooden doors have large, heavy latches and the gallery—in the style of the Munstead gallery—is an important feature. It is all excellent in workmanship and in design. The garden planting was in Miss Jekyll's charge—and she herself visited the castle a year or two later.

But there were many collaborations with Lutyens which included Folly Farm, Sulhamstead, Berkshire, Hestercombe, Taunton, Somerset, and—perhaps one of the most exciting for them both—Millmead, Bramley, a small house with a small garden.

In 1906 came the death of H. B. Brabazon—a sad loss to Gertrude Jekyll—and in 1907 a further publication, *Flower Decoration in the House*.

Two more books were published in 1908, one of them suggested by Edwin Lutyens. He felt that his family should be brought up from an early age in the gardening faith, and it seemed sensible that a reliable and interesting guide to gardening for children should be written. The result was Gertrude Jekyll's *Children and Gardens*.

Miss Jekyll's book for children would have been of little use, however technically accurate, if it had not been written in the language that children would understand and appreciate. Her capacity for entering into the world of a child was one of her greatest accomplishments. There are constant references throughout the book to humour, adventure and magic, and descriptions of some of her cats, which were her constant companions.

A quantity of expensive and rare plants in a garden, with long Latin names written across their labels, would not have impressed Miss Jekyll, even though she was familiar with the names herself. Affectation in any form was outside her province and she had no patience with it. The best illustration of this is her advice given and the trouble taken over a factory boy in Rochdale who wanted help with the planting of his window-box.

The boy had advertised in a mechanical paper for help in planting a window-box. Miss Jekyll wrote years later: 'He knew nothing—would somebody help him with advice? So advice was sent and the box prepared. If I remember rightly the size was three feet by ten inches. A little later the post brought him plants of mossy and silvery saxifrages, and a few small bulbs. Even some stones were sent, for it was to be a rock-garden, and there were to be two hills of different heights with rocky tops, and a longish valley with a sunny and shady side.'

The days spent as an art student and the painting accomplished later, until her eyes troubled her too greatly, now bore fruit in the other book which she published in 1908—*Colour in the Flower Garden* (subsequent editions entitled *Colour Schemes for the Flower Garden*). This book, as far as it is possible to judge at this distance of time, is her great contribution to English gardening. Her ideas on colour stand in a class apart. In this book the essence of her artistic training is distilled and here she is first an artist and then a gardener.

Speaking of the impossibility of continuous colour everywhere in the garden, she says: '. . . it is even undesirable to have a garden in blossom all over, and groups of flower-beauty are all the more enjoyable for being more or less isolated, by stretches of intervening greenery'.

Probably her biggest contribution to the study of colour is that she established that no colour stands alone and that it can only have real value if it is thought of in relation to the colours close at hand.

This was a time in English history when the cottage gardens were keeping the flag flying. In some of the estates and the larger gardens there was little imagination, only a good deal of ornamental bedding-out. The shape of the flower bed was described as being more important than what went into it. Some of the precious flowers we love and treasure today were to be found only in cottage gardens, having been turned out in many cases in favour of half-hardy plants cosseted through the winter in Sir Joseph Paxton's greenhouses.

Throughout her writings Gertrude Jekyll acknowledges not only her love for but also her debt to cottage gardens. She was a gardening genius largely because she was alert and interested and ready to learn. And she went to the cottage gardens for much of her knowledge because she felt that 'they have a simple and tender charm that one may look for in vain in gardens of greater pretension. And the old garden flowers seem to know that there they are seen at their best; for where else can one see such wallflowers, or double daisies, or white rose bushes; such clustering masses of perennial peas, or such well-kept flowery edgings of pink, or thrift, or London pride? (*Home and Garden*).

But it was not only the plants in the cottage gardens that she noticed on her drives with Lutyens. He must have learnt from her about the setting of a chimney, the different uses and patterns of tiles, the right proportions of windows and doorways—all matters essential to his work. As Robert Lutyens wrote: 'The influence of this wise, eccentric and cultivated woman on her generation in general, and on my father in particular, has been on the whole insufficiently acknowledged.' Mr Harold Falkner was aware of this influence: 'Miss Jekyll had . . . a knowledge', he wrote in a letter to me some years ago, 'of the very finest building practices which she transferred to Lutyens, and that "sense of material" made him different from all other architects of his time.'

Sometimes a restoration can be more difficult to effect successfully than an original design. Lindisfarne Castle and Great Dixter, now the home of Christopher Lloyd, the well-known plantsman and writer, are examples of Lutyen's application of the lessons learnt from his mentor.

Frequently in her writing, Miss Jekyll refers to the importance of the smell of a flower. Apart from the enjoyment and the love of a scented garden, she maintains that to recognize the smell of a flower is to get to know it. Writing in *Children and Gardens*, she says: 'one finds out a great deal about flowers and plants by smelling them and it is one of the most important ways of getting to know them'. She writes in *A Gardener's Testament* of 'the sweetness of a sun-baked bank of wallflower' and 'the sweet-scented leafing of sweet briar', and, of wild honeysuckle, 'It throws out its crowns and garlands of sweetest scent'; and in *Wood and Garden*, 'For mignonette is and always should be a plant of modest colouring and sweetest scent; both these qualities belong to the older kind. . . .'

Apple blossom, small pansies, myrtle and the cabbage rose, a twig of bay, a tuft of thyme or a sprig of rosemary—all are mentioned, with many others. Pinks and carnations are an obvious selection, also lily of the valley, gardenia and jasmine. She comments particularly on the smell of dying strawberry leaves.

The final appeal may to be the stirring up of memories. Miss Jekyll mentions especially her travels in the islands of the Greek archipelago, recalled 'in a way far more distinct than can be done by a mere mental effort of recollection' by the scents of shrubs in her garden, 'many of them at home in dry and rocky places in far-away lower latitudes. . . .' (*Wood and Garden*).

To have a well-remembered garden it seems that some sweet-smelling plant will do more than paved terraces, colourful borders or ornamental pools. 'The sense of smell has also its peculiar province, a strange power of conjuring up the past . . . and we shall therefore carry away a lasting recollection of the garden, if . . . the air is heavy with scent of some particular flower. . . .' (Sir George Sitwell, *On the Making of Gardens.*)

William Nicholson had been a personal friend of Ned Lutyens for many years, and since the First World War he had also been a neighbour in Apple Tree Yard, the mews of 7 St James's Square where Lutyens had the Delhi office. It was through Lutyens that Getrude Jekyll was eventually persuaded to sit for William Nicholson, which was an achievement in itself. The persuasive charm of her old friend and the adaptability of the artist won the day and throughout October and November of 1920 the rather unofficial 'sittings' took place. In most of them the painter was condemned to work in lamplight, as Miss Jekyll insisted on working during the best hours of the day. In the intervals Nicholson gave his attention to an old pair of gardening boots, gratefully using for them the valuable daylight which she refused to waste on herself.

The portrait, which now hangs in the National Portrait Gallery, is important as a work of art but also on account of its picture of Miss Jekyll's character. The artist wrote that he hoped he had put 'a little of her serene charm' into the painting. But the

portrait of the boots has in some ways become almost more
significant. Miss Jekyll's boots have acquired over the years the
position of a kind of symbol in the gardening world.

*19 William Nicholson's painting of Gertrude Jekyll's boots. He produced this while
waiting for Miss Jekyll, who was making the most of the daylight in her garden*

Gertrude Jekyll has been described both as gentle and fierce.
She had little patience with indifference or stupidity and could
settle both with quiet but devastating remarks. She was deeply,
but unfussily, religious and at the same time she had a keen sense
of fun and delight in adventure with children, understanding their
love of magic and make-believe.

If all this is linked together there emerges a composite picture
which has been clearly caught by William Nicholson. In spite of all
the hard work accomplished and her respect for the good use of
time she still gives a feeling of serenity. She sits in her chair, a
stout, round figure, dressed in her usual style of voluminous blue
serge. (Unfortunately there cannot be seen a piece of string
hanging from the back of her chair with a piece of cork at the end of
it. Lady Emily, wife of Edwin Lutyens, told me that it was always

there for the benefit of any cats in the household to play with—
frequently there would be about six.)

During her last summer, 1932, she was only able to see her
plants from the wheelchair which Lutyens had given to her, and
she was apologizing to a friend in a letter dated 26 August for not
having written earlier in reply: 'The delay is because of my
infirmities—my years are eighty-eight and there are times when
my doctor keeps me very close on account of a worn-out heart, so
that many things that I ought to do have to be set aside.' She died
on 8 December after a short illness, having celebrated her eighty-
ninth birthday on 29 November.

Miss Jekyll has been described as the first horticultural
Impressionist, translating gardening into terms of painting. But
she was not only a gardener in colour—she understood as an artist
the use of light and shade.

In 1934 her memorial, designed by Sir Edwin Lutyens, was
erected in Busbridge churchyard. The inscription reads: 'Artist,
Gardener, Craftswoman'. The order is significant as it implies
that the second and third qualifications depend on the first. More
important is her permanent memorial in the ideas and designs
which she has passed on to all future generations.

It is difficult to keep a garden as it has been kept by someone
else; however much one tries to copy ideas small personal
differences will creep in which give an individual character, but one
of the most exciting restorations of a Jekyll-Lutyens garden has
been taking place in Somerset. Hestercombe House stands at the
foot of the south-facing slope of the Quantocks, overlooking
Taunton Deane. (It is at present owned by the Crown
Commissioners and has been leased by the Somerset County
Council since 1953 as the headquarters of the County's Fire
Service.) Of the original design Christopher Hussey wrote: 'The
Hestercombe gardens represent the peak of the collaboration with
Miss Jekyll and his [Lutyens's] first application of her genius to
classical garden design on a grand scale.'

Under the combined direction of the Chief Fire Officer and the
County Architect, extensive investigation into the possible
restoration of these historic gardens, using the original plans, was
begun in 1970, copies of some of the plans being kindly lent by the
Department of Landscape Architecture, University of California,
Berkeley. The gardening was worked out to take place in phases

over a period of about five years. Research for the replanting was carried out by the Somerset County Architect's Department, and although the gardens are being furnished exactly according to the original plans, it has been found necessary in certain cases to substitute perennials where annuals were indicated before. The stonework is being restored by the Crown Estate Office and this, with much of the planting, is now almost completed.

Eventually it is hoped to open the house and garden officially to the public on certain days in the year, a fitting tribute to an enlightened gardener.

Miss Ellen Ann Willmott

1858–1934

*. . . as you know, my plants and my gardens come
before anything in life for me, and all my time is
given up to working in one garden or another, and
when it is too dark to see the plants themselves I
read or write about them.*

AUDREY LE LIÈVRE
Miss Willmott of Warley Place

Miss Ellen Ann Willmott, FLS, VMH, described as 'ambitious,
proud and beautiful', was the unmarried daughter of Frederick
Willmott, a prosperous London solicitor and financier, and his
wife Ellen. From her godmother, later Countess Tasker, a relative
of her mother, she received and then inherited considerable sums
of money. After her parents' death, Warley Place in Essex, near
Enfield, became hers, and she was then able to spend as much and
as extravagantly as she pleased on the large house and extensive
gardens, and also on the properties she bought in the south of
France and in Italy.

She will probably be remembered most for her scholarly work
The Genus Rosa. Published by John Murray in 1910–14 in two
volumes, it is a classic composed of Miss Willmott's notes
accompanying the illustrations by Alfred Parsons, ARA. She
gives a detailed biography of each rose often adding her own
comments and mentioning particular points of interest. It is the
kind of book which took up years of work and cost the author more
than she ever got back on it. She had valuable help from
knowledgeable friends which she acknowledges in the Preface:

July 1910

I have had the inestimable advantage of criticism, of help and of
encouragement from several competent authorities, and especially
from the Rev. Canon Ellacombe of Bitton, who has given much kindly
encouragement throughout, and helped on many occasions; Mr. J. G.
Baker, FRS, late Keeper of the Royal Herbarium at Kew, who has been
of especial service in drawing up the specific characters, Professor
Sargent of the Arnold Arboretum, Harvard University, USA, who has

131

read the whole book and given much valuable criticism and advice; the late Rev. Charles Wolley Dod of Edge Hall, Cheshire, who encouraged the work at its inception, and made many useful suggestions; Major A. H. Wolley Dod, Sir George Watt, Lord Redesdale, and Lieutenant-Colonel Prain, Director of the Royal Gardens, Kew . . . to all of these my grateful acknowledgements are due. But for the first I should never have undertaken the book at all; but for the last it might never have reached the stage of publication.

Ellen Willmott

Like Miss Jekyll, she could champion the cause of a flower as long as it was properly grown and placed. For instance, discussing in this book the rose *Rosa wichuraiana*, which came to England about 1890 by way of the United States, she refers to the hybrid 'Dorothy Perkins'. 'Perhaps the greatest favourite of all the Wichuraiana hybrids is the charming Dorothy Perkins, whose beautiful pure pink flowers resemble a clustered Rose de Meaux.'

She remarks (also like Miss Jekyll—'one expects every rose to be fragrant') on the scent of roses: 'Roses vary as much in perfume as they do in colour; each has its own distinctive scent, except in the instances, sad to say far too frequent among the newer roses, where the flowers are absolutely devoid of any fragrance whatever.'

She was always closely connected with the activities of the National Rose Society—frequently accompanying the Queen when Her Majesty visited the Rose Show. (*The Genus Rosa* is dedicated to Queen Alexandra.) But roses were not by any means her only horticultural interest. She was a life member of the Royal Horticultural Society and a committee member of its Narcissus, Tulip and Lily Groups. Photographs of her garden at Great Warley, Essex, show her interest in spring flowers, alpines, harebells and foxgloves, a lily pool, a nutwalk. There are roses, of course, but not to the exclusion of everything else.

Her massive book of the garden at Warley Place *Warley Garden in Spring and Summer*, gives an impression of orderliness and planning, but now and again there are variations on this theme. Orderliness there should have been as it is recorded that at one time she employed nearly a hundred gardeners. But though most of her gardening was precise she could branch out into unexpected extravagance to the tune of ten thousand bulbs of *Camassia esculenta* for the borders of her lake.

132

Miss Willmott kept up the custom of wearing fresh flowers and at the RHS meetings she would take a subtle pleasure in selecting something uncommon from Warley to try out the knowledge of the committee members. Her delight in confounding those who could not identify the flower was only equalled by her genuine pleasure in finding those who could.

20 Miss Ellen Ann Willmott, owner of extensive gardens in Essex, Italy and southern France

She was awarded the Victoria Medal of Honour in Horticulture and made a trustee of the RHS Gardens at Wisley when they were handed over by Sir Thomas Hanbury. She was also the first woman to be elected to the Linnean Society in 1904 and in 1912 the French Société d'Acclimatation honoured her with the rare Geoffrey St Hilaire medal. She was also appointed a Patron of the Glynde School for Lady Gardeners, organized by the Viscountess Wolseley in the early years of the century.

Miss Willmott knew and visited most of the gardening giants of the day. She stayed at Edge Hall in Cheshire as the guest of the Revd Charles Wolley Dod. It was here that an argument took place over the nomenclature of a certain narcissus and Mr Dod suggested that she should visit Canon Ellacombe's garden in Gloucestershire. This introduction resulted in a long friendship.

She writes:

> On my first visit to Bitton, I went from Paddington by the nine o'clock
> express, having ordered a good pair of horses to meet me at Bath to
> take me out to Bitton. Just as I was getting into the victoria at Bath, a
> voice said: 'I am sure you are Miss Willmott, and coming to see my
> vicarage garden. You are very welcome and your visit is one to which
> I have been looking forward. I travelled down by the same train and
> looked out for you at Paddington, but expecting to see one of more
> mature years, I missed you.'

She describes the drive out to Bitton and her first sight of the
church tower as it appeared over the tops of the trees. This was the
beginning of many visits either of hers to Bitton or of the Canon's
to Warley. His weekly journeys to London to attend the meetings
of the New River Board meant that he was also in the vicinity of
Warley and Miss Willmott recalls that his interest was especially
for the old roses in her garden.

In May 1904, Miss Willmott's sister, Mrs Berkeley of
Spetchley Park, near Worcester, also a good gardener, was
staying with her in her house in the south of France, when they
received a visit from Canon Ellacombe. 'Spent the day at
Tresserve', the Canon wrote in his diary. 'Went up after breakfast
and found Miss Willmott and the Berkeleys ready for us.' The
house must have been idyllically situated as it stood on a low hill,
the garden running down to the edge of Lake Bourget with hills
behind the lake, separating it from the Rhone valley. 'The garden
is intersected throughout by long shady walks and there is a
marvellous abundance of flowers revelling in the soil and climate.
We had come at the exact time for the irises of which there is a
splendid collection, also a great variety of roses, but we were too
early for the great collection.'

There is also the following description of the same scene a few
years earlier in a letter from Lady Wolseley to her husband.

Aix-les-Bains 18/9/1900

> We are all very happy together. On Sunday we drove out to see Miss
> Willmott and her garden. It is on the side of a hill sloping down to the
> Lake (Bourget), with views of exquisite mountains on the other side
> of the Lake. The flowers, shrubs, vines, are most beautiful, a wild
> tangle of loveliness, the most artistically natural, or naturally artistic,
> thing you ever saw. Of course, there is a great deal of labour and art in
> it all, but it *looks* as if Nature had her own way. A nice old house. We
> had tea on a hard, stone, creeper-hung verandah.

There is mention in Gertrude Jekyll's *Children and Gardens* of Miss Willmott's visiting Munstead. Miss Jekyll, who was a friend of long-standing, described her as early as 1908, when Miss Willmott would have been about fifty years of age, as 'the greatest of living women-gardeners'. Like Miss Jekyll she was talented and intellectual and had other interests besides gardening.

They had affection and appreciation for each other throughout their lives as this letter from Miss Willmott, written to Mr Cowley, at the time of Miss Jekyll's death, shows:

> *Warley Place,*
> *Great Warley,*
> *Essex.*

Dear Mr Cowley,
I have just had a telegram from Lady Jekyll [Gertrude Jekyll's sister-in-law] with the sad tidings of Miss Jekyll's death. I am sure it will grieve you deeply and I am full of sorrow at the loss of one I admired so greatly and loved sincerely. She was such a sensitive and great personality. I so thoroughly realised it, perhaps more than others.

In her were all the qualities I most admire, for apart from being a great gardener and lover of plants, her sense of beauty and the picturesque in a garden combined with horticulture and cultivation at its best is very rarely found. In fact I have never known it except in my sister Mrs Berkeley of Spetchley.

I was 15 when I first knew her. Then the awe she inspired in me in the course of years became admiration and affection. You who knew her so well had so many opportunities of knowing her great attainments. I saw her last in August just before I was taken ill with bronchial pneumonia. It was a great effort to go to Munstead but I had a feeling I must go. Her last letter was upon Sir Herbert's death. On the occasion of my last visit she mentioned that the notes I made about her and which you published had given her more pleasure than anything else written about her. I gave an evening about her at the Garden Club with slides of views in her garden. Several of her family were present and they all seemed pleased.

Although the present generation of so-called gardeners knew her only as a name, to all of us who knew her she was always a living force, an example and an inspiration.

It was Sir Herbert's death which must have hastened her death for her last letter to me was very pathetic.

(Perhaps I may see you at the R.H.S. on Tuesday.)

> [Yours faithfully,]
> E. WILLMOTT

Miss Willmott painted some of the roses she grew with the touch of a Fantin-Latour and was an ardent supporter of the Bach Choir. After her death the sale of her music and herbals at Sotheby's took the best part of three days. It was a collection of musical manuscripts and early works on horticulture which showed the interest of an educated mind. There were early printed editions of Purcell and Handel, manuscripts of Bach, Mendelssohn, Schubert and Liszt and autographed letters of Wagner, Liszt, Rossini and Mendelssohn.

21 'Dorothy Perkins', the rambling rose which is still grown and which was described by Miss Willmott as 'perhaps the greatest favourite of all the Wichuraiana hybrids'

The sum of her education taught her to study the rose, particularly the older and the wilder ones, as a scholar as well as a gardener. She was generous too to other gardeners. It is related that when being shown round a garden she would comment: 'I see you have no . . . You must have some. It does well at Warley.' Presently, some time after her visit, a bulging sack would arrive full of all the plants she had mentioned, with extra ones. It was obvious that her presents exceeded her promises in generosity.

To return to the magnificent publication, *Warley Garden in Spring and Summer*: it includes among others, illustrations with the following captions: 'Planting of Rocky Slope': 'Dog's Tooth Violets amongst large stones and pieces of rock': 'Alpine Primroses': 'Path to Alpine Garden': 'Ramondas in Alpine Garden': 'Foxglove Time': 'Slopes of the Alpine Garden': 'Outer Fringe of Alpine Garden': 'Lily Pool': 'Pool in Alpine Garden': 'Rocky Pathway': 'Alpine Garden, (Path like Wisley)': 'Border of Hardy Flowers': 'Cranesbill and Rock Flowers': 'In the Alpine Garden': 'Flowers growing between Rocks': 'The Garden House': 'Alpine Harebells':

Among forty entries there are two devoted to roses and one to lilies. In fact, the greatest interest from this list of headings would appear to be the alpine garden, so that to think of Miss Willmott as a rosarian, without any other knowledge, would be a misrepresentation of her gardening interests. It was the period of interest in alpines and she took this up with some energy. Many were being collected abroad and sent home for propagation, and Miss Willmott's sunken alpine garden was almost as much of a feature as E. A. Bowles's rock garden at Myddleton House was to become later.

The influence of William Robinson was evident in her planting and, although there were already many fine specimen trees—the garden was much as the diarist John Evelyn, a former owner, would have remembered it—the alpine and wild gardens were her creation and were greatly admired. M. Henri Correvon of Geneva, the judge of alpines, was especially complimentary. Miss Willmott also established a large garden at Boccanegra, near to La Mortola, Sir Thomas Hanbury's world-famous garden in northern Italy. At one period, early in the century, she became involved in the plant expeditions of E. H. Wilson in western China and Tibet, cultivating successfully some of the plants he sent back to this country.

Beautiful, extravagant, eccentric, scholarly to a high degree, Miss Willmott was one of the most colourful of all the lady gardeners. Queen Alexandra and Queen Mary both visited at Warley and it must to many people have seemed like a termination to a way of life when Miss Willmott died at the age of 76.

The Times obituary notice remarks on her physical powers,

which were astonishing: '. . . had she to visit a friend's garden she would rise betimes to catch an early train to her destination, walk about all day, and catch the last train from Liverpool Street to Warley station, walking thence about a mile to her house, as often as not with a knapsack of plants on her shoulders'.

Her portrait shows a face of great character and beauty, remarkable for the dark eyes, softly waving hair and charm of regular features.

Mrs Francis (Louisa) King
1863–1948

Charm in gardens is as uncertain as acoustics in a
room. Both are longed for, neither can be
harnessed; therefore the capture is all the more
precious.

LOUISA KING
From a New Garden

'In the three decades between 1825 and 1855, Downing, disciple
of Repton, planned many beautiful places along the banks of the
Hudson River and elsewhere, estates which still stand in
wonderful dignity and beauty.' So wrote the American Louisa
King in the 1930s in a chapter on 'American Gardens' in Eleanour
Sinclair Rohde's *The Story of the Garden*. She could also have
written of the many references to Downing's 'Landscape
Gardening', published in 1841 in the *Encyclopaedia of Gardening*
by J. C. Loudon, and of the fact that in 1852, the year he died,
Downing edited Mrs Loudon's *Gardening for Ladies*.

Many years later in this transatlantic interchange of thought
and ideas we find another American, Beatrix Farrand, designing
the North Forecourt and rhododendron walks at Dartington Hall.
We discover, too, her admiration for Miss Jekyll's ideas to the
extent that Beatrix Farrand is sometimes spoken of as 'the
Gertrude Jekyll of America'. There was also the mutual regard, of
some importance to both countries, of Gertrude and Louisa King.

Born on 17 October 1863, Louisa Boyd Yeomans was the elder
of two daughters in a family of five children, whose father, Alfred
Yeomans, was a well-loved Presbyterian clergyman. The child
grew up in the lively, cheerful atmosphere of a New Jersey
parsonage where there appears to have been plenty of light-
hearted fun and irresistible jokes to counteract the strict
admonitions from the pulpit relating to heaven and hell.

She thrived on this slightly unusual mixture and developed into
an intelligent young woman, warm-hearted and receptive of new

ideas. Life in the parsonage was not luxurious, and meals might even be skimpy as well as plain, but there were books everywhere and reading them became a natural part of existence.

Louisa Yeomans went, in her early twenties, to visit a friend in Chicago. Staying also in the house was a young man, Francis King, and they fell in love. There were no serious problems—financially her future husband was well equipped, holding a senior post in his father's established business—but the usual social obligations of such an event had to be fulfilled and it was June 1890 before they were married.

In the first years of their marriage she and Francis went to live with his parents on their estate at Elmhurst, Illinois; it was then that Louisa came into close contact with serious gardening. Quite apart from her flower garden designed on the lines of Mt Vernon, formerly the home of George Washington, Mrs Henry King (Louisa's mother-in-law) had a large area given up entirely to herbs and was reputed to have had over 200 varieties—a similar collection to those in the garden of Acorn Bank, Sowerby, West Yorkshire. (The herb garden here is open to the public.)

In the early 1900s the young couple moved into their own home, Orchard House, Alma, Michigan. By now they had three children whose upbringing had obviously taken up most of Louisa's time and interest, but in the background there had been conversations about herbs, details of selections and planting, walks in the gardens to look at the box-edged borders, and indoors well-stocked shelves of botanical books. Louisa had become familiar with the hand-coloured lithographs in Mrs Loudon's books standing together with volumes of *Curtis's Botanical Magazine* and with many of the new books being published, some of them from England. Between sessions with the children she had read of the gardening revolution led by Gertrude Jekyll and William Robinson, of the more natural designs, contrasts in planting, a painter's use of colour—all competing with Reginald Blomfield's Victorian bedding-out.

So it was at a reasonably early age that Louisa King, already influenced by her mother-in-law's interest in herbs, also settled for many of Miss Jekyll's gardening ideas. In her chapter on 'American Gardens' she selects two contemporary examples: the small herb garden at the Mission House, Stockbridge, Massachusetts, and the garden of Ithan House, Rosemont, Penn-

sylvania, which had a fine vista looking down the steep terraces
to Ithan Creek. Miss Jekyll, when drawing up a garden plan for a
new client, frequently hoped to introduce a vista. Francis King's
part of their new garden at Alma was centred in planting an
orchard, while his wife's flower garden was formal in design as
indeed were many of those to be found in Miss Jekyll's book *Wall
and Water Gardens*, published about the time of the Kings' move
to Alma. But there were also contrasts of natural planting, such as
spring bulbs flowering under and around shrubs that edged the
lawn.

*22 Mrs Louisa King with her three children, about 1902, shortly after the family
had moved to Alma, Michigan*

Mrs King had written her appreciation of various of Miss Jekyll's books. On one occasion, in February 1912, Miss Jekyll had replied: 'You make me blush—in fact I have been blushing hard ever since I had your letter—now a few days ago—at all the delightful things you say about my books . . .' In the summer of the following year Louisa King wrote again, to ask if Miss Jekyll would write a foreword to her publication, *The Flower Garden Day by Day*. The spread of gardening interest across the States would have made it a simple matter for Mrs King to have found someone in her own country to write her foreword. The fact that she invited Miss Jekyll to do so was a tribute not only to her books and to the esteem in which they were already held across the water but also to the appeal which the English style of gardening, as expounded by the owner of Munstead Wood, must have had for Americans at this time.

Miss Jekyll wrote, in August 1913, to thank Mrs King and to accept 'with the greatest pleasure. . . . All your garden ideas are so sympathetic that it will be an easy and pleasant task. I am so glad you are taking up the colour question and trying to show what you mean by colour words. . . .'

It must, by now, be obvious that Mrs King and Miss Jekyll had so much in common in their writings either could usually be speaking for the other. For instance, in the American's *The Well-Considered Garden* the preface is by Gertrude Jekyll. I quote from it now:

> What is needed for the doing of the best gardening is something of an artist's training . . . for gardening, in its best expression, may well rank as one of the fine arts. But without the many years of labor needed for any hope of success in architecture, sculpture, or painting, there are certain simple rules whose observance, carried out in horticulture, will make all the difference between a garden that is utterly commonplace and one that is full of beauty and absorbing interest.
>
> Of these one of the chief is a careful consideration of color arrangement. Early in her gardening career this fact impressed itself upon the author's mind. . . . A few such lessons put in practise will assuredly lead on to independent effort; for the learner, dilligently reading and carefully following the good guidance, will soon find the way open to a whole new field of beauty and delight.

In Chapter I, entitled 'Color Harmony', Mrs King writes:

> The past mistress of the charming art of color combination in gardening is, without doubt, Miss Jekyll, the well-known English

writer; and to the practised amateur, I commend her 'Colour in the Flower Garden' as the last word in truly artistic planting, and full of valuable suggestions for one who has worked with flowers long enough to have mastered the complications of his soil and climate.

Later in the same publication, she continues:

Yes, in the matter of books necessary to garden knowledge, Bailey [Dr L. H. Bailey, the American gardener designer] is undoubtedly the keystone of the garden arch. Every other book may go—this cannot. And the arch thus firmly held together, let us proceed to decorate it appropriately by mentioning as our second necessary book Miss Jekyll's masterpiece, 'Color in the Flower Garden'. Given these two publications, any intelligent man or woman with time, money, and the wish to do it need have nothing ugly in their gardens. . . . Bailey furnishes us the sound knowledge, the structure for gardening. Miss Jekyll—who better? provides the structure with a more exquisite and carefully considered garnishment than has ever to my knowledge been given before by man or woman. With her ingratiating pen, too, she is so happy in creating pictures that the garden-lover cannot choose but hear . . . Can anything surpass the beauty of description of the various gardens at Munstead Wood in the 'Color in the Flower Garden' . . .? Yet there is something here better than beauty; there is suggestion which amounts to inspiration—Miss Jekyll has the faculty of setting all sorts of plans going in one's head as one reads what she writes; and I will venture to say that most of her readers in this country do not attempt to copy slavishly her ideas but use them as points of departure for their own plantings. Miss Jekyll has succeeded not only in so charmingly showing us what she has planned and accomplished in her Surrey garden, but in giving a great impulse toward the finest art of gardening—gardening as a fine art.

We hear it said: 'Miss Jekyll's books are written for England, and the English climate and conditions.' Yes; but here is Bailey to set one straight culturally for one's own spot in America. . . .

In *From a New Garden* she is writing of fragrance:

I cannot pass by that old rose, Zephirine Drouhin, often named in Miss Jekyll's books, and always with affectionate mention of its fragrance. For this is surely the sweetest scent of any rose. . . .

I must name too, Madame Gregoire Staechelin, a beautiful pink and fragrant climbing rose from Barcelona, Spain.

And then about the colours of tulips:

One glimpse of what is done with them by our greatest gardener, Miss Jekyll, I had at Munstead Wood two years ago. Here in the 'Spring Garden' I, alone and in the rain, saw such a picture as only her hand could create. A great drift of spring colour was here, formed for the most part of the single early tulip White Swan, and tulips Thomas Moore and La Merveille, richly intertwined with a superb purple sage which Miss Jekyll uses to perfection (but which I have never seen growing in this country), 'a charming accompaniment to anything of pink or purple colouring, 'and with which Miss Jekyll often uses tulips Clara Butt and the early pink Rosamund. Here were brown and orange wallflowers and foregrounds of dark heuchera leaves, arabis, and forget-me-not, with aubretia of pale and deeper purple. Crown imperials stood in their orange glory at the back of this border, and beyond all was a fine shrub in full clear orange bloom, *Berberis Darwini*, a shrub that we cannot grow in our part of the country, but which one covets for its beautiful orange bloom. All was green about this picture when I saw it; that rich ineffable green seen only under the English sky and brightened by the English showers; but there I stood and wondered at the beauty of the right use of the tulip, as often I have wondered at the charm of the descriptions of such uses in the books of this best of all garden writers of our generation.

23 *Part of Mrs King's garden at Orchard House, Alma*

She describes in the same book how her friendship with Miss Jekyll started—through delphinium seeds:

> Well do I remember the first flowering of the delphinium in a garden of my own. It was, to be sure, an annual, *D. chinense*, a clear light blue. The seed was sown in a parallelogram which had been dug, but not specially enriched; for this was virgin soil of the Illinois corn belt or near it; the resulting flowers were amazing in quality and colour. So remarkable were they that, on sending a photograph of them to Miss Jekyll, I was asked by return mail for some of the seed, thus beginning an acquaintance which has become of the warmest of friendships.

The garden of Orchard House, Alma, was well on its way, and Mrs King must have been getting material ready for her own book in which she describes its making. She emphasizes three foundation stones on which it was built: it must have a plan, it must have privacy and its colour must be handled as an art. She loved using colour as a painter loves to employ his paintbox. She wrote, in *The Well-Considered Garden*:

> My latest joy is my white border connecting two sets of beds where many old and some new fashioned flowers are massed according to a plan which does change somewhat every year, as my visions of colour combinations vary. What a lot of white flowers one can find to crowd in front of the background of tall white phlox. . . . Here are all the white-flowering bulbs, and rock-cress, sweet william, columbine, lilies, peonies, Japanese anemones, achilleas, the lovely *Campanula pyramidalis*, summer hyacinths, feverfews; and after the bulbs have faded away every spot is filled with white annuals. This border has just had its first birthday. . . .

(Perhaps a forerunner of Miss Sackville-West's grey and white garden at Sissinghurst.) As she suggested various colour groupings she was also aware that 'taste in colour is essentially a personal matter'. She was deeply indebted to Gertrude Jekyll but it is obvious from the groupings described that she also had ideas of her own.

Their correspondence flourished into closer friendship, and we find Miss Jekyll writing to thank Mrs King for sending her a book on American gardens. She commented on the Italian influence, especially at Drumthwacket, New Jersey.

> A very capable architect has been at work and has reproduced some genuine Italian feeling. The success of Drumthwacket is that of the artist, although it is fairly far North. I think the true Italian character is only suitable or completely possible in a corresponding climate such as that of California and others of the Southern States.

In *Old Time Gardens* by Alice Morse Earle, there are references to gardens all over the States from Georgia to Pennsylvania, from Massachusetts to South Carolina and Drumthwacket is one of those illustrated. The author writes, 'This garden affords a good example of the accord which should ever exist between the garden and its surroundings'. (A point that is especially emphasized by Miss Jekyll and illustrated by Gledstone Hall, a house near Skipton, North Yorkshire, designed by Lutyens with a garden planned by her, although she was too old at the time to visit it.)

Mrs King's comprehensive chapter on 'American Gardens', in *The Story of the Garden* by Eleanour Sinclair Rohde, mentions the early days of Mt Vernon, Virginia. She writes:

> The diaries of General Washington give a number of references to the garden and from these allusions we are obliged to draw our conclusions. The first of these references to the flower garden in its present form is in the diary for February 4th. 1786. ... The next information on the development of the garden is recorded for April 10th. 1786. General Washington mentions here the construction of the fence surmounting the wall: '. . . and also began to put up my palisades (on the wall).'

She goes on:

> Among the gardens which have been made today with great feeling for the past is a highly interesting small one, that of the Mission House, Stockbridge, Massachusetts, the first built in that town and now set up and perfectly furnished for its period. It is close to the street and near one side of the lot. Between it and the highway is a small fenced-in herb garden. Behind the house is a little yard. . . . This garden of the Mission House is not restoration but a recreating of an early American garden as it was supposed to exist. . . . The gardens mentioned or described in these pages such as Mt. Vernon, and that of the Old Mission House, at Stockbridge, are two notable examples of restoration and recreating, and are of untold value to our people. . . .

Mrs King makes frequent references to Miss Jekyll's books and, I am pleased to say, gives special mention to one of my own favourites. In the final three pages of *The Beginner's Garden*, she writes:

> And here, since Miss Jekyll's name is constantly appearing and re-appearing in current gardening literature in this country, it may be interesting to say that 'Color in the Flower Garden' is one of eight books from Miss Jekyll's pen issued within nine years' time. The others are: 'Wood and Garden,' 'Home and Garden,' 'Wall and

Water Gardens,' 'Lilies for English Gardens,' 'Roses for English Gardens,' 'Flower Decoration in the House,' and 'Children and Gardens.'

Since I have lately been re-reading Miss Jekyll's book, 'Children and Gardens' (Miss Jekyll is the foremost amateur in and writer on gardening in England), and since each chapter of this book has in it something of value for parents and children alike, I will give here a digest of the book for those who may not have seen it, since it has unfortunately been allowed to go out of print.

Published in 1908 and with over a hundred photographs and drawings by Miss Jekyll herself, this book has many practical suggestions looking toward gardening for children. 'I think,' writes the author, 'that the best way to help children to love and value a garden is to give them a pretty one ready-made. The actual planting, though it must be learnt in time, would seem to come better a little later. The daily tending of an already made garden is better to begin with; it is more interesting and inspiring, and the needs of the flowers can be seen and attended to with immediate result. It is in every way more delightful and encouraging to a child to have the lovely flowers to tend at once than to have to flounder through a mass of failure and mistake, and then to wait the best part of a year before there is anything whatever to be seen.'

Here was, for me, a new idea. I had always thought that a child should begin at the very beginning. But this other plan is so reasonable, above all, as Miss Jekyll says, so encouraging, that I have quite changed my mind and believe this to be best.

The first chapter of 'Children and Gardens' gives some account of Miss Jekyll's own childhood, and of the way in which her own attention was drawn to flowers; first by the dandelions in a London Park, then by the water forget-me-nots by ponds in the grounds of her father's country place, and the gay marsh Marigolds there in April. Where there is money, and room, Miss Jekyll advises giving children a playhouse, with a little garden before it. This, one may say, is a pleasure for the rich alone. No, it is not. While the little house can be of costly materials and even designed by an architect, any man with a hand for tools and a little lumber can build a sample house for his children's fun. To a child a shack is as good as a palace. The same amount of fun can be had in and from it; and any one who remembers how, on rainy days, with chairs and shawls they built houses for themselves and played at living in them will realize what the delight is of having a little playhouse of their own. All children adore the feeling of remoteness, of independence if they have only a place of their own. . . .

Then near the playhouse, says Miss Jekyll, a little vegetable strip should provide lettuce, radishes, and other things that could be prepared in the playhouse kitchen for a little salad, while the flower-beds would provide for the table decorations. Some good recipes then follow in 'Children and Gardens' for 'playhouse soups,' Julienne and white milk soups, and for a French salad; also for scrambled eggs, scones, and for little cakes called 'Fairy Cakes.'

147

Chapters follow on Early Weeds, on Seeds . . . on Cowslips—
where the making of cowslip balls is described—Smells and Shapes,
Botany, My First Garden, Flowers from Your Own Gardens,
Adventures on the Lawn, Amusements, and last of all a charming
disquisition on 'Pussies in the Garden.' One more quotation:

'It is amusing to see the different patterns that kittens lying in a
round basket will sometimes get into. I have seen five kittens almost
symmetrically arranged like cutlets in a pigeon pie. It was almost
impossible to believe that only four small people could have so many
little toes. Three kittens at nearly equal distances round a saucer of
milk make quite a pretty pattern. The architect said it was an
equi*cate*ral triangle.'

This book now nearly twenty years old, is as new and as delightful
as though published yesterday. That it is out of print is one reason for
this endeavor to communicate something of its substance and quality.
It is a book for old and young, a guide, a friend, and a delight.

In 1913 the Garden Club of America was formed in Philadelphia.
On 30 April twenty-four women were invited to attend this first
meeting, and one of the four vice-presidents elected was Mrs
Francis King of Michigan. In January 1914, after a visit to
England where she had met members of the Women's Farm &
Garden Association, she was instrumental in founding a similar
group in Philadelphia, of which she was its first President. Today
it has a membership of over 8,000 and through its membership of
the Association of Country Women of the World it helps to
maintain a United Nations representative.

There were still more publications and in her mid-sixties
(1927) came *The Beginner's Garden* followed, in 1929, by *The
Gardener's Colour Book*, which was a joint venture with John
Fothergill. It was highly original, being in the form of charts, and
Mrs King was anxious for her co-author to have the chief credit for
the idea. In his introduction he writes:

And now, Mrs Francis King, one of the few fascinating and suggestive
garden writers, is going to let her compatriots have the benefit of her
uncommon knowledge by adapting this tabulation to the needs and
conditions of the United States. Henceforward there will be no excuse
for a jumble of colours in the gardens of either this or that country.
The Spreadeagle, Thame, Oxon.   *John Fothergill*

A year later, in 1930, one of her most successful books was
published in New York—*From a New Garden*. She must by now
have been getting on towards seventy-five but her book shows no
sign of advancing age. It is fresh with enthusiasm if also now
packed with experience. The foreword and the introduction to

From A New Garden are both tinged not only with appreciation, but also with real affection for the author. She has made her contribution to the American way of life without any doubt. She is bereft of her garden at Alma, Michigan, and she is starting again. I should like to quote from the introduction by A. P. Saunders of Clinton, New York:

> It would be impertinent to undertake to introduce Mrs Francis King to the gardening public of America. No other writer is more widely known and to no other do the lovers of plants in this country turn with a more affectionate admiration. She has made a place for herself in the library of every intelligent person sensitive to beauty in the garden. . . .
> When Mrs King was awarded the George Robert White medal by the Massachusetts Horticultural Society—the most signal horticultural honour that can come to anyone in America—Professor Sargent stated that the medal was given to her in recognition of her service to horticulture by increasing the love of plants and gardens among the women of the United States . . . by the example of her enthusiasm and industry. . . . Having once seen her aim in life and grasped it, she has never let go. . . . Not only has she told us how it should be done, but as long as she had her garden at Alma, Michigan, she showed how her ideas worked out when they were put into practice. Now that the well-known garden is no longer hers, she still carries on undaunted. . . . And therefore our admiration goes out to her for what she has done, but even more for the constancy which has been back of the doing of it. . . . with an admirable resolution she continues to put her thoughts and her visions before her public; a public which because of her writings cares, I am sure, somewhat more for the things of the spirit than if her books had not been.

Like Andrew Jackson Downing before her who wrote: 'The love of country is inseparably connected with the love of home', Mrs King's greatest contribution must surely be considered the lessons learnt from her own garden and her love for it. Again, like Downing, who is described in *An Introduction to Landscape Architecture* as having, by the mid nineteenth century, 'Established himself as a tastemaker in gardening on the East Coast in America', Mrs King, who died in 1948, made a similar impact, always with generous acknowledgement to the English taste. Louisa King summed up her own thoughts on the subject when she wrote:

> From our gardening forebears, English, Dutch, Spanish, we have a great inheritance of interest in this art, an art which I hold is almost divine. Let me confess my devotion to the English tradition in gardening.

E. A. Bowles
1865–1954

It is pleasure and a privilege to be asked to write
about a real garden. . . . It is not so very long since
carpet bedding went out of fashion. . . . But now the
accursed thing is once more rearing its head. . . .
For the rich must have their money's worth in
show: . . . better a hundred yards of Arabis than
half a dozen vernal Gentians. . . . What would they
say now if they were led into the garden through
which we are now going to be conducted by its
creator?

REGINALD FARRER
Preface to E. A. Bowles, *My Garden in Spring*

Myddleton House, near Enfield, Middlesex, was the home of the
Bowles family, and was where the young Edward Augustus grew
up. He used to say that not only was his interest in gardening first
aroused by Canon Ellacombe, but that the Bitton garden was the
most interesting he had ever seen. There have been many cases of
direct gardening influence from one generation to another, but
this was surely one of the most outstanding—the firms of Paul,
Tradescant and Veitch are all obvious examples but these are
family ones, understandable from heritage and background. The
link between Canon Ellacombe and E. A. Bowles began through
the New River Scheme.

The history of this scheme goes back at least 300 years to when
Sir Hugh Myddleton (*c.* 1560–1631) founded the company and
was to supply London with clean water. The canal was constructed
and was no small undertaking, being about forty-eight miles in
length. Professor W. T. Stearn comments: 'Within the garden
itself the New River is a pleasant landscape feature rather than an
aid to gardening', and E. A. Bowles writes: '. . . of water there
seems to be plenty for the New River runs through the very centre
of the garden, but though it may carry many millions of gallons
through it, clever Sir Hugh Myddleton made its clay banks so
strong that even after 300 years they let no water soak away.' In
any case the water was chiefly derived from chalk wells and Mr
Bowles describes at least one disaster: 'A liberal dose of New

River water, given in a spirit of kindness to a collection of dwarf rhododendrons during a time of drought killed all but one in a fortnight.'

But more important even than the New River with all its hazards was the fact that Henry Carington B. Bowles (father of Edward Augustus), who was the last Governor of the New River Company, had as a fellow member on the board Canon Ellacombe. Could there have been a more important stroke of good fortune for the younger man? Meetings were held at Myddleton House every week, and the Canon attended them regularly. In his article in the *Royal Horticultural Society Journal* for August 1955, Professor Stearn writes of Mr Bowles as being 'one of the last direct links with the great amateur horticulturalists of late Victorian times, with H. N. Ellacombe, C. Wolley Dod, Ellen Willmott, H. T. Elwes and others.' In his book *My Garden in Spring* there are frequent references to the Canon's generosity, and several of these are quoted in Chapter Three. Referring particularly to the Myddleton Garden, Bowles writes:

> I grew mine [Citrus trifoliata] from pips taken out of an orange given to me by Canon Ellacombe, that had ripened in his garden and two of the resultant youngsters planted side by side in the rock garden have grown wonderfully quickly. They are now 10 feet high. . . .

and of *Anemone blanda*:

> It must by this time be quite apparent to my readers that half of my choicest treasures are due to visits to Bitton and the generosity of Canon Ellacombe, and they will not be surprised to learn that both a pale and a dark form of this glorious miracle are now thriving in a bay of my rock garden. . . .

and so on, and so on.

As anyone who has ever received gifts from a gardening friend knows, it is not just the actual plant which is of value. In the first place, a great deal of trouble may have been involved in its propagation. It may have been tried out in different locations, and 'a few seasons' may have gone by before it was advanced enough in growth to propagate. It is, in fact, often on these seemingly small bundles of earth and roots or thin stems of cuttings that some of the best gardens are built up, forming a kind of linked chain which ensures that many precious plants survive, and many of the old roses, pinks, sweet peas, etc., are saved from extinction.

But Canon Ellacombe gave more than plants to the young gardener, and two of the most important gifts were based on spiritual guidance and could have been remote from gardening.

24 E. A. Bowles, who readily acknowledged the gardening debt he owed to Canon Ellacombe

First he taught him that 'it is more blessed to give than to receive' and that one of the greatest pleasures in having a garden is in giving plants away whenever they can be spared. The other was perhaps more practical—how to form a good library and how important this can be as a background to the actual planning and planting of a garden. To select even one book for guidance can be a valuable acquisition or it can be a disaster. To have a book behind one, or at any rate an author, to whose work one can turn in any emergency for information which one knows to be *completely* reliable is probably half of the success of making a good garden. And Canon Ellacombe showed E. A. Bowles how to look out for standard works, how to collect notices of sales and which authors were dependable in different branches of horticultural knowledge. Anyone with even only a few books on their shelves will know the value of such advice.

In the second chapter of *My Garden in Spring* Mr Bowles describes the garden at Myddleton House, rather than the individual plants, as it is the type and situation of ground which has enforced the type of gardening—

> climate, soil (and trees) contrive to make it the driest and hungriest in Great Britain, and therefore arises the line of gardening I have been driven into. . . . many find the garden too museumy to please them. I plead guilty to the charge, knowing there is more of the botanist and love of species and natural forms and varieties in me than there is of the florist or fine cultivator..

Certainly there are fine trees, vistas across water and plantings of flowering shrubs for which one might well feel envy. But the fact that it is a collector's garden emerges even now, nearly thirty years after it has ceased to be his personal possession, and a repository for rare bulbs and plants collected from friends in this country as well as from many parts of the world.

Perhaps most of the plants and shrubs from abroad were sent or brought back by, or collected with, Reginald Farrer. Sometimes they came from Farrer's home at Ingleborough in North Yorkshire, as in the case of *Galanthus elwesii*, sometimes bulbs went north to Ingleborough from Myddleton House as in the case of the short-stemmed variety of the same snowdrop, christened by Farrer 'Fat Boy'.

Together they hunted for rare primulas in the Tyrol and at Myddleton House there soon appeared a large area of rock garden to take Farrer's alpines. It was the 'Moraine Magician' himself who helped Mr Bowles to plan his 'plain granite chip arrangement'.

EAB loved the spring-flowering colchicums, the many varieties of narcissi, various hepaticas, cyclamen and anemones—'There is a charm in the simple form of a single Anemone that goes straight to my heart' is his opening sentence for the chapter on anemones. A well-earned tribute comes to him from America in a book by Mrs Francis King. She is writing of spring flowers and especially here of the yellow crocus: 'As for the yellow crocuses, I never look at them if I can help it!' In her book, *The Well-Considered Garden*, she goes on:

> Mr E. A. Bowles, of Waltham Cross, England, tells us that the more delicate and subtle tones of yellow are to be found in several varieties of crocus species; it is to these that I plan to turn my attention with

great ardor another season. Few of these species crocus do I already know in my own borders—only half a dozen—and as I believe readers will rejoice as I have done in some of Mr Bowles's enthusiastic comments on or descriptions of these flowers, I offer no apology for quoting from him, as I mention the flowers of which he knows so much, through years of collecting, growing and study.

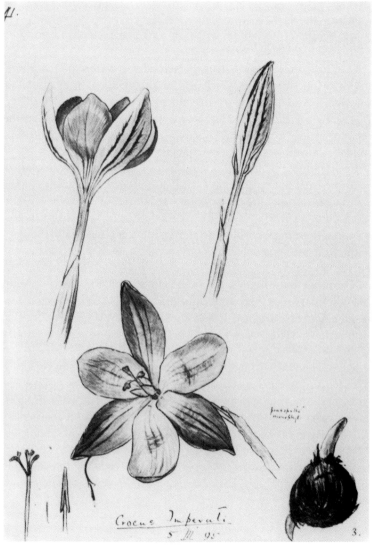

25 Crocus imperati: *a pencil drawing by E. A. Bowles*

He had a great affection for plants with variegated foliage of which he introduced many into his garden, periwinkle, box, acer, iris, elder, laurustinus. But perhaps the most unusual collection was what he called his 'Lunatic Asylum', a bed to hold shrubs of 'abnormal tendencies'. The first crazy inhabitant was the twisted hazel which came as a sucker from Bitton. The strange but characteristic appearance of this tree in the summer, when it seems to be malformed and diseased, contrasts with the almost beautiful effect of the interlacing stems in winter. There were other strange incumbents of the bed: an elder with congested growth, two laburnums, a dwarf ash and two forms of Butcher's broom.

The idea of such a bed seems to fit better into the garden of Wuthering Heights than the almost suburban garden only ten miles out of London and Mr Bowles does not expect it to be attractive to everyone. 'Does my Lunatic Asylum appeal to you, or appal you?' he asks. 'I cannot tear some visitors away from it, and others who do not care about the demented inmates are pleased with the effects of the surroundings.' It cannot be denied that the idea has botanical interest, although it holds no attraction for this biographer.

Known especially for his love of fragrance in the garden, Mr Bowles began a talk to the Royal Horticultural Society in 1952 with a quote from Milton:

> . . . fragrant the futile earth
> After soft showers.

'That is the very thing I wanted,' he went on,

> because I am not limited to the fragrance which comes from flowers. There is a general outdoor fragrance which is one of the most delightful of the experiences that make life worth living. Take, for instance, the first time that you really smell spring in the air—it is hard to define what sort of scent it is, but it conveys the idea of fresh and young growth, and when we get it we feel 'Now we have got rid of the winter.'

This is almost word for word what Miss Jekyll writes in her first book *Wood and Garden*:

> There is always in February some one day, at least, when one smells the yet distant, but surely coming, summer. Perhaps it is a warm, mossy scent that greets one when, passing along the southern side of a hedgebank; or it may be in some woodland opening, where the sun has coaxed out the pungent smell of the trailing ground ivy, whose blue flowers will soon appear; but the day always comes. . . .

Like Miss Jekyll he comments on the various reactions of some people to the same scent. With *Jasminum polyanthum*—'my housemaid thinks it a horrid sickly smell', and like Miss Sackville-West, he does not 'care much for Phlox, which smells like a combination of pepper and pigsty'. Some of his favourites are: Farrer's *Viburnum fragrans* (now *farreri*), japonica, violets, snowdrops, Mount Etna broom and newly opened evening primroses. Perhaps the most unstinted praise is for cowslips—'I believe that if heaven smells of anything it will be of cowslips.'

Characteristically the list ends with a reference to Canon Ellacombe—'I have left the Californian Bay, *Umbellularia californica* for the end. . . . The fragrance is as pungent as cinnamon sticks. . . . the fallen and dried leaves still retain their powerful odour. . . .' He describes his own tree planted on the south side of a stout holly hedge for shelter—'It is a self sown seedling of the fine old specimen which used to grow, and I hope may still do so, at the right hand side of the porch at Bitton Vicarage. . . .'

About the man himself Professor William Stearn writes in warm friendship: 'Of him it could be truly said that he was "the soul of honesty and the enemy of humbug—a steadfast friend . . . and no time-saver" who did with a whole heart whatever he undertook.' Professor Stearn ends with these words:

> Lest it should be thought that, in bringing together these notes on his long and beneficial life, affection has given a false perspective, it seems fitting to conclude with some words about him from a letter written by a California botanist and horticulturist: 'In America he was held in the highest esteem by myself and all others who knew him personally or came into direct contact with him through his writings. To us he ranked among the best that England could produce.'

Happy memories come from a friend—some years younger than Bowles—who lived for many years about two miles away at Enfield. Later in life, when 'Gussie', as he was known to his friends, could only read with the aid of a large magnifying glass, this friend used to read to him. He met EAB through church services and they both sang as tenors in the choir. Frequently he was invited to tea on a Sunday afternoon and then they went on together to evensong. This friend remarked to me that he liked the atmosphere of Myddleton House—its friendliness and welcome, its homeliness and its jolly games which made everyone feel at ease. He himself sometimes sat down at the piano and played while

Gussie and whoever else was there would join in the singing. It was informal. If it happened to be winter-time, and there was ice that would 'hold', EAB would produce spare pairs of skates for those without any. Then they might skate on the lake in the woods belonging to Gussie's brother. This friend remembers especially the scent of the balsam poplars when they were walking through these same woods in early summer.

As a young man, in his Cambridge days, Gussie was a great bug-hunter and collector of moths and butterflies. Some of these collections were made with an undergraduate later well known throughout the land—Stanley Baldwin. EAB had many, many friends and acquaintances, but fundamentally he was shy and reserved. For this reason it might be expected that he would enjoy Reginald Farrer's company—both of them virtually 'only' children, highly intelligent, with many of the same interests with regard to plants and the same scholarly approach to their study. 'I once thought I did not care greatly for Alpine Primulas. . . .', he wrote, 'but a few weeks among them in the Tyrol, with Mr Farrer as interpreter of their charms, converted me. . . .' On a similar occasion: 'A few days later Mr Farrer took me to another ridge just to look at other interesting primulas. . . .' Writing specifically of *P. bowlesii*, he says: 'A whole morning of careful search this June rewarded Mr Farrer and me with three plants of it.' He even repeats a compliment (unusual for him) when he mentions Farrer's looking round the Myddleton House garden and his reaction to a dwarf almond, among rare crocuses, primulas and the blue *Anemone blanda*. 'Mr Farrer always lingers lovingly over this corner, and declares it to be his idea of good gardening.'

Among the Hills, Reginald Farrer's planting-hunting book published in 1911, was dedicated to E. A. Bowles. Theirs had been a friendship which had grown unusually quickly. They might almost have known that time was not on their side. Whereas Gussie's first important friendship had been with Canon Ellacombe, who died during the war years (1916) at the age of ninety-two, Farrer and Bowles had only met very recently when this dedication appeared. Shortly Farrer was to be invited to write the Preface for *My Garden in Spring* (1914), which he did with the greatest pleasure. One sentence from the Preface shall illustrate in a few words the feeling that Farrer had for the Myddleton House garden.

'Come', he writes, 'into Mr Bowles's garden and learn what true gardening is, and what is the real beauty of plants, and what the nature of their display.'

Bowles himself wrote: 'I have no wish to see Niagara or New York skyscrapers, but I should like to stand in a wood full of Bloodroot when the flowers are wide open.' (*Sanguinaria canadensis*, about the third week in April.)

Viscountess Wolseley

1872–1936

Bring some mignonette, some sweet pea, some hops, some wallflower, some heartsease seed, and a few dozens of crocus roots; anything and everything will grow here. . . .

FROM LORD WOLSELEY
The Letters of Lord and Lady Wolseley, 1870–1911

As a small girl the Viscountess Wolseley, years afterwards to become the founder of the Glynde School for Lady Gardeners, often stayed at the Kentish home of Alfred Austin, author of *The Garden that I Love*, *In Veronica's Garden*, among others, and later to become Poet Laureate. According to Marjory Pegram in *The Wolseley Heritage*, it was evidently largely due to Mr Austin that

> she learned the love of country life which later brought her much happiness. . . . together they explored the cool depths of bluebell woods and ransacked the hedgerows for flowers; he told her wonderful legends about flowers, and was keenly alert to hidden birds' nests, and the homes of rabbit and mole; and the memory remained with her of those blissful days. . . .

She was born on 15th September 1872, in Belgrave Road, Pimlico, the only child of Colonel and Mrs Garnet Wolseley, and lived the typical existence of most soldiers' daughters—that is, her father was often away from home in some far-off area of war and her mother either stayed in London leading the social life of the day or travelled to be as near to him as possible. *The Life of Lord Wolseley* tells how, in February 1874, as Major-General, he was leading a campaign on the Gold Coast and with the fall of Kumasi one of the terms of peace 'required the payment of 50,000 ounces of gold'. An auction was held of the king's treasure which included the king's crown and orb. These Major-General Wolseley bought, 'the latter to become his infant daughter's rattle. . . .' Frances, at the age of two, was already involved with her father's life-work:

From the day that he received his commission to Cyprus (1878) he determined that sooner or later, and the sooner the better, Lady Wolseley should join him there. He was equally determined that he would deprive himself of this pleasure until adequate accommodation could be found for her and his little daughter. . . . By Christmas the modest building which was to do duty as Government House was ready, and Wolseley could resume the family life which he preferred to everything . . . The wooden building stood on a flat-topped hill a little more than a mile from Nicosia. . . . The panorama, for a distance of nearly thirty miles, was superb, and Wolseley's interest in afforestation, which his daughter was to inherit and give expression to in horticulture, was agreeably exercised in planting acres of eucalyptus, in ordering every sort of seed and root from England, and in transferring fully grown date-palms to the natural terrace which fronted and flanked the house. . . .

An example of his ordering 'every sort of seed and root from England' comes in his letter (I quote here extensively from *The Letters of Lord and Lady Wolseley*) to his wife from Camp Nicosia, Cyprus, 24th November 1878:

> Bring some mignonette, some sweet pea, some hop, some wallflower, some heartsease seed, and a few dozen of crocus roots; anything and everything will grow here. Also enough good seed to sow an acre. . . .

Frances accompanied her mother on many of these excursions and must have been aware, in a childish way, of her parents' deep affection for each other and for her, and of their interest in plants and the countryside. She stayed variously in Cyprus (when her father was appointed Governor), in France where she learnt to speak the language fluently, at Freshwater (while her father was in Russia) where she and her mother visited Tennyson, and in 1885 went on a long visit to Egypt and Italy. Quiet country intervals with the Austins, walking through bluebell woods in Kent, hunting for birds' nests, must have provided welcome relief from so much sightseeing and bustling about. The future Poet Laureate and the small girl became fond companions, and in March 1877 he wrote the following poem to her:

'Impromptu' To Frances Garnet Wolseley

> Little maiden just beginning
> To be comely, . . . and winning,
> In whose form I catch the traces
> Of your mother's gifts and graces,
> And around whose head the glory
> Of your father's growing story,
> O'er whose cradle fortune guided,

Mars and Venus both presided,
May your fuller years inherit
Female charm and manly merit; . . .
Fate no fainter heart allot you
Than the brave one that begot you,
So that you a race continue
Worthy of the blood within you,
Handing down the gifts you bring them,
With a better bard to sing them.

March 1877
Soliloquies in Song

A few extracts from letters at this time follow.

(From Lord Wolseley)   *Government House, Cape Coast.*
6.10.73.

I wonder as I pray for you every morning and evening if you are at the same moment praying for me. Tell me when you write that you do not forget me in your prayers. . . .

17.10.73
. . . I trust that God will spare me to carry out this campaign successfully; but the personal ambition of which my very heart was at one time so full, has in great measure died out within me, and I have often of late wished that I could be taken. Don't vote these thoughts gloomy. I never was in better health or in better or higher spirits *outwardly* than at present, but I feel a sort of relief and comfort in telling you just what I think and feel. . . .

3rd. Nov. 73
. . . Please send me out a box or two of really good Havanas, for many sailors dine with me here and make large hauls upon my tobacco. I smoke three or four cigars myself every day, and find they agree with me.

(From Lady Wolseley)
Tours. Hotel de l'Universe. 21.10.1878.
The French papers have it that you are to be Commander-in-Chief against Afghanistan. . . . I heard this morning from Lady Sligo. . . . I am longing to hear from you, that my plans may be a little more definite. I feel doubtful about Malta for an indefinite time; the 'sociability' of it would be rather too much for a Trappist like me. At the same time, if there were any chance of your going to Afghanistan, I should fly to Malta at once, to be near at hand to rush over and see you. Please recollect you must not go on to Afghan without seeing me, *if I even see you only for five minutes and go thousands of miles to see you.* I hope you will like some cretonne I have bought here; though pretty it is scarcely *Morris.* . . .

18th Nov. 78.
Your letter of the 5th., detailing the Naples plan and desiring me to be there on the 10th. December, has just reached me. If our house has no heating apparatus ready, and fireplaces are not finished when I get to Malta, I think I would leave Frances there for a few weeks, as a new cold house might lay the child up. . . .

(From Lord Wolseley)

On board the *Calabria*, *Wed. 2.8.82.*
. . . Give Frances a kiss for me and tell her she must have her pony. . . .

(From Lady Wolseley)

Homburg, 30th August, 1882.
Frances was delighted with her letter. This pear she has drawn entirely alone from nature. She has a drawing master, and a little German girl comes to play with her for an hour every day, so she is not quite idle. I miss you so very much I cannot take interest in anything but Egypt or even read other things in the paper.

In February 1885 Frances was first presented to Queen Victoria, an event she registered in her diary. In April of that year she and her mother went to Egypt to spend two or three weeks with her father. They left England on Good Friday and arrived at Alexandria six days later. From Egypt, Lady Wolseley and Frances went on to Italy, arriving at Bologna on 26 April. They afterwards visited Ravenna, Florence and Venice, and Lady Wolseley appears to be delighted with her daughter.

F is really the most charming companion to travel with. She reads Murray day and night and looks at everything. So unlike most children who would be tired of galleries and churches. I let *her* make our plans for the day, because it increases her pleasure, and she does it well, too.

She was thirteen. In July her father was granted leave and Frances and her mother went to Dover to meet him. They all returned to London together, where they were given a rapturous welcome by hundreds of people assembled to meet them. In August her father, by now Sir Garnet Wolseley, was made a viscount. She writes in her diary: 'Papa called me to Mamma's room and there read me a letter from the Prime Minister, Lord Salisbury, which said that Papa was to be made a Viscount, and that by special request of the Queen, the title should descend to his daughter. I had to write my first letter to the Queen.'

By the next year, aged fourteen, she was already going to semi-grown-up parties. She had become much interested in painting

and, after having some lessons with Mrs Helen Allingham
(1848–1926), 'she was taken one day to the house of John Sargent
for his advice. He was painting in his garden, upon a six-foot
canvas, a sunlit table and a bowl of scarlet geraniums, and
suggested that Frances should make a sketch of the same model.
. . . she never heard the verdict.'

26 Frances, Viscountess Wolseley, with her cairn terrier puppies in 1919

She also had literature lessons from Edmund Gosse. Then came an important move of the Wolseley family from London (Hill Street) into the Surrey countryside and it was here that her interest in a garden, as something to be planted and cared for, really began. Her schoolroom days were, in any case, coming to an end and her mother impressed upon Frances that she must 'not live solely for amusement. . . .' Her diary went on: 'Young women, I was told, must learn to love some solid hobby. . . .' Although she already loved riding, painting, and had studied languages in no small degree, the 'solid hobby' in her case soon appeared to be gardening as she was put in charge of the home garden at their new home.

'Beyond the fact of having always loved country things', she wrote in her diary, 'I knew little about gardening. What kinds of shrubs and plants were suited to our soil? What were we going to grow?' From these queries developed the contact with William Robinson of Gravetye, whose garden she visited with her mother in 1888. As she wrote in some detail of this visit and as it led to a friendship of great importance to her gardening life, I will quote the diary extracts as she wrote about it.

It was about the year 1888 that I first saw lovely old Gravetye Manor, and my visit came about in this way. My schoolroom days were drawing to a close and my mother, very wisely, decided that I must not live solely for amusement. Riding and dancing were fine things, she said, but they must not take up all one's time. Young women, I was told, must learn to love some solid hobby; they should become engrossed in it, so that it held deep interest for them right on into the later years of life. Being an active-minded woman herself, my mother could not brook having a daughter who did not throw herself whole-heartedly into some department of our busy lives.

The charge of the home garden was accordingly given over to me. Candidly, I must confess that at the outset I felt hopelessly ignorant of what was expected of me. . . . What were we going to grow? Merely flowers to cut for arranging in the house, or was our garden to look well in regard to colour and lay-out at every season of the year? These were some of the questions that had to be answered.

A gardening paper, studied each week, seemed to be the quickest way of learning the long Latin names and of finding out what plants were annuals and which were perennials. For this purpose we subscribed to one of the gardening papers edited by Mr William Robinson. Great was my delight to find that one or two of my questions, asked through the columns of this paper, were answered by the editor himself in a kind and encouraging way. After this a personal correspondence by letter commenced, and seeing how anxious I was to learn, Mr Robinson invited us to spend a day at Gravetye Manor.

Accordingly, upon a sunny day in spring-time, we travelled from our home at Ranger's House to Kingscote Station in Sussex. In those days a village fly had to be ordered to meet the train, and I recall how the weary horse pulled us up the lower road; for Mr Robinson had not then made the perfect entrance-drive of gentle gradient that was later engineered upon high ground to improve his property.

We turned sharp to the left beyond the little railway station, and driving through some beautiful woods belonging to his place, we ascended to higher ground still, until, passing some farm buildings, we reached his terraced orchards, with distant views of surrounding country. Here, beneath apple-trees in full blossom, were carpets of dancing daffodils. This was the first lesson that I learnt; for in those days it was a novelty to combine bulb-growing with fruit-culture.

A plain farm-gate admitted us to the private gardens; for the impressive stone-built posts and wrought-iron gates of today had not then been thought out. We knew that we were going to see a beautiful garden; but as the driver turned right-handed and flicked his whip for the final exertion of the old horse, a most perfect stone-built Elizabethan Manor House was exposed to view. This was indeed a joy to my mother, who loved old houses.

Our host, a six-foot tall, black-bearded, keen-faced man, then shewed us round the many surprise gardens that he was laying out. First there was the small paved and walled-in forecourt garden beneath the south windows.

This entry of the 'paved . . . forecourt' is of special interest, bearing as it does on the whole concept of Robinson's natural gardening combined, *where suitable*, with formal design. He has been mistakenly accused of only recommending 'wild gardening', but if his works are read carefully it will be appreciated that he constantly advised doing what would be best in any certain situation, certainly with emphasis on natural design but never to the complete exclusion of paved areas when necessary or desirable.

The gables of the house with their well-modelled stone pendants and the stone-mullioned windows looked down upon this. Here I learnt that stone-edged beds filled with sweet-smelling flowers should be close under the windows of the house; also that bedding-out was wholly unnecessary. Nothing could give greater pleasure than fragrant roses grown on their own roots and carpeted with low-growing Herniaria glabra, Aubretia, etc. Small bulbs could find homes near the edges of the stepping-stones that were placed at intervals upon the beds. These, and the low-growing plants and happy-faced pansies, all helped to retain moisture round the roots of the roses. They were new ideas in the 1880s.

Then, as we wandered between the further rose-beds on the long terrace to the west of the house, there was clematis growing upon a clever criss-cross arrangement of bamboo sticks, thus forming a climbing background to the roses. We mounted higher and higher up the hillside, passing beneath vine-clad pergolas, similar to ones seen in Italian gardens. On the terraces between these winding paths, I was shewn how groups of one or two flowering shrubs tell far more if massed. Here was no 'spot and dot' medley of many different kinds; the choice was restricted to perhaps two, and of these there were many in one group, so that thus their effect was accentuated.

Mr Robinson prided himself at that time upon having no glass for forcing. His great ambition was to demonstrate to an ignorant Victorian public that bedded-out geraniums and calceolarias, hitherto planted out in heart or star-shaped beds, were unworthy of the large amount of labour that had to be expended upon them. A natural arrangement of hardy plants, besides being of greater interest, could be permanently planted; accordingly they were labour-saving. His famous book, *The English Flower Garden*, stresses this, and at Gravetye Manor each terrace garden exemplifies it.

Frances has rightly been described as a 'most assiduous diarist', and how especially grateful can we be for this account—not only of the visit to Gravetye but also of the many lessons that were waiting there to be learnt from that garden by their example. Small points were emphasized as much as big ones and from the detailed description we are privileged to read it does not appear that anything was missed by this impressionable teenager. Later on we shall find William Robinson being consulted about further gardening matters so that the 'solid hobby' could be developed and its scope broadened as much as possible. Her next diary mention of him is in lighter vein: '. . . at 6 the guests and Papa arrived. Miss Willmott (aged 40, rich and great gardener) Mr R. aged 55, rich and a great gardener, why not marry them up!'

But there were other ways of living her life 'not solely for amusement'. In 1891 she mentions a letter from a girl friend who had been asking advice from Octavia Hill (known perhaps chiefly now as a founder of the National Trust, she was also a leader in social reform and a partner with Ruskin in the difficult work of slum clearance) on useful books to read. Among the books she recommended were *Report on Cases of Children Wanting Food; Homes of the London Poor; Life and Labour of the People, East London*. Frances does not mention how many she read herself but she was interested enough to make a note of the titles. In this year, too, she became the Honorary Secretary of the Irish Branch of the

Soldiers' and Sailors' Families' Association, and in 1895 she was appointed honorary secretary for their East End of London Branch where she was helped in her work by the Baroness Burdett-Coutts, who must have been about eighty at this time.

However, social life was still an important part of this young woman's timetable and was made, at the turn of the century, slightly less formal (and therefore more attractive) by the advent of the bicycle. Young ladies and gentlemen were still invited to country house parties but no one now went without taking with them their 'machine'. Frances was invited to Clarence House, with her bicycle. A diary entry for October 1896 opens with the following note: 'Papa and I out at 8, with a master for him to learn biking. . . .'

The same day she also recorded her other activities which make rather sad reading for an intelligent, attractive girl in her early twenties:

> Had a hairdresser to teach Blanchette a new way to do my hair and explain my fringe and its difficulties. . . . *En suite tête-à-tête* dinner with Papa. Both much bored and not knowing what to talk about, surrounded by the powdered supcriors! To bed at 10.40, feeling I had spent a selfish day—and rather a lonely one. . . .

A compliment meant much to her and this one is confided to her diary: 'Sir Evelyn [Wood] told me his daughter has told him she thought me lovely. Not that I'm fool enough to believe this—but it was nice of the girl saying so.'

> Early in 1898 the Wolseleys rented Glynde Place from their friends the Dudley Smiths and were so enchanted with it that they decided to take the little dower house called 'Farm House' for a short time with the option of a term of years later.

They all three loved Glynde. Frances in her diary comments on 8 March 1898: 'Another long interval. Now at Glynde for some weeks more—and love it.' And on 10 March her diary entry reads:

> Mr Robinson, the great gardener, came to spend the night. He arrived at luncheon time and was good enough to spend some hours of the afternoon in our new little garden at Farm House, giving me advice. Mostly about planting trees to hide the cowshed roof. I think I grasped his meaning. . . .

And of her father's feelings there is this biographical comment:

> . . . the farmhouse Glynde—the place he loved better than any other—
> he had lived in many houses, but Glynde alone seems to have been the
> home where he was on easy terms with life, and where no unwelcome
> visitor intruded. The house lay in the folds of the Sussex Downs and
> Wolseley loved to climb to their heights with some friends—or more
> happily still with his daughter—for a companion. The keen air acted as
> wine to his veins, and his friends would say that so exhilarating was his
> talk that he would infect them . . . with his own enthusiasm. . . .

There is unfortunately no suspicion of a hint of romance in the
visits of Mr Robinson. The gap in years between them—
approximately thirty years—was not impossibly great and they
had the interest of gardening in common, although knowledge of
the subject was abundant on one side and barely existing (at this
stage) on the other. She was charming and anxious to please and
he was good-looking and intelligent. But that seems to be as far as
it went, and in the meantime she was seeing a good deal of Lord
Castlemaine and considering seriously whether she should accept
his proposal of marriage. Finally she decided against it.

It was only five years later, in 1903, that a gardener was
needed at Glynde and Lady Wolseley happened to see a
newspaper advertisement of someone in 'distressed circumstances'. She wrote off immediately, feeling sorry for the
applicant, who turned up shortly afterwards for an interview.
Lady Wolseley describes the historic occasion in her letter of 22
February 1903 to her husband:

> The applicant for the gardener's place dined and slept here while I was
> away. Frances was much struck with her. An *absolute* lady *and* didn't
> flinch at manure stirring, or scullery drain, or anything! An unhappy
> marriage, and failing in market gardening has brought her to this.
> Dean Hole most strongly recommends her, and has known her all her
> life. She says, 'I think I have forty years' work still in me.'

The importance of this engagement of a lady gardener to work the
Farm House garden lay in the fact that it was from this happening
that the idea was born of having women students who would come
to learn gardening. According to Frances's diary it was on
Saturday 14 March 1904 that the first two students arrived—Miss
Dodd from near Birmingham and Miss Haymes from near
Leamington—and the preliminary stage of the Glynde College for
Lady Gardeners had begun. Frances, who was to teach them, must
have awaited their arrival with some nervousness.

In her book published in 1916, *In a College Garden*, Frances Wolseley writes: 'My College of Gardening was founded at Glynde in 1902, but in the late autumn of 1905 it was necessary, owing to an increase of students, to supplement the ground. . . .'

27 Students at Viscountess Wolseley's Glynde School for Lady Gardeners

This date of 1902 must have been due to a slip of the pen, or the typewriter, according to the letter from her mother quoted above, unless she was dating the foundation from before the arrival of any students or the lady gardener, when the scheme could not have actually matured, although it might have been seriously considered.

Although Frances's first interest in country things may have come from visits to Alfred Austin's home in the Kent countryside, some credit must be handed to her mother for the idea of gardening. Frances was herself greatly interested and took every opportunity of visiting other people's gardens, but did not pursue gardening to the exclusion of all other activities.

The muck-raking and sheer hard work of the Glynde garden was well-leavened at this period with outside events. For instance, Frances had recently been included with her parents in an invitation to be present at Queen Victoria's funeral. Some years later, in February 1905, Lady Wolseley writes to her husband:

Frances has just been here to luncheon and evidently enjoyed her
Ireland. Lord Roberts was unfortunate at the Investiture and offended
the Knights. . . . She told me many delightful things of her fellow-
guests. The Iveaghs were so kind and anxious their guests should be
happy, but Lady Iveagh herself never appears till 2, and retires to rest
3 to 5—so they did not see much of her. The Castle party was a fine
show of Duchesses and diamonds. . . .

This was one side of the coin. Frances was meeting people from all
walks of life, many of them of real interest. Her mother recorded a
vist to Lord and Lady Brownlow for tea where they met the Oscar
Wildes, and Lord Wolseley mentions dining at the Athenaeum
when he sat next to Henry James—'He had been writing all day
and his appetite was prodigious in consequence'—and it was only
about five years later that Frances received a letter from Henry
James encouraging her in her gardening venture at Glynde.

But visits to gardens are mentioned whenever they take place as
being events of equal importance with other highlights of the
social round and, after joining Lord Wolseley in Mentone later in
1905, her mother wrote to Frances: 'Yesterday we went to Lady
Hanbury's "At Home Day" at La Mortola. . . . Such pergolas and
flowering shrubs, and aloes and agaves. . . .' and her visit to Miss
Willmott's garden in 1900 had been described in just as much
detail to her husband as his to her of the decorations from the
Sultan at the Pera Palace, Constantinople, 'beautifully enamelled
and made up of diamonds, rubies and emeralds'—one for herself
and one for Frances.

Meanwhile at Glynde, where it had become necessary to
enlarge the area of ground 'owing to an increase of students',
Frances now rented a cornfield of about five and a half acres called
Ragged Lands and it was here that the new garden was made.

Although Lady Wolseley must take credit for lighting the
gardening spark in her daughter's life, it must now be admitted
that she could not understand that the Gardening School had
grown to such dimensions that it was necessary to expand, that
independence was essential. The hostility of many Victorian
parents towards their children who showed enough character to
want to break away from their home background now became
evident and there was an uncomfortable breach. In her letters to
her parents Frances seems to have been a most dutiful daughter
and was only carrying out to its fullest extent the enthusiasm
which they had begun. Miss Jekyll never had to contend with this

situation and it must have been a sadness for Frances that what had now become her life's work was unacceptable to her mother and father. But she was a pioneer in her efforts to train women in gardening, and pioneers must expect difficulties.

The first presented many problems. 'We were very poor in those days', she writes, and explains that for a school of gardening many different types of design and planting must be included. The garden must be 'filled with decorative flowers of every description such as are to be found in most gardens, otherwise employers might later on be disappointed with the knowledge and experience of their women-gardeners.' This principle applied equally to fruit as to vegetables, to greenhouse work, to path-making and terracing, to rock gardens, rose gardens and herbaceous borders. There must be a lecture room and 'expert lecturers and teachers have to be engaged'. All this had to be paid for and involved a considerable expense at the outset.

28 *Starting town gardens. Viscountess Wolseley was particularly interested in the project which early in this century provided London children with small plots to cultivate*

There were other problems: 'Until quite recently many looked down upon the profession of gardencraft for they imagined it to be a narrow life, restricted as regards its intellectual possibilities; others considered that women were physically unsuited to it. As in all new professions, there were a certain number of failures at the outset. . . .' One has only to recall some of the hazards that beset Elizabeth Garrett Anderson when she passed 'for the first time through the gateway of the Middlesex Hospital' in 1860, or Madame Bodichon in the early days of Girton, or, for that matter, the classic case of Florence Nightingale and the Crimea.

The course was a two-year one—'a gardener cannot hope to be really useful under a two-years' course of training, and then she will only be suitable for a small post'. But there were encouraging signs before too long. One of these concerned 'a masterpiece this week at a garden in Sussex, when between the hours of ten and four' over 2,000 plants were safely settled into their places in a large herbaceous border, 'according to a colour scheme arranged by our College'.

And then came the war and she wrote: 'my young women realised that at last their chance had come and that if they could work with precision and method, those doubts so often cast upon their capability would once and for all be dispersed'.

This is, in fact, what happened. Much of the garden was given over to produce, and most of this was not only cared for and propagated by the students but also distributed by them, on what was known as 'The Vegetable Trolley', to the villagers. This was a side of gardening which had not before been thought suitable for women. Growing flowers was one thing, rather delicate work which needed gentle fingers and patience, but digging potatoes, spraying fruit trees, turning over heavy soil ready to take such crops as celery, cauliflowers and cabbages, this was different.

In the middle of all this activity Frances somehow made time to write her book entitled *Women and the Land*, published in 1916. The start in this country of the Women's Institutes is one of the bigger subjects dealt with in some detail, while one of the smaller and most attractive ones is that of gardens for London children. These started in 1911 by

acquiring a vacant building site in Paddington and in the summer of 1915 there were eight gardens all working in very poor districts. . . . each child has a plot of his or her very own, the produce of which, both flowers and vegetables, they take home in due course. . . . More and more, both for boys and girls, is a thorough, practical training necessary in . . . the hygienic feeding and proper handling of cows, pigs, and other live stock, poultry-keeping, jam-making, bee-keeping and all that appertains to the wealth to be attained for our nation by means of the land.

The fame of the Glynde School began to spread abroad and more and more applications for training began to come in. As early as September 1904, she had received this letter from the Massachusetts Agricultural College:

Dear Madam,
I have noticed with much interest the announcement of your school in the *Gardeners' Chronicle.* As we are trying to develop something along the same lines in this country, I am anxious to have all possible information on what is being done elsewhere. If you can send me any further facts regarding your work, I shall be greatly obliged.
    I shall be glad to reciprocate you further in any possible way.
Yours truly,
F.A.W.
(Professor.)

Lady Wolseley was by now just as interested in the school as Frances and

suggested that a prospectus should be designed bearing names well known in the gardening world. This brought much interesting correspondence from famous gardeners and heads of gardening colleges, and the little school at Glynde was well on the road to becoming an established success.

Visitors from interested concerns came to look round, to ask questions and to find out what was going on, and sometimes to lecture on branches of women's work overseas. One of these was Mrs Watt, who came to talk to the students about the Women's Institutes which had been formed as long ago as 1897 in the province of Ontario. It may be significant that the first Women's Institute was founded over here in North Wales, 1915, and the second in September of the same year in West Sussex.

Later on came a Royal Warrant and some financial support, followed by a stand at the Chelsea Flower Show with the presentation of a bronze medal 'as a mark of approval for the produce shown'.

The influence of William Robinson is to be felt in this Glynde garden and it is stated that his *English Flower Garden* was always consulted for the planting of a colour scheme in the borders. As Miss Jekyll wrote most of the section on colour, her ideas also were incorporated, so that 'one part consists of blue flowers, merging gradually into white, which is followed perhaps by a pale yellow, leading to stronger shades and then to reds'.

But what were Frances Wolseley's own ideas on garden planting and design? Her fame rests, and rightly so, on the success of her great experiment of training young women in gardening so that they could face the world with knowledge behind them and the ability to earn a living. But little is reported of her own gardening ideas. These may be found in her book *Gardens, their Form and Design*, published in 1919. In it she combines the formal with the informal, paved gardens with 'surprise' gardens, and writes with as much enthusiasm of ornaments, sundials, garden seats, fountains, steps, treillage and topiary as she does of trees and shrubs planted to look like the natural hillside. Miss Jekyll is quoted in the introduction as the 'one great pioneer' and 'since she was brave enough to lead the way others have also taken up garden design seriously'. Students are urged to study all her books 'and in especial her *Gardens for Small Country Houses*'.

Frances writes warmly and at length on the gardens of Bagatelle in the Bois de Boulogne, finding that the outstanding feature is the unusual height achieved by arches for climbing roses or clematis. These almost give another dimension to the garden: 'There is much that can be copied from this garden and much that has never yet been sufficiently studied in our English gardens', she comments. 'We are so apt to make our arches and pedestals too stumpy.'

She has suggestions for a great variety of garden ornaments, some of them thought of previously only in connection with formal design. Like Miss Jekyll she could contemplate the marriage—or contrast—of natural gardening with the introduction of formal ideas. For instance, she gives some lyrical notes on the selection and placing of garden seats. The question of seats—placed either to be out of the prevailing wind, hot sun or sheltered from a shower of rain—brings us automatically to ideas for seats for an arbour, seats for an arch of treillage, seats to form a feature at the end of a walk or a vista, seats by a pool or fountain and seats for rest on a steep stone staircase. On the subject of paved gardens she writes:

Real York slab is what we like best; but, since it is expensive and difficult to get, let us consider what other material can be used in its place. A pretty arrangement is where a line of red bricks alternates with irregular-shaped grey stone paving. Sometimes a few hundred bricks are left over after a house has been built, and although not sufficient in themselves to make a long path, they will do so if some pices of York slab are used too. The bricks are practical also, for wheeling a barrow over. . . .

Her suggestions for rock gardens are in agreement with Charles Wolley Dod and Reginald Farrer, especially with the former who would have agreed with her note: 'a rock garden, once planted, cannot be left to itself. It needs careful yearly, even twice yearly thinning out.'

She writes delightfully of 'shadow-houses' and garden 'houses', some of them to be found located in formal gardens, others in 'surprise' gardens, water gardens, or flower gardens.

Frances was initiated into gardening by her parents and by William Robinson, but she could also write in warm appreciation of the brilliant French garden designer, Le Nôtre. An enthusiastic admirer of his work, she contrived to hold the balance between his school and the more naturalistic teachings of William Robinson—especially with regard to the selection and planting of shrubs—and the tolerance of Miss Jekyll. Students are advised to read Robinson's *English Flower Garden*, especially the chapter intitled 'Flowering Trees and Shrubs and their Artistic Use'. Of Gertrude Jekyll's many books, *Gardens for Small Country Houses* is especially recommended. This is full of architectural detail and garden adornments, together with plantings of borders, roses, lilies, climbers and so on.

The last ten to twelve years of Frances Wolseley's life were spent in consolidating much of the work that had gone before. In 1925 a site at Ardingly was bought and her last home, Culpepers, was built. From then until 1934 she was a committee member of the Sussex Archaeological Society, in company with—among other illustrious names—Rudyard Kipling. In 1926 the Wolseley Room at Hove was opened. In June 1934 'her stiffness, as she persisted in calling it, had increased so much that she could not even climb the short flight of stairs to her bedroom, and had to have a lift installed: she also had handrails in various places to help her to steady herself. . . . [Finally] she could not stand and was forced to take to a wheel chair; and then slowly, her sight was affected, and she could no longer see to write, read or type. . . .'

Apart from her two important books already discussed, she had others written. Three of these were essentially inspired by Sussex, her beloved countryside: *Some Sussex Byways, Sussex in the Past*, and *Smaller Manor Houses of Sussex*, illustrated from photographs specially taken under the author's supervision.

The Viscountess (she had inherited the viscountcy when her father died in 1913) died suddenly during the night of Christmas Eve, 1936, of heart failure, and the funeral service took place at Beddingham Church, near Glynde, on Tuesday 29 December. *The Times* obituary notice remarked especially on her ability to combine the two opposite schools of gardening ideas: 'Steeped in the traditions of French landscape gardening and an enthusiastic admirer of the work of the famous Le Nôtre, she contrived to hold the balance between that school and the more naturalistic teachings of William Robinson and Miss Gertrude Jekyll.' In her own words, from *Gardens: their Form and Design*:

> There still remain in England some few—fortunately very few—gardens where geraniums and calceolarias are bedded out and look the picture of regimental discipline. . . . There was a time, not so very long ago, when this style of planting was greatly in vogue, and it is probably to Mr William Robinson and some few pioneers of the new school of garden craft that we owe its almost total abolition.

The Garden Steward of Girton College, Cambridge, wrote:

> The death of Lady Wolseley means the loss of a great pioneer as well as of a great woman and a great gardener. . . . By founding a horticultural college, by writing many books, by originating propaganda, she did much for women workers on the land—but her public activities were only a fraction of her work. Myself a student at her college in its early days . . . I am only one of very many women who have frequently drawn on her immense experience. There seemed no limit to her rural interests. . . .

Let us be grateful that through the Glynde School of Gardening the enormous influence she had over so many students was of a high calibre, and interpreted with such integrity.

The Revd
William Keble Martin
1877–1969

We should like to make two suggestions about
gathering flowers: first that it should be done
sparingly, and secondly that collectors should be
fully courteous to the owner of enclosed land.

W. KEBLE MARTIN
The Concise British Flora in Colour

The Revd William Keble Martin, author of *The Concise British
Flora in Colour*, was born at Radley, Berkshire in July 1877.
Educated at Marlborough, he took his BA at Christ Church,
Oxford, in 1899 (with botany as a degree subject), his MA in
1907—going meanwhile to a theological training college—and
was ordained in 1902.

Keble Martin was one of a clergyman's family of nine children,
each one of whom showed individuality of interests. Edith, the
eldest, became a court dressmaker and Dora, the second daughter,
was a watercolour artist and also played the cello. Nellie and
Katherine both gave violin lessons and played in the Exeter
Cathedral orchestra for some years. Of the boys, Charlie was a
fruit grower, a consultant of some standing, and the second son,
Jack, took an Oxford degree before being ordained. Arthur
trained as an architect, rebuilt the chapel at Sandhurst and
designed various churches in South London. He also designed the
pulpit in the church at Wath-on-Dearne, near Rotherham in
Yorkshire, Keble Martin's first parish, 1908–21. Dick took a
training in engineering and probably had more excitement than any
of them. Among other activities, he surveyed the Angola railway
for the Portuguese Government in the South West African desert.

Keble Martin, like his brothers and sisters, enjoyed a wide
variety of interests. Although he is rightly known and remembered for his *Concise British Flora*, there were many other
facets to his life which may not be so familiar to his readers but

which, nevertheless, must have made their valuable contribution to this book.

Perhaps the first and most obvious facts relating to such a *Flora* are that it must have taken hours of hard work, much keen and intelligent observation and a determination to overcome all obstacles to his collecting while still fulfilling most conscientiously his varied obligations as a much-loved parish priest, firstly at Wath-on-Dearne, then in Haccombe and in Torrington, both in Devonshire. His self discipline, for instance, must have been of a high order, and his interest in plants and wildlife as intensive as it was in people.

29 *The Revd William Keble Martin, whose* The Concise British Flora *made him a best-selling author at the age of 87*

He would go miles out of his way to find a special flower, moth or butterfly, just as he would make tedious journeys by bus or bicycle or on foot to visit his parishioners. He travelled long distances, often in some discomfort, to go on bird-watching

expeditions. He was the sort of person for whom life is filled to the
brim with fascination, awe and wonder; so much to see, to notice
and observe and even 92 years were not enough time in which to
do it all. Flowers, mosses, moths, butterflies and birds, his
knowledge and observation of these were all part of an intensive
training on the one hand as, on the other, were his parish visits of
which he writes frequently: 'For this visiting I kept careful
abbreviated records. I have done this all my life. It enables me to
use common sense in visiting, and to pray intelligently. . . .'

These contrasts appeared throughout his life. As a schoolboy at
Marlborough he was in the Rifle VIII competing at Bisley for the
Ashburton Shield, and later was in the Oxford University Rifle
VIII. This needed practical skill and sound judgment. He attended
the summer camp at Aldershot for ten consecutive years. Here,
among other things, he was asked to set an example of kneeling
for prayers and was selected to be a hare in a paper chase, and there
is a note which says: 'the camp was on that wet Laffans plain where
large gentians grew in the marsh'.

Of his holiday activities in the large rectory garden at
Dartington, where he also collected mosses, he wrote:

> I had a secret path in the laurels near some box bushes where the
> dormice slept all through the winter. They were tightly curled up in
> their nests with the long tail curved over the head and right round the
> body. One early morning I saw a tug of war. . . . a dormouse and a
> long-tailed fieldmouse both had hold of a hazel. The nuts were in much
> demand. . . . the nuthatches stored them in some old hollow trees and
> the squirrels carried them out to the pastures and buried them under
> some tussock or a dock plant. We have seen them go out in two inches
> of snow, scratch it away, and find the nuts without fail.

He comments on the fact that these were red squirrels: 'the grey
squirrels had not yet been imported.'

It appears that, in some ways, birdwatching had been his first
love. He writes of his schooldays when

> on fine summer mornings we sometimes went to bathe in the river
> Dart. . . . The pool was reputed to be very deep. We were told you
> could sink a church tower in it. Young kingfishers used to chase one
> another in circles over the water or a dipper would sing with full rich
> notes.

And again of an early summer trip into Lincolnshire: 'This was
made more for the birds than for the flowers.'

At midnight on 16 June 1896, he set out on his push-bike to see the sunrise from Rippon Tor on Dartmoor.

> The sunrise was truly beautiful. . . . the skylarks and pippets were singing that beautiful morning. I knew of a snipe's nest in the marsh below . . . and tried to snap . . . the bird leaving the nest. . . .

Gardening appears to have taken an important part in his childhood occupations. He describes one of the various rectory gardens which he recalled in later life. This one was large, or seemed so to a child of five years, and had 'a shrubbery with bluebells, where we each had our little garden bed to look after'. He refrains from commenting on the success or otherwise of such an early venture, but there were tears over a planting incident a year later:

> I was given some geraniums to grow in my garden bed at the end of the summer of, I think, 1883. I was six years of age. I lifted these geraniums into a box as we were to move house. I wept because, of course, the removers did not go down the shrubbery to fetch them, and they were left behind.

The children greatly enjoyed visits from Edward Moberly, a kind uncle who stayed with them frequently and went out of his way to interest the whole family in various pursuits.

> He was musical and started my sisters' training in the violin, in which they became very proficient. And he fitted up the boys with all that was needed for collecting butterflies and moths, nets, setting boards, store boxes and even cages for rearing them from caterpillars. For this purpose it was necessary to find the correct food plants. This led to the earliest effort to know some wild plants.

He describes the fun of chasing a butterfly which they thought was new to them—to the annoyance of the gardener more often than not, as they ran heedlessly across the flower-beds. He concludes:

> In the evening we 'sugared' the trees as an attraction to moths, especially two beautiful tulip trees on the lawn. It was a life full of interest and activity. We had our little garden plots to cultivate. . . .

Oh, for all children to have the blessing of an Uncle Edward, to brighten the lives of a young family and to provide the wherewithal to enable so many hobbies to be encouraged.

In his autobiography *Over the Hills*, published in 1968, there emerges a portrait of an industrious, intelligent and happy man, a man of strong principles and great strength of character. It also shows him as a hard-working parish priest, conscious that while preaching the word of God was important, so also were his daily contacts with his parishioners. His sense of humour emerges in the writing as does his attention to small incidental sidelights of social history. For instance there was the time in 1889 when they were lost in darkness, mist and driving rain on Dartmoor and could not see to consult a compass. 'Electric torches had not been invented'. Then came the advent of bananas. He wrote of seeing big bunches in a shop, 'the first bananas I ever saw'.

He also mentions Professor Dodgson (Lewis Carroll), who was retired but still around in Oxford when Martin was there. 'We were told that Queen Victoria was so pleased with *Alice* that she asked him to send his next book which he did. It was on *Differential Calculus*. He was a mathematics professor.'

Another much younger man was also in Oxford, working in a bicycle repair shop. Keble Martin bicycled everywhere and his brakes were often adjusted and punctures mended by this young man whose name was Morris, 'later Lord Nuffield'.

In his usual practical way, he later noticed various details of the life of a young woman 'in her twenties living at Dove House in Ashbourne. She was an active, outdoor person. I saw her in Dove Dale. She was a member of the hockey team and a good tennis player. She was a very regular worshipper at the Parish Church, and I happened to discover that she played the piano beautifully (another valuable asset).' Soon after he writes: 'I ventured to invite Violet and her elder sister to tea in my room to meet Dora (his sister). After tea I told Dora my thoughts, which she had not guessed. Soon after this I proposed to Violet . . . and was met with the reply: "I do not even know you, Mr. Martin."' At this stage one would feel that Violet was justified. However, things moved on towards a slightly closer relationship and in 1908 they became engaged to be married. His future wife was evidently introduced early in their courtship to the type of life that might lie ahead. Reaching down a steep bank for Jacob's Ladder (*Polemonium caeruleum*) he was saved from disaster—'my fiancée holding me by an ankle to prevent my falling'. Whenever possible the important aspects of his work and happiness were shared with his wife; holidays, church events and visiting, family outings and collecting expeditions.

Their marriage took place at Ashbourne on 8 July 1909, and

after a honeymoon on which they encountered the D'Oyly Cartes and were given a lift to Dartmouth in their enormous, very fast car, being driven at hair-raising speeds, they 'came safely' to their new parish at Wath-on-Dearne, in Yorkshire. They remained there for about twelve years.

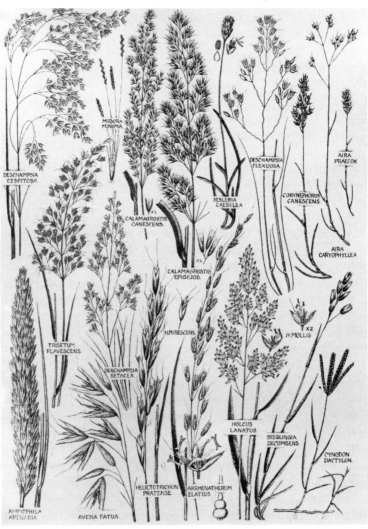

30 A selection of grasses: one of Keble Martin's drawings from
The Concise British Flora

There were problems connected with the new vicarage at Wath, as the old one had been condemned and until the new one was built they had to stay outside the parish and to come in either by bicycle or by walking. He tells us that 'In the early days at Wath-on-Dearne very little was attempted in the way of flower-drawing. We were both very much occupied with the parish and the gardening.' His wife was involved in parish affairs but also was kept especially busy with the arrival of four children who, in 1917, were Patrick, aged six, Barbara, aged five, Vivienne aged four and the baby, Henry. In 1917 there was an urgent call for more chaplains to serve with the army, and Keble Martin volunteered to go 'as a temporary Chaplain to Forces'.

Starting a new family, settling into a new parish and a new vicarage, with four small children at home and the First World War taking place across the Channel—this was hardly an atmosphere conducive to collecting, growing and drawing wild flowers. Everyone was overworked, tired, desperately worried. Some years were to go by before a more settled way of life was possible.

He continued adding to his plant collections, sometimes in spare time which was saved carefully and conscientiously from what might be described as 'leisure' periods, but often packed into a few minutes here and there, in an already busy programme. He describes, for example:

a hurried visit to Perthshire. After a full Sunday, 24, July, 1933, the midnight train took me to Killin and Ben Lawers. There the clouds were down to 1,000 feet. I went straight up in the clouds and rain and chanced to find two nice saxifrages, one especially which is very local and flowers sparingly. It was in flower. I took it down and made a drawing and coloured it. The next morning, up in mist and rain again, I luckily found its own niche, and replanted it firmly in its own place. A few other little alpine species were gathered, and these were in cigarette tins. They were all drawn in the train during Thursday night on the return journey.

He adds, sadly, 'I was sorry to have had to go without my wife. At a later date, she was free to go there with me.'

In 1938 he describes a plant-hunting trip in Devon: 'We were really very fortunate in having so much help from kind friends to take us out. In the following January we were given a lift, and we led our friends to the rock on which the tiny fern *Asplenium septentrionale* still grows. We found it in good condition, showing no likelihood of dying out. This is in the southern half of Devon; there is a little of it on the North Devon coast too.'

He mentions this plant in a conversation with the head botanist, Mr Wilmot, at the British Museum (Natural History) who remarked that 'its existence in Devon is a proof that the climate there was once of a more arctic type.' (Botanists will know that the name *septentrionale* means northern. It is a plant of sub-arctic regions.)

He goes on, still connected with the collecting of plants, but in rather a different context:

> . . . four months later, on 23rd. May, we went off to attend the 150th. Anniversary of the Linnean Society in London. I did sometimes attend the ordinary meetings at Burlington House and exhibited drawings at them. But this anniversary gathering was held in Albemarle Street for more accommodation. So we wrote in the June Parish Magazine: 'It has been the writer's privilege this week to attend a long series of addresses describing some of the latest discoveries and conclusions of a dozen of the greatest biologists of Europe, drawn from nine different countries. If some of our members fancy that modern science is not compatible with the Christian faith, it may be of some help to them to be assured that this is not at all the case.'

(Perhaps Gerald Priestland, of the radio series 'Priestland's Progress', would also agree.)

During the war years 'no flower drawing was done' but

> as soon as the war was over we started little outings. In July, 1945, my wife and I went to Newbridge on the Dart and *Sibthorpia* and its flower enlargement were drawn; another day to Landscove for a mullein. And at the end of July, I went with my cousin [Willy Martin] . . . on a brief visit to Teesdale, staying with Dr. Murphy at Whistle Crag, a very windy spot. *Lysimachia ciliata* and *Serratula* were drawn. In Novemeber my wife and I went to Berry Head and *Solanum nigrum* was added. . . . But the Parochial work was kept up.

Sometimes the elements produced the worst difficulties for locating and collecting the precious plants still needed to be drawn. For instance, at Combe, Keble Martin noted:

> Early in 1947 a few weeks of serious snow had made the steep hills almost impassable. I mostly walked, but when I went to the expense of a taxi home, the driver refused to go down into Combe, saying he would never get up again. At other times in fog the auto-bike travelling was terribly cold.

He describes an incident on a climb that he took with his wife in Scotland in midsummer 1952:

From Ashbourne and Derby we went by train to Edinburgh and Killin Junction. There the expected train from Oban had not arrived. It was late. We asked how long it would be and met the answer: 'a wee while.' We timed the 'wee while' and found it 43 minutes. . . . We arrived at the Ben Lawers Hotel. We attended the kirk on Sunday and explored the walk to the Lawers burn. We received kind help and guidance from Mr. Stelfox of Dublin. . . . On Monday, two days before my 75th. birthday, we walked together up the burn. . . . I went on up past the Lochan to the top and gathered alpine plants as directed by Mr. Stelfox. . . . I was alone on the top admiring some little mountain woodrushes when suddenly we were wrapped in dense mist; in a minute drenching rain began and a severe thunderstorm burst. The lightning was much branched, striking the ground all around. A wonderful sight, it was a noisy bombardment, quite continuous. This lasted for what seemed many minutes. . . . there were waterfalls everywhere. When I had gone down 2,000 ft. the sun came out. . . . I'm afraid some had started out to look for me. . . . I had promised to start back at 5 o'clock . . . and eventually ran down in another storm about 10.30. . . . Two days later we had a long walk together in the Tayworth Castle area.

The pattern of their lives became more regular as the years went by, but the work and industry, the application and the enthusiasm never diminished.

Keble Martin's effort to find a publisher for the *Flora* is something of a saga in itself. The details are clear in the mind of Sir David Checketts who, in the early 1960s, was Equerry to Prince Philip, to whom Keble Martin wrote after trying several book publishers in vain.

Sir David recalls: 'Prince Philip was certainly interested enough to pass the letter to me with instructions to look into it and, as a result, Keble Martin and his daughter-in-law, Margaret, came to see me bringing with them a selection of his original drawings. They were quite remarkable and I was so impressed with their quality and detail that I showed them to Prince Philip, who was of the opinion that Keble Martin's incredible artistry and effort deserved to be published and told me to do what I could to help.

'The publishers whom Keble Martin and his daughter-in-law had previously approached all saw it as a "drawing-room" type of book, I suppose similar to the Redouté book of roses, at a price of about ten guineas (I seem to remember) which was an astronomical sum in the early 1960s, and well beyond the pockets of most enthusiastic plant lovers. I felt its real value would be more as a field guide similar to the pocket guide books of birds more readily available to all plant and wild-life lovers in the United Kingdom.

'It took me about eighteen months to two years to get it published, having contacted several publishers without success. Most of them saw the cost of colour reproduction as being the biggest obstacle to low cost production, bearing in mind that to do Keble Martin's drawings proper justice would need several colour applications and the new technique of colour reproduction, which I believe was French, was still not in general use in the UK.

'Luckily, two coincidences occurred. My wife and I had dinner one evening with Sir Robert Lusty, at that time managing director for the Hutchinson Publishing Group and a governor of the BBC,

31 Examples of evergreens, from The Concise British Flora

and she mentioned the subject to him. He, in turn, put me in touch with Mr George Rainbird, who, by chance, the very day I contacted him was considering the publication of a book of American wild flowers.

'When Rainbird saw the selection of illustrations he at once decided to publish Keble Martin's *Flora*, as a type of working manual, and it was subsequently published at about thirty-five shillings a copy. I have no idea whether the book of American wild flowers was eventually published but Keble Martin's *Flora* was certainly an incredible success.'

So Keble Martin, at 87, became a best-selling author overnight. *The Concise British Flora*, which contained nearly 1,400 colour reproductions of his drawings, was published in 1965 and sold 100,000 copies in the first year. In 1967 he won the distinction of being asked by the Postmaster-General to paint some stamps with wild flower designs.

How much his contribution can account for the renewed interest in wild flowers and the possibilities of growing them in the natural garden cannot be assessed. The love of wild flowers is nothing new. Collections have been made over hundreds of years—some the great and historic ones known throughout the world, others small and amateur like that discovered recently, made by Joshua Gosselin of Guernsey (1739–1813). Affection and delight have gone into them all, perhaps engendered by the foundation and growth of the Wild Flower Society, founded in 1892 and happily flourishing. Perhaps it is significant that at an RHS show in the summer of 1980 there was a particularly attractive stand of wild flowers, exhibited by John Chambers of Kettering, Northants, which drew a good deal of attention.

Literary achievement had come late to Keble Martin and had taken most of a lifetime to produce, but must have been sweet when it came. However, Keble Martin was a man who could stand up easily enough to success of that kind and, as he said himself, he 'enjoyed every minute of it'.

Reginald Farrer

1880–1920

Few things are more annoying than dogmatism; and dogmatism is nowhere more misplaced than in horticulture. The wise gardener is he whom years of experience have succeeded in teaching that plants, no less than people, have perverse individualities of their own, and that, though general rules may be laid down, yet it is impossible ever to predict with any certainty that any given treatment is bound to secure success or failure.

REGINALD FARRER
My Rock Garden

The mountain stream that rushes down the hillside by the grey stone cottages of Clapham in Yorkshire gives visitors the impression that they are wandering into an alpine village. The village is on an incline and the lower slopes of Ingleborough Fell descend into it: the air is clear.

This was the home of Reginald Farrer, plant collector, explorer, author, gardener and scholar. Anyone enthusiastic about alpines could hardly have lived in a more suitable situation and the Farrer rock gardens were eventually to provide varieties of alpines for gardens all over Europe.

He was born at Clapham in 1880, son of J. A. Farrer, a Liberal MP, and Mrs Farrer, who was described as 'strikingly handsome', cultured and a plant lover. The background was auspicious but one physical handicap affected his outlook and perhaps helped to dictate his way of life—he was born with a cleft palate (hare lip). Accounts vary about how much this really altered him as a person, but there seems little doubt that he felt he must strive to be witty when he was in company, and to be content in solitary occupations. His parents were keen gardeners and had a rock garden at Ingleborough House. He is reputed to have rebuilt the rock garden when only fourteen. At Oxford his letters home contained instructions to his mother about maintaining it and collecting plants from neighbouring rocks and screes.

Farrer grew a heavy moustache to conceal his upper lip, but nothing could alter the unfortunate timbre of his voice. It says a great deal for his personality that he overcame this, and people talking to him were so taken up with his conversation and enthusiasms that it often went almost unnoticed.

As a young man he was comparatively free, although the restrictions of his home life were those of a Victorian household. He had enough money to enable him to travel when he came down from Oxford. His second cousin, Osbert Sitwell, in *Noble Essences*, comments:

> Reginald had been brought up in an austere if opulent world, where you could have possessions so long as you did not enjoy them, and where each Sunday dragged after it a weary, weekly train of charitable village functions . . . and the more purely domestic orgies of Missionary meeting and simple family prayer. . . .

32 Reginald Farrer, plant collector, explorer, author, gardener and scholar

It was these family prayers that lined Reginald Farrer up in sympathy with Sir George Sitwell (father of Edith, Osbert and Sacheverell), who never attended them, and who did not conceal his delight when a rumour went round that Reginald had become a Buddhist missionary. Sir George took infinite trouble to commend his activities warmly, whether it was writing novels—'which

produced consternation' and 'frigid grief'—or his conversion to
the Buddhist faith, which was thought equally shocking and called
forth prayers from the relatives that 'the heathen might be
permitted to see the true light'.

When he stayed with the Sitwells 'his mere presence in the
house struck a chill to the bones of the faithful' and the young
Osbert was sent away. Being twelve years Reginald's junior it
must have been thought that there might be contamination of
ideas for the boy, although Edith Sitwell had stayed frequently at
Ingleborough House and not only liked Reginald but much
appreciated his lively conversation and talent.

In his twenties Farrer was hunting down plants in the
Dolomites, sometimes with E. A. Bowles, propagating them at
Ingleborough House or sending them to friends. In botany he was
almost entirely self-taught, although whenever opportunity came
for learning he took it.

What may sometimes be overlooked about him is his youth. He
had an adult mind, and was experienced enough in his twenties to
publish *My Rock Garden* and to write in it with the wisdom of a
Gertrude Jekyll in her fifties,

> The wise gardener is he whom years of experience have succeeded in
> teaching that plants, no less than people, have perverse individualities
> of their own and that, though general rules may be laid down, yet it is
> impossible ever to predict with any certainty that any given treatment
> is bound to secure success or failure. There are so many possibilities to
> be reckoned with, so many differences of soil, climate and aspect.

This might have been Miss Jekyll speaking, or William Robinson
writing in *The English Flower Garden* when he was twice Farrer's
age.

In *My Rock Garden* there are frequent references and
acknowledgements to other people's gardens, which show that he
must have travelled a good deal when still young, studying things
to do with his subject. He writes:

> Kew offers everyone a model which it would be impertinent to praise.
> The Glen form is apt to be monotonous, perhaps, but climatic
> conditions make it necessary at Kew and in many other parts of
> England; and Kew has triumphed over the problem of how to make a
> glen perpetually various and interesting.

He then mentions Miss Willmott's extensive alpine garden: 'At
Warley, again there is the gorge-design to be studied—to my

own personal taste, a trifle too violent to be altogether pleasant, but still a noble example of definite purpose definitely carried out.'

But perhaps the garden most frequently mentioned is that of Edge Hall, Cheshire. Farrer regarded Wolley Dod as the alpine expert of the time, referring among others to *Omphalodes lucilla*, and who was Lucilla? (Mr Wolley Dod had told him once, but he had forgotten.) 'She owns the Glory of the Snow as well, the grasping Lucilla.' Mr Wolley Dod died in 1904 at the age of seventy-eight, and Farrer must have known him as a close friend; and as he would have prepared the material for *My Rock Garden* well ahead of its publication in 1907, he could have been little more than twenty when he first studied the Edge Hall garden. Even allowing only one year before publication date he was young in years but old in experience to have written as he did.

He had also travelled in the Alpes Maritimes, Austria, Germany and Ireland, as well as knowing well the flora of Durham, Yorkshire—above all of the Ingleborough and Pen-y-Ghent Fells, round Malham Tarn—and the Isle of Walney, off Barrow-in-Furness. By this time he had also made three rock gardens at Ingleborough, no small achievement for a young man of the time with all the opportunities for a life of leisure.

Writing in one of his spring chapters in *My Garden in Spring* (for which Farrer wrote a Preface), E. A. Bowles discusses the whole question of 'moraines' in relation to Farrer:

No one would read a gardening book nowadays that did not deal with this latest fashion in gardening. The name and popularity and prattle of the thing are new, but many good cultivators had their porous, gritty, raised or sunk beds for alpines, whatever they called them, long ago. ... Then arose the prophet. The abundant rainfall of Ingleborough and the local limestone (three or four lumps of which make any sort of rock gardening a thing of beauty if only one side of the block be bedded up with earth), aided and abetted by river silt from the lake's mouth and chips of all sizes from the mountain side, were only waiting for Mr Farrer's master mind to plan their combination and lo! a new era dawned. The most discontented of his alpine treasure flourished, the great news went forth to the world, a series of books in slate-coloured covers became the foundation of conversation, even at dinner, to the great annoyance of those who wait and therefore should expect all things to come to them. This is a fact: a head gardener, in speaking of the extraordinary wave of the fashion of gardening, told me that the men in the house complained bitterly that, whereas once upon a time they picked up innumerable sporting tips and had much interesting gossip to listen to, nowadays the talk at

dinner was all Latin names and about soils and gardening books. Now
the moraine holds the field. . . .

Of course I was an early victim of the moraine measles after my first
visit to Ingleborough, and when next the Moraine Magician came to
see me, he helped in planning my first attempt at a granite chip one.
My previous experiments had not been over successful. . . .

There are further references to Farrer and his garden at
Ingleborough, and he ends this dissertation in a summing up:
'That, then, is the history of my moraines. I call the first granite
chip one the "Farrer" moraine, the second the "sand" moraine,
and the "lead pipe bed" and "fish hatchery" will refer to the
others.'

Farrer's next important publication was *Among the Hills*,
dedicated to E. A. Bowles, in 1911. Like all his horticultural
writing, it is an enjoyable book; again it shows a mind mature
beyond his years. In it he says:

> For, into the actual seeing and enjoying of a thing there always enters
> the personal element of the moment; and with the personal element,
> incompleteness. One sees too much, or one is tired, or one is cross and
> hungry; or one cannot notice the world because of the plants that
> abound in it. . . . the whole thing is too big for us at the time. But
> distance and absence clarify the view; wipe out the confusing touches
> and reduce the chaos to a composition of bare essential lines. The Alps
> or the jungle are never so near or so clear as when one is standing on
> the shore of Pall Mall or the Mediterranean.

In 1912 Farrer's *The Rock Garden* was published and in February
1914, Farrer and William Purdom set off on their first year of
plant hunting in the Chinese province of Kansu, on the Tibetan
border. *On the Eaves of the World*, in two volumes, is Farrer's
record of the first year of this expedition. He notes: 'I had the very
great luck of happening on an absolutely perfect friend and helper
in Mr Purdom, formerly of Kew, and he and I with three untrained
Chinese lads from Shansi, made up the whole of the Caravan that
left Peking.'

What an effort it must have been to write about these
adventures, making notes at the time so that precious material was
recorded accurately and safely despatched home, together with all
the other work necessary to keep the expedition going. There was
also the fatigue of climbing under difficult conditions (in one
situation he describes seeing a plant or shrub with his field glasses
and estimating that it should take about half an hour to reach it; in

fact it took nearly twenty-four hours). Yet his lively prose is sprinkled with humour; there is seldom total depression.

His gift for understatement is illustrated in his descriptions. He approached a 'typical Tibetan bridge of poor class arching high' to cross a ravine. It was not only in poor condition, it was hardly in existence at all,

> with the rails all gone and half the planks also. . . . Purdom's pony disliked the look of it. . . . I meanwhile sat philosophically quiet on *Spotted Fat*, waiting on his mood. . . . However, all went well. *Spotted Fat* sniffed at the bridge for a moment, and then began solemnly to advance. . . . Beneath me, far down between the gaps of the planks, I could see the boiling, ice-grey water of the racing torrent and in my ear there was a general roar and suddenly I became aware that *Spotted Fat* was sidling out towards the unprotected edge. . . . A Paralysis possessed me. . . . Purdom's frozen face of horror advancing to meet me remains photographed on my mind. . . . I was conscious of a stumbling subsidence behind me, a splintering crash . . . *Spotted Fat* and I, no longer one, but two, were falling through 20 feet of emptiness, and down into the glacial abysses of the river. Down and down into the icy water we sank. . . . There was no swimming possible and no struggling. . . . Desperately I struck out at each rocky headland as it raced into sight, and raced away behind me again, out of reach.

Farrer eventually waded ashore but the shock and buffeting must have beaten him almost into unconsciousness. However, he recalled that as he was rushed through the roaring waters of the torrent he could 'study the Primulas as, in their crannies, they fled blandly by'. Later he adds ruefully that as *Spotted Fat* swam directly across to the opposite bank, he could have reached safety without any dramatic dash down the river if only he had hung on to his horse's tail.

During this expedition he was painting in water-colours and an exhibition of these works was held in 1917 at the Fine Art Society's galleries.

A meeting of Farrer and Osbert Sitwell in 1918 was described in *Noble Essences*. The cousins were guests of a mutual friend near Bath. By then Farrer, having returned from his Kansu expeditions, was working in the Ministry of Information. 'It was a day of early spring' and they came to an inn and sat in the sunshine drinking peach brandy. Sitwell describes how Farrer entertained him and another guest,

> talking, telling us of many things, homely or exotic, for the conversation ranged from his parents to the uplands of China and

Tibet. . . . he had already discovered—and this was a year before his last journey—an amazing number of new plants, including the famous gention named after him. And he brought to bear on every flower, and on even the most ordinary pleasure of everyday life, what I can now see, after my visit to China, to be a Chinese gift of appreciation. It was precisely this quality which made his company often so delightful.

33 Gentiana farreri, *the flower named for Reginald Farrer and discovered by him in north-west China in 1914*

The acount goes on, as the level of the brandy fell lower in the bottle, to describe an 'impromptu bacchanale'. 'We twined for our heads, I remember, garlands of ivy, as a plain British substitute for the authentic vine.'

The Rainbow Bridge, published posthumously in 1921, was described by Sitwell as being 'in some ways the most interesting and representative' of Farrer's writing. This was the account of the second season in Kansu, which he completed in 1918. Perhaps even more than *On the Eaves of the World* this is a book which, in the hackneyed phrase, it is almost impossible to put down. There is rapture when a new plant is found and safely collected, there is gloom when the search ends in disappointment.

> Very cold blew the wind along the topmost *arete*. And very cold was my mood, as I roamed its sharp dells of turf and examined its dorsal fins of rock, only to find nothing new whatever; far along I roamed, and up and down, and nowhere came on any better luck.

There is also the unusual approach of a botanist who understands that there may be readers who do not want too much botany and others who want botany and not too many details of social conditions:

> Be patient, then, you who don't like plants and do like prattle; and you others, bear up against the prattle for the sake of the plants. . . . in my rainbow bridge there are many colours, of which you must accept those you don't like as the price of those you do. And if you like none of them you are very welcome to stay at home and not set foot on my bridge at all.

He apologizes for notes on foods and feasting, but explains that

> the countless cross-examinations I have undergone since my return at the hands of the more intelligent have left me with a conviction that people's prime interest in one's travel experiences lies in learning what one had to eat and drink.

This does not surprise or offend him and the statement is not a criticism.

As he can also write, 'there are no joys in life, I suppose, more restfully rapturous than the discovery of a new lovely flower' his attitude must seem unusually tolerant towards those concerned only with food and drink.

The book is much more than a day-to-day diary of events. As Sitwell writes, 'a most genuine love of beauty permeates his books; they are stamped with his unusual individuality and in all of them is to be found a powerful surge of original humour and of wit.'

Let us see what he has to say about *taking exercise* (in *My Rock Garden*), for instance:

> It was a steaming hot morning when I and my party alighted in the Rhone valley, that Turkish bath of prostrating heat. And immeasurably far above rose the awful mountains. Is there any weak vessel who will sympathise with my feelings of crushed despair when I stand at something like sea-level and gaze with craning neck up, up, up to those peaks a thousand feet or so straight overhead? . . . I must

evidently make a clean breast of it here, or the shameful truth will leak out. I am lazy. I can walk, I suppose, as well as most. On the open fell I can go on perpetually without much food or fatigue. But I don't really like walking for its own sake; I had rather not walk. I walk only where there is something to be got by walking that could not be got in any other way, and never for the mere sake of the walking itself. I regard the British craze for exercise as a superstition, and, of all Mr. Chamberlain's ideas, am proud only to share one, in our common prejudice against unnecessary exertion. Therefore, it will easily be seen how hard a fate it is that has dowered one so sedentary with a passion for plants. Walk I must and walk I do. But whenever I needn't I frankly don't. I have no shame whatever in availing myself of any funicular that may happen to be handy; and when there is a railway up the Matterhorn, I may faintly deplore it, but I shall certainly go up in it. . . .

And about *bulbs*:

The shameful truth must now come out. I am utterly afraid of bulbs. With ordinary plants I have no such qualms, for they have no wish to disappear underground and keep you in the dark. The moment the plant feels poorly you note its symptoms, and diagnose the disease, and heave up the whole thing with your trowel and give it repeated changes of soil and situation until you have either killed or cured. But how underhand and secretive a thing is a bulb! Your priceless daffodil, your gracious lily, blooms in glory; two months later there is nothing left of them above ground, perhaps, and you have not an idea what dreadful things may be going on under the surface. In all probability a mouse or a slug is having a word with that bulb, and you may say a last goodbye to your lily and your money and your happiness all at once. Therefore I maintain that there is something ominous and terrible about bulbs. . . .

There is the sale of *Spotted Fat*, 'clotted in incorrigible laziness, one eyed, sullen and demoniacal', and the unusual use of strange words that fit to perfection the description needed: 'I only know of it as . . . rather dull and squinny of flower', 'the next few days after all were rather niddering', and 'up we moiled, panting'. And there are, of course, many references to his favourite Jane Austen characters: on finding a special primula, 'in singing dancing, exclaiming spirits like Emma'.

Emma was embarking on the love affair of her life, while Farrer was illustrating his contention that 'there are no joys . . . more restfully rapturous than the delivery of a new lovely flower.' He and Jane Austen were completely in accord.

The following letter to Sir Francis Younghusband is given in full. It appears to be unpublished and gives a kind of summing-up of Reginald's hopes and activities very shortly before he died. It also gives an impression of future plans and aspirations—there is not the slightest hint or suggestion that these may not be fulfilled. His ideas are clearly outlined for the next few years and include at least one, and perhaps two, to be spent at Ingleborough. He is thinking aloud, and his thinking is full of the happiness that made him 'in singing, dancing and exclaiming spirits', like Emma.

c/o T. Cook & Sons
Rangoon
(After Dec. to H.B.M.'s
Legation, Peking)

Nyitadi, above Konglu, above
Fort Herts, above Myitkyina,
Sino-Burmese Alps.
Sept. 13, 1920

Dear Sir Francis

I hope you have not thought me ungrateful for all your help, because I have been so long in letting you have news of my progress? But I have been waiting till I could give you a more or less complete account of my two seasons. For the first did not take me into country of any special interest, since Hertz (then at Putao) said it was too late to arrange the stores & coolies necessary for an expedition up the Adung Long. So that I was reduced to making for Hpman instead. And, of course, in such country as this one looks on a spot already visited by a half a dozen white men, as almost as populous and overtrodden as Piccadilly! However, I had an exceedingly successful and happy time, both with plants & with people: so that all was well. But then an awful alarm arose. Barnard, who had by that time succeeded to Putao, declared he couldn't have me in the district at all, as he would want all the available coolie-labour for himself. You may imagine what a crisis then arose! However, I kept my head, & pulled strings, & behaved prettily, & diplomatised: until finally I'd won him, in ten minutes of talk after months of futile correspondence, to allow me away East, up here, on condition of employing mules only. This I did: with the result that when I came to the unbridged furies of the terrible N'Mai Hka, they all, with one accord, immediately forsook me and fled, so that for the rest of the way I had to employ coolies after all. However, after days of absolutely desert and lifeless jungle, I had then come into a country quite populous with Lissus, a people with whom I get on extremely well. So that in due course, after nearly six weeks of hard travel, I came at last successfully into this ultima Thule, a 'terre vierge' if you like, where no white man has ever visited, except the two who came up here on the Akhyang Expedition, & took over (entirely without rhyme or reason or excuse, of course) this whole district from the patient but indomitable Empire of China. Here, then, in high happiness, I have been spending the summer, collecting flowers, & tending the local sick. Though this, indeed, is the last edge of nowhere, my own chief work has really lain almost over the edge. Since the city of Nyitadi, (which consists of three chalets,) has been, & is, my Capua: while up on the high passes overhead into China I have spent the chief of the summer, in cloud that never lifted, & rain that never ceased. It has been, indeed, a wonderful and most delightful season: quite alone as I am, this year, but for my beloved Staff Of Gurkhas, I have been far happier than in the beaten ways of Hpman. But I will not now trench upon the tale which perhaps the R.G.S. or the Alpine Club may call for: except to warn you that, happy as is the country with no history (like this one, indeed), so also is the explorer. No White Wolves this time, no Squinting Abbots athirst for blood, no sieges of cities like many-towered Ilion: no, nothing but peace & goodwill all round, and an ample sufficiency of what the labourer described as 'muck & 'ard work'. And so may things continue until I quit this scene of primeval cordiality, uncontaminated by what we chose to call 'civilisation', (because, to our own undoing, we invented it.). I start down-country again, I hope, about Nov. 15; leave Rangoon for Peking about Jan. 6: & thence, in a fortnight, steer a straight homeward course, where I shall hope soon to see you and unfold my tale at leisure. I hope, in fact, that you will be so well satisfied with your protégé, as to help him yet again, to visit parts remote? In 1921 I shall be at home, & in 1922, I should *like* to stay there: but in 1923 I feel I may be ripe for another expedition. Now, could you, & would you, give me your help towards either Nepal or Tibet? I suppose, though, that an invitation, or a mission to Holy Lhasṣa [sic] (I don't know how to spell the Holy City!) *would* be quite out of the question, even for one of His Holiness's own flock? In Rangoon I had a long talk with the Venerable Bhitikhu (ne Mr McKechnie, of Hull: & you will agree that the change of name was felicitous): and he told me that not even he, professed religious of the Yellow Robe, would be allowed within sight of Lhasa. But then, of course, he *is* of the *Yellow* Robe, & I don't suppose the Three Abbeys would stretch points for *him*: whereas, with times & policies always changing, it *might* be that Authority at home might now be in favour of making acte de presence at Lhasa, by means of some unofficial person of quality, who by this time, I hope, has acquired a good reputation as a discreet & not unpopular traveller? My scheme may be wild: but it is not outside the bounds of human possibility, so I though I would put it to you. The botanical haul would be of course be prodigious: but fades into utter insignificance, even to me, beside the thought of setting my eyes on the inside of the böring, & the outside of the Potala! But Nepal would be a glorious second-best, &, as I see that you are lending your countenance to an expedition that once more aims at violating Gaurisankar, I have hopes that you might do as much for me. I gather that neither Nepal nor its Maharajah are quite as intransigent about strangers as Lhasa & His Holiness: nor, I think, would O'Connor, a friendly acquaintance of mine, (I believe,), be hostile to the scheme. In any case there are tracts of time before us, though, of course, if opportunity insisted on my seizing 1922 instead of 1923, seize it I would indeed, & with both hands. But, aiming for preference at 1923, we have space before us in which to talk things over, & interview people, & all the rest of it:—always supposing, of course, that you don't turn down both me & my proposals as hopeless. In fact, though I head my letter with an address for correspondence, I do not really expect an answer, but only ask you to revolve my ambitions benevolently in your mind till I return: &, if you are favourable, lend me your good word meanwhile with the right people. To Nepal, certainly, & to Lhasa, probably, my faithful Myitkyina Gurkhas would, I know, be all agog to follow me: and, *if* matters should shape as I hope, I should depend greatly on high authority to have the pair of them detailed to my service again, out of their poking little Battalion at Myitkyina, for *what* a life is this, of the hills: even in country so uninhabited as this, & so curiously inviolate by either history or religion. Lonely, lonely, not so much dead, as never having lived: that is the impression one gets as one stands on one of these peaks & looks out Northward, over an uncharted sea of undistinguished mountain ranges, broken only by two or three tremendous peaks, very far away indeed, up in Tibet, or away over East in China. One has two Empires in view, India & China's & the last two theocracies of the world, Burma & Tibet. Not that the climate often allows so stimulating a prospect! It is, in fact, so foul that though I long to visit every one of those peaks & passes, I never really want to visit the Sino-Burmese Alps again. Besides which, the lone country is quite untravellable, clothed entirely in jungle, as Hertz puts it, of a positively Malayan density. Happy though I & my flock have been, collecting flowers & seeds (they are adepts now, & as keen as myself), I have often given a sigh to the clear air & sunlight of Siku, the roads, the facilities, the immemorial geniality of China.

This is a very long letter, which I can only hope our community of enthusiasms may excuse, from yours v. sincerely & gratefully Reginald Farrer.

To realize the physical privations, the exhaustion, the problems with the natives about supplies and transport, the difficulties in finding a plant in flower and then recovering its seed, the labelling, the waiting on the weather—even a lively imagination cannot be fully aware of so many taxes on strength, patience and fortitude. But all these were intensified on Farrer's last journey into upper Burma. Mr E. H. M. Cox, who shared in some of his expeditions, in his introduction to *Farrer's Last Journey*, emphasizes the depression of the perpetual rains as contrasted with the climate on the Kansu expedition.

Above all, it must be remembered that conditions in the Burmese Alps are entirely different from anything that Farrer had experienced before. In the past he had travelled in countries that had a background of an ancient civilization. . . . Also, he had never had to experience a monsoon; for in Kansu the climate had been that which exists among the high hills throughout most of the world; whereas in Upper Burma

it rains, almost without ceasing, from the end of June until October.
. . . Life is so difficult that the inhabitants . . . have to wage ceaseless
warfare against nature's encroachments.

Even so, the plant-collecting went on. For the first year (1919) he
was with E. H. M. Cox, but for the last eight months he had only
orderlies and Burmese guides. Still, articles were written for the
Gardeners' Chronicle at about fortnightly intervals.

He became ill on 1 October 1920 and died on 17 October. In a
letter to a friend, written about six months earlier, from the
village of Nyatadi, he says:

Not but that everything does well; so far all my fears have been
falsified and I continue a great deal happier and more serene of heart
than I ever felt last year. And solitude proves not a trial but a most
blessed comfort. August is now ending and the discovery work of the
year is now practically over, yet . . . I am still in far heartier fettle and
less fagged that I was in July in the infinitely less trying conditions of
last year. This defies reason, for certainly both climate and country are
heart-breaking.

The story of his last illness is now well known. Bhaju, one of his
servants, was devoted and wrote to Cox (by dictation),

I beg to state that [Burra Sahab Bahadur] was suffering from cough and
chests pain from 1st October to 13th October, 1920, but not so serious,
also he never tired up to 13th October, 1920 which he converses
between us distinctly and properly.

But it seemed that after this date

he discontinued to take his food except soda water, whisky and
medicines for his benefit . . . and without giving any pain or trouble to
us he breathed his last on the morning of the 17th October, 1920.

Bhaju had made 'a wonderful journey' (*Farrer's Last Journey*) to
Konglu to try to get medical help, taking only three days over
difficult terrain and refusing to stop for rest either on the route or
even at Konglu. He got back shortly before Farrer died.

From Bhaju's report it seems that although the last few days
were those of a very sick man, perhaps the preceding time was not
too distressing or painful, apart from all the usual discomfort
under such conditions. Perhaps Farrer did not realize how near the
end was.

In *The Times* obituary there were these revealing sentences:
'He was not a scientific man. He was first and foremost an artist,
not merely looking at things from a new angle, but creating a new
idea.'

Miss Eleanour
Sinclair Rohde

1883–1950

The very word 'Herb-garden' has a pleasant sound,
for it suggests seclusion and peace; it conjures up
visions of a quiet pleasaunce full of old-fashioned
colours and perfumes, and plants with homely yet
musical names, such as Sweet Cicely, Lovage, Balm,
Lad's Love, Woodruff; of humble plants such as
Thyme and Foxglove.

ELEANOUR SINCLAIR ROHDE
Herbs and Herb Gardening

In the *Gardeners' Chronicle* of 1 July 1950, there was recorded with
deep regret 'the death, at Reigate, on June 23rd, after a long
illness, of Miss Eleanour Sinclair Rohde'.

She was probably one of the most scholarly as well as one of the
most prolific writers on gardening matters of this or any
generation, with an especial emphasis on herb gardening. Her first
publication, entitled *A Garden of Herbs*, was published in 1920
followed two years later by *The Old English Herbals* and, in 1936,
by *Herbs and Herb Gardening*.

But herbs did not by any means constitute her only approach to
gardening, and two of her most valuable books dealt with the
history and the scents of the garden, namely, *The Story of the
Garden* and *The Scented Garden*. These two books are full of
information, interwoven with literary references and quotations
from a catholic taste in poetry as well as from many of the early
herbals. Her writing shows that it is the product of 'a polish'd
mind'.

Eleanour Sinclair Rohde was the only daughter of the late John
Rohde of the Travancore Civil Service, and was educated at
Cheltenham Ladies' College and at St Hilda's Hall, Oxford. She
grew up in Surrey in late Victorian times and one of her first
memories was connected with herbs. This was the cry of a London
flower-seller calling out the familiar street cry: 'Sweet lavender,
six bunches a penny.' Years later she wrote of a bank of lavender
as being 'one of the pleasantest sights of late summer'.

Her chapter on old roses in *The Scented Garden* is full of references to most of the famous rose books that have ever been written. She quotes from Dean Hole's *Book of Roses*, from William Paul's *Rose Garden*, from Miss Willmott and Miss Jekyll, from Gerard, Loudon, T. Rivers, H. C. Andrews, Parkinson, Redouté and Miss Lawrence. Her reading of such works included also the French rosarians, and her knowledge of the history of each rose and of its introduction to this country make their contribution to a store of valuable information.

There is special reference to 'Stanwell Perpetual'. 'This fine pink rose has a fine rich scent' which was at first puzzling, but later she describes 'The centre as rather flesh colour, the outer petals paler. . . .' (I have always found it to be the palest of pale pink, with a gentle scent, but perhaps it has altered like 'Madame Pierre Oger', with the weather). Writing of the difficulties in obtaining the 'Yellow Provence' rose she quotes Andrews, who, in 1810, says of *R. sulphurea* that it was not to be met with in flower in any of the nursery grounds very near London. 'We have not seen it even in a budding state nearer than Brentford in the collection of the Duke of Northumberland at Sion House.' Writing fifty years ago, Dean Hole said it was almost extinct and that he had seen it only at Burghley House. This rose, which is still there, was brought from France by a French cook and was formerly called either the Burghley rose or the Yellow Provence rose.

It is these small comments, thrown in for good measure, that help to fix in one's mind the name or colour or scent of the rose in question. Like Miss Willmott she could find interest in a rose which is now regarded as too popular for many people's taste:

> R. Wichuraiana, named after the German botanist, Wichura, came to England by way of the USA. It was sent to Brussels in 1886 from Japan. An American named Perkins crossed this rose with the old Hydrid Perpetual, Madame Gabriel Luizet, thereby producing the formerly popular but now much maligned Dorothy Perkins. R. Wichuraiana (the type) has the wild rose perfume. . . .

One of her favourite roses seems to have been the old Bourbon rose 'Zephirine Drouhin'. She writes that however small a garden she had it would be grown there:

> And what an array of virtues this rose has! It is very vigorous, it blooms from June to October, its fragrance is delicious, it will thrive on a chalk soil, and it is one of the few roses which will grow near the smoky atmosphere of a large town.

She remarks also 'its lovely deepish pink petals'. It may be of interest to mention here that it is known from present-day experience to be a reliable rose for flower arrangements if cut when still in bud.

34 Miss Eleanour Sinclair Rohde (in hat) with some of her war-time 'circus' members

The historical aspect of most of her work and her scholarly approach to the subject, which at once unites it with its origin and social history, make for absorbing reading. It is interesting to know, for instance, that the rose shown in the early stained glass windows of cathedrals is almost always the *Rosa gallica*; that acanthus leaves are embroidered in the tenth-century stole made in memory of St Cuthbert to be seen in Durham Cathedral; that sweet bags were stuffed with lavender, verbena, scented geranium leaves, mints and rose leaves, and hung on wing armchairs 'to smell unto for Melancholy or to cause one to sleep' and that lilies of the valley were first planted in this country in 1568 and were recorded as growing wild on Hampstead Heath in 1807 by Philip Miller. Also rosemary used to be highly valued as a cosmetic and cowslip leaves were eaten in salads and tarts; St Bride 'lights the kindly flame of the dandelion'; the poet's narcissus has grown here since the Roman occupation and the Huguenots brought auriculas to this country. Then there is a note too on the drying and preserving of flowers in hot sand, as found in *Delights for Ladies* (written by Sir Hugh Platt, a courtier to Queen Elizabeth), and, at about the same time, a quotation from one Richard Hakluyt in a book published in 1582 which tells of the introduction of the tulip: 'And now within these foure years there have been brought into England from Vienna in Austria divers kinds of flowers called Tulipas, and these and others procured thither a little before from Constantinople. . . .'

It is to be expected that many of these miniature picture backgrounds of detail should be provided for various herbs and, although there is much valuable information about many, perhaps two of the most loved are rue and rosemary. Of rue we are told that it likes a chalk soil and is usually poor in growth unless lime or chalk are present. The soft blue-grey colour of the *Ruta graveolens* foliage is well known and especial mention must be made of its scent because this is strong and repellent to some people, whereas there are others who regard it with affection. 'It is frequently mentioned by Shakespeare, and both Ophelia and the gardener in *King Richard II* speak of it.' (Gardener: 'Here did she drop a tear: here, in this place,/I'll set a bank of rue, sour herb of grace'.)

There is so much history attached to the rosemary— *Rosmarinus*, 'dew of the sea'—that we are given almost an essay on this shrub alone:

> Hentzner mentions in his *Travels* (1598) that in English gardens the walls were frequently covered with rosemary, and at Hampton Court he says 'It was so planted and nailed to the walls as to cover them entirely.' Both in cookery and medicine the uses of this herb were manifold. The flowers were candied, a conserve was made of them and rosemary cordial was used in every household. . . . Above all rosemary was the herb of friendship. 'As for rosemary,' wrote Sir Thomas More, 'I lette it runne all over my garden walls, not onlie because my bees love it, but because it is the herb sacred to remembrance and to friendship. . . .'

Friendship must have been a key word in Eleanour Sinclair Rohde's life. She never married and lived most of her life on her own, at Cranham Lodge in Reigate, after both her parents had died. Her only brother was killed in the First World War. An elderly cousin, a dame at one of the Eton colleges, came to live with her in retirement. This cousin was never seen to emerge from the house and certainly not to walk round the garden, and she died during the same war.

It was the war period which probably drew on Miss Rohde's skill with friendships more than at any other time. Some of the people she had to work in her gardens were strange to say the least, and she is credited with this comment on the unusual mixture of material she had to depend on: 'I don't engage my wartime staff. They engage me. During the last two years we have asked each other at intervals "Who next will join the circus?"' At this time there were for the most part: two land army girls; two secretaries; three others, including a mysterious titled lady in a caravan; three men who were conscientious objectors. Among this contingent there were two Czechs—one a racing motorist who also played the violin, and one who appeared to live on wild rose hips.

A close friend of the Messel family, Miss Rohde worked frequently in the library at their home, Nymans, in West Sussex. The very beautiful garden there, open to the public from April until October, was that most known and loved by Miss Rohde. She would most surely have agreed with the description of the garden in the National Trust booklet of West Sussex gardens opened every year: 'One of the great gardens of the Sussex Weald, rare and beautiful plants, shrubs and trees from all over the world.' It is situated at Handcross, near Crawley.

She also catalogued Lord Curzon's library when he lived at Reigate Priory, before the Second World War, and knew well both Sir Oswald and Lady Moseley. He, in fact, sent orders for herbs from prison, so that they could be ready for him when he came out. Lady Eve Balfour, founder of the Soil Association, was another great friend.

There is fascination in glancing through the index of Miss Rohde's various books. Who, for instance, was Dr Butts? One cannot resist turning to the page indicated to discover that he was a physician to Henry VIII whose recipes are preserved in the Sloane Collection at the British Museum.

But all her references are not to early history—Mr Reginald Farrer is mentioned in connection with the discovery of *Viburnum fragrans* (now *farreri*) and Captain Kingdon-Ward with the cowslip-scented primula, *P. florindae*.

It is interesting to compare her comments on the scents of the garden with those of Miss Jekyll, Mr E. A. Bowles, or Dr Hampton (Jason Hill). All three begin the year with *Chimo-*

nanthus (*fragrans* or *pralix*), mentioning in turn the scents and flowers through the spring and summer, primroses, cowslips, wallflowers, honeysuckle, sweet-briar, carnations, but they all recognize that individual scents may appeal in different cases and that for example phlox may seem sweet to one gardener but smell of pig sties to another, and some flowers smell sweet in the open air but may become suffocating in a warm room. For instance, Mr Bowles particularly mentions the introduction by Reginald Farrer of *Viburnum fragrans* (now *farreri*) and that he found it difficult at first to persuade other gardeners of its value, and showed it for several years before it was given an award. Miss Rohde writes that '*V. fragrans* opens its richly scented, wax-like, pinkish cymes sometimes as early as November, and this shrub should find a place in every scented garden. . . .'

There is special mention of a scent which was once mentioned to me by a blind gardener as being a favourite one. Miss Rohde writes: 'Few people appreciate the scent of broad bean flowers, simply because the broad bean is a vegetable, yet it is one of the most beautiful of flower scents.' My blind friend emphasized the pleasure of walking near a beanfield in full flower—'One of the best scents of all,' he said.

It would be difficult to include all the scents of flowers, leaves and the countryside generally. Miss Rohde mentions especially the nostalgia of new-mown hay for town dwellers, calling up pictures of hayfields 'for surely no other smell makes them realize with the same poignancy that their lot is that of prisoners, no matter how gilded their cages may be'. Then there is Francis Bacon declaring: 'That which above all yields the sweetest smell in the air is the violet, especially the white double violet which comes twice a year, about the middle of April and about Bartholomewtide.' Wallflowers cannot be omitted, and Miss Rohde quotes Gervase Markham writing over 300 years ago. 'The husbandman preserves it most in his bee garden, for it is wondrous sweet and affordeth much honney!'

But, however incomplete the list must needs be, it would be hard to leave out the scent of mignonette. Its history reveals that 'in the library of Sir Joseph Banks there is a note to say that the seed of mignonette was sent in 1742 by Lord Bateman from the Royal Garden at Paris to Mr Richard Bateman at Old Windsor.' Miss Sackville-West's reference to 'small but scented spires' in

The Garden is the perfect description of the mignonette we want to see and smell.

Eleanour Rohde's knowledge of the scents of herbs must have been probably the most extensive of anyone of her own time. She grew few flowers, according to the workers of the war years, but concentrated completely on herbs and unusual vegetables relating either to Shakespeare's time or before. She had three gardens, all well stocked. One was her own, quite a small one, but she also took over during the war years two large Victorian gardens—they must both have been about two acres in size. Here were grown quantities of angelica which, it was understood, was sold to the makers of gin, but this is not clear. Endless borders and clumps of Hamburg parsley are remembered, as well as pennyroyal, the latter grown for medical use. There was also a fine collection of mints and peppermints, among them the black peppermint. (At this mention of these particular herbs the story was told of 'A young man pushing his mother—a visitor to the "peppermint" garden—in her wheel chair. It was explained to him that this collection was a very rare one, especially the black peppermint. He then had to relay this information down the old lady's ear trumpet. Her reply was: "Rare indeed, grows like a weed round my garden,"')

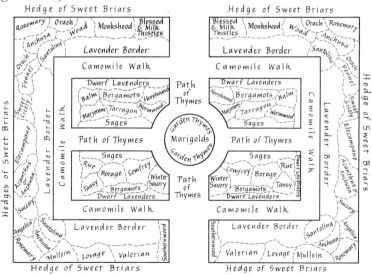

35 *A plan for a herb garden by Miss Rohde*

The herb garden was recognized as a war effort— to encourage home cooking—and included many other than those herbs already mentioned. Among them there were dill, purslane, Mexican blackbean, endive (for the Canadians). In her own garden Miss Rohde grew a 'strawberry' called Black Prince, sent to her from France. This was a fruit between a raspberry and a blackberry. She was also successful with melons and aubergines, asparagus peas and many other different peas and beans. She often used the roots of the Hamburg parsley in her cooking, and sowed bergamot in drifts of purple, Cambridge scarlet, white, mauve and rare pink.

One of the wartime helpers recalls helping to 'pack seeds and plants for sale'. She especially remembers washing seeds and thinks that Miss Rohde sorted them into small envelopes herself. These were sent off by post as orders (there was a catalogue) and the helper does not recall that people went frequently to the garden to give orders.

This brings us to the heath and heather garden at Lullingstone Castle, Kent. The little note on the Lullingstone catalogue for autumn 1948, and spring 1949, explains what happened about the herb garden there only a short time—perhaps a matter of months— before Miss Rohde's death. In the introduction to the catalogue there is this note: 'The Herb Garden at Lullingstone was designed by Miss E. Sinclair Rohde and based on plans of an old herb garden from medieval monasteries. The garden is probably one of the largest of its kind in the country [about three-quarters of an acre].'

Of all her gardening interests, the making of a herb garden was perhaps the most important to her. She would probably like to feel that this is why she is most remembered. So here are some ideas for a herb garden, mostly taken from her book *Herbs and Herb Gardening*, full of practical suggestions and lists of plantings.

The Making of a Herb Garden and some Recipes
(from *Herbs and Herb Gardening* by Eleanour Sinclair Rohde)

The chief considerations in making a herb garden are soil and aspect. Nearly all the herbs mentioned in this chapter require a light, warm soil and full sun. The most decorative herbs are the Lavenders, tall-growing herbs, such as Angelica, Succory, Lovage, Fennel, Woad, Elecampane, Aconite, Sweet Cicely, Anchusa, and Orach, and herbs with vivid colours, such as the Bergamots and Marigolds. To make an effective Herb Garden, the general design should, I think, be laid out chiefly with the evergreen or nearly evergreen herbs. In Plan I, designed for a garden ninety feet long and sixty feet wide, the whole is encircled with a hedge of unclipped Sweet Briars, lovely throughout the summer with their twelve and fourteen feet long, graceful stems and deliciously scented foliage, in June with flowers and throughout autumn and winter with red berries. Between this outer enclosure and the broad belt of Lavender (either *L. spica* or *L. vera*) are the stately herbs, none of which are evergreen. This bed is ten feet wide and the Lavender will occupy about five feet of it. Unless planted two and a half feet back from the edge, vigorous Lavenders, such as the Grappenhall variety will grow almost across the path, ruining the Camomile walk and leaving no room to walk. The remaining five feet behind the Lavenders is sufficient space for the Sweet Briars and the tall-growing herbs, though there will not be enough room for more than a few of each of the stateliest herbs.

The four inner beds are also outlined with evergreen herbs—the Dwarf Lavenders on the outer borders, Sages on four of the inner borders, Winter Savory and Horehound the other four. Within, the centres of these beds are filled with 'herbs of middle growth', to quote Lawson's phrase. In the centre is a circular bed ten feet across, Pot Marigolds in the centre, surrounded with a three feet wide belt of Garden Thymes. It will be noted that all the outlines are laid out in evergreen, fragrant herbs so that at all seasons the garden is pleasant to behold and to smell.

Naturally, this plan will have to be modified according to climate and soil. In many parts the Rosemary I have marked at the four corners will not flourish in the open. In this case it will be advisable to fill the corners with *Anchusa italica* and to interplant the Anchusa with the slender Orach. When the Anchusa's flowering period is over, the plants are untidy, but the tall, blood-red stems of the Orach, especially in seed, will be decorative in late summer and autumn. Until the Santolina has made bushes four and five feet across, the space behind might be given to any of the minor herbs. I have purposely not marked spaces for the less decorative herbs, such as Anise, Coriander, Dill, Cumin, and so forth, as room can be found for them in odd spaces. Again, until the Lavenders have attained maturity, the spaces behind and in front of them might be given to colourful herbs, such as the Bergamots, Clary, Herb Bennet, Bastard Dittany, etc.

Where there is sufficient space the further entrance might lead to a garden devoted to the old Roses. As most of these are vigorous growers they do not take kindly to formal beds. They might be grown in a broad bed encircling the garden and the centre could be filled with Carnations. The old Roses flower only in June and the Carnations would carry on the interest of the garden till they were cut by frosts. Other flowers used as herbs, such as Madonna Lilies, Primroses, Honesty, Winter Cherry, etc., could also be grown in this garden.

In an article entitled 'How I Made My Herb Garden' appearing in *The Countryman* in July 1935 Miss Rohde describes not only exactly how she made the garden but many of the various plants she put into it and where they came from. She especially mentions the Aldenham House garden in Hertfordshire.

> I have a handsome, broadleaved variety of Salvia officinalis, which I value greatly because I had it from the late Mr Vicary Gibbs. My red-leaved sage is descended from cuttings given me years ago by a very old friend, a post-mistress in Devonshire. My original Salvia schlarea, which we used to call Salvia turkestanica, I received as a seedling from one to whom it was presented by a gardener in the Vatican garden. This old-fashioned clary varies greatly, but the true Vatican strain is by far the handsomest. It certainly is a striking plant in flower, with its big, rough leaves and four feet high stems of mauve flowers with large pink bracts. It would be ideal for big jars for indoor decoration, but unfortunately—apart from the fact that the smell is disagreeable and overpowering—it fades immediately when cut. Tastes have changed, for in the seventeenth century clary leaves dipped in batter and fried were commonly eaten. The smell is so coarse that I have never had the courage to try eating them.
>
> My chervil came from Hatfield. This herb, with its lace-like leaves and delicate fragrance, particularly charming in autumn when the foliage turns mauve pink, always fascinated me when I saw it growing in French herb gardens. But, though I sowed diligently every year, not a seed germinated. At Hatfield I saw chervil growing in masses and from Mr Hall, the head gardener, I learnt that the seed must be sown as soon as it is ripe. I think every seed in the large packet he kindly sent me must have germinated and ever since it has sown itself in our garden.

If one had never seriously thought of making a herb garden before, one would surely be tempted to make a start after reading her suggestions. First of all, a herb garden need not occupy much space although is is possible, if the area is big enough, to have ample opportunity for experiment and the inclusion of many flowers and plants which were used in early recipes but are not commonly connected with the present-day use of herbs. A garden designed by Miss Rohde for one of her clients (Mr Appleton of Birmingham) included chives, borage, tansy, chervil, lavender, rosemary, balm and sages as well as marigolds, mulleins, foxgloves, anchusa, meadowsweet, valerian, santolina and southernwood. She especially mentions the Munstead dwarf lavender with its 'large spikes of richly coloured, deliciously scented flowers'.

In another plan for a herb garden Miss Rohde includes 'a hedge of unclipped sweet briars' and a camomile walk, and suggests that where it is possible an entrance might lead from the herb garden into one of old roses. These were another of her loves.

Miss Sinclair Rohde knew and visited many gardens of her time and two of the ones she mentions most with gratitude and affection are Nymans and the Hon. Vicary Gibb's garden at Aldenham House. The name Munstead appears less frequently, but it is in connection with Miss Jekyll that *The Times* obituary compliments her. Of Miss Rohde's book *Gardens of Delight* (1934) the writer says it showed 'by its combination of the literary-historical with, for the first time, the practical-illustrative, that the mantle of Miss Jekyll had fallen on her.'

Dr F. A. Hampton
(Jason Hill)
1888–1967

I was glad . . . that you like Herb Robert and its
rough, rank smell, but, although I expect that
you know it and grow it, you did not mention the
albino variety, which, I believe, has been raised
to specific rank as 'Geranium Celticum', so I am
sending you a few plants of it. It was given to me
many years ago by Mr Bowles . . . and I wonder
whether you could find a home for the little 'St
Helena' violet, which I am also sending. It was
given me by Miss Jekyll. . . .

(Part of a letter to a friend)

Dr F. A. Hampton, alias Jason Hill, provides a link with at least
three distinguished gardeners and writers, Mrs Margery Fish,
Miss Jekyll and Miss Alice Coats. He must have known of the
prevalence of variegated-leafed plants at Mrs Fish's East
Lambrook garden as the following letter, dated 24 June 1965,
from her indicates:

Dear Hampton
I am very thrilled with the variegated rose. Thank you so much for
sending it. The scent of the flowers was coming through the parcel and
the leaves are delightfully variegated. I promise I will take the
greatest care of it. . . .

He also corresponded with Miss Jekyll frequently on the subject of
scent in flowers and leaves, and had visited her at Munstead Wood
late in her life when she was nearly blind. Dr Hampton described
how, in spite of this, she still carved a leg of mutton with skill and
dexterity, feeling the shape of the joint with the back of the knife,
and how she could detect the slightly wrong shade of colour in a
hollyhock from which she had meant to take seed. After meeting
her, he commented that the Nicholson portrait, which he described
as 'rather wooden', did not do her justice.

Dr Hampton, formerly on the staff of the Maida Vale Hospital,
London, was born in 1888 and died on 28 March 1967, aged 79.
He was educated at Charterhouse and New College and did his
medical training at Guy's Hospital, graduating in 1913. He was
on holiday in Spain when the First World War broke out and, on

hearing the news, sold his gold watch-chain in order to afford his ticket and get back as quickly as possible to join up. He served at the front as a doctor throughout the war and was awarded the Military Cross. He was an honorary psychiatric consultant resident at the Maida Vale Hospital for Nervous Diseases during the years between the wars, visiting the hospital twice weekly. It was in giving treatment here that he was credited with introducing fish tanks into the psychiatric wards on account of their therapeutic value. In later years he suffered from severe arthritis.

On being invited, in 1939, to join the Royal Naval Medical Service (at that time he was 51), his reply was 'that he would be delighted to serve anywhere, in any capacity and in any ranks'. As a surgeon-commander, RNVR, he gave valuable service 'looking after naval officers with psychiatric breakdowns or any other nervous troubles through the war years'. The writer of his obituary in the British Medical Journal claims for him: 'I think that all his professional colleagues, first at the Maida Vale Hospital and later in the Navy, would agree that he was the most personally gifted psychiatrist in their experience. . . . He was perceptive, immensely civilized, most kind and yet firm.'

He must have been a delightful man to meet. The obituary notice describes him as an 'entrancing talker' and his many friends testify to his charm and humour. Miss Alice Coats, to whom I am indebted for much firsthand material, writes: 'Perhaps his outstanding characteristic was his highly discriminating taste— not only in plants, but in literature, music, painting and cookery, in all of which he was interested. He was intolerant of what he considered vulgarity, in any form, but he did not confuse the 'common' with the vulgar; he had, for example, a special strain of the ordinary nasturtium, in a rather subtle shade, which he kept and propagated year after year. She also wrote: 'Dr Hampton was a most lovable person; a warm-hearted and affectionate man with a delightful sense of humour.'

Regarding his sense of humour, there is the story of how he persuaded 'an old bleary-eyed boffin of a regular surgeon-naval captain' to give invalid leave to a hypomanic officer. Without moving any facial muscles he was heard to explain: 'I think I should report, Sir, that this officer gets up in the morning to pick flowers before breakfast', which produced the required response: 'Good God, the man must be mad and should be invalided.'

✦ Dr F. A. Hampton (Jason Hill) ✦

Dr Hampton took the name of Jason Hill from a hill near his home at Chesham Bois. He wrote to a friend: 'On the opposite side of the Chert Valley to our little house there were two small hills, Venus Hill and Jason Hill, which caught my eye one day when I was trying to think of a name to sign an article with.' His two chief and invaluable contributions are *The Curious Gardener* and *The Contemplative Gardener*, both published by Faber and illustrated with line drawings by his friend John Nash.

In these his sense of humour is interspersed with his sense of poetry and appreciation of what might seem to be insignificant detail. Writing in *The Contemplative Gardener* of highly coloured flowers, Siberian wallflowers and others, he says: '. . . it is doubtful if we like mere brightness in flowers any better than we do in people' and '. . . there is a great deal of beauty in the garden during winter, if only we do not insist upon flowers and if we are willing to regard green and brown as colours'. He continues:

> . . . so much can be gained by looking at the garden as though we were seeing it for the first time, an attitude that often reveals a hitherto unseen harmony of green and, wherever plants have become fully established, balanced groupings of mass and volume, which, if only by reason of their mechanical stability, are satisfying and restful to the eye. There is still more to be discovered by narrowing the field of vision, even, if you like, to an ant's view, and exploring the patterns formed by a few pebbles and the rosette of a plantain or by a cushion of moss or an old brick. It is rather surprising that painters do not more often take a close-up landscape or still-life for their subject—Durer found a good deal of interest and beauty in a piece of turf.

And then there is his plea for what may be regarded as unremarkable:

> Among the plants, whose good qualities we most often fail to appreciate, are those robust and self-sufficient ones that claim no cultural attention and seldom get any other; we know so surely that the clump of Fennel will reappear where it was planted (and probably elsewhere), that the sculptural beauty of its sea-green columnar stems and the moulding of its pale bracts usually develops and passes unnoticed.

Alice Coats mentions Dr Hampton's interest in pebbles, of which he made a fine collection, and he introduced into his small Bampton garden some 'Sarsen stones' (transported by ancient glaciers). He had also collected some pebbles taken from the gizzard of a fossil dinosaur. (Evidently these creatures needed stones for breaking up their food, as a chicken requires grit.)

36 In the garden of Jason Hill (Dr F. A. Hampton) at Bampton,
Oxfordshire

His interest in cooking is recorded in a book he wrote with X M Boulestin, *Herbs, Salads and Seasonings*, illustrated in silver-point by Cedric Morris, a gardening friend. To another such friend he sent a receipt for Tansy Pudding (the complete recipe is given in *Wild Foods of Britain*):

White breadcrumbs	3 oz
Sugar	1 oz
Butter	$\frac{1}{2}$ oz
Eggs	2
Milk	$\frac{1}{2}$ pt

Tansy leaves, young and finely chopped, 1 dessert sponfl.

Among the many gardening friends who were fortunate enough to have had letters from him were Miss Jekyll, E. A. Bowles, Sir Stephen Tallents (to him also went a first edition of *The Curious Gardener*), N. G. Hadden, W. Ingwerson, to mention only a few. So often these letters reveal other facets of his nature. In one he writes to a friend in Scotland and is referring to the robbing of the osprey's nest: 'Perhaps you know the inside story. I'm interested because I always like things and situations which are not quite what they appear to be—people, too.' To the same friend he gives a description of his garden:

> This little garden is full at present of my flowers of 60 years ago—the dusty, dusky old columbines, the lolling, opulent double crimson Paeonies and lilac smelling sentimentally of old-fashioned face powder, but this evening a cold wind is blowing across the garden (we know where it comes from) and the stately irises are swaying like dowagers who have had a gin too many.

Perhaps a sentence in a letter I received from Mrs Hampton sums up his attitude to gardens and gardening: 'In a way, I think Tony was more interested in plants than in gardening. I mean he would be enormously interested in a cottage garden—with some unusual plant in it, say an old rose, or even a small plant. . . .' I asked her about his choice of gardening books, about his gardening friends and his affection for any specific gardens. Gertrude Jekyll, Reginald Farrer, E. A. Bowles and Kingdon-Ward were the authors he chiefly read, but Mrs Hampton emphasized that he would '*read* and keep good catalogues, e.g.: Hilliers, Scott's, Murrell's, Fielden and Crouch'. Among his gardening friends Miss Jekyll came high on the list—especially through their correspondence on scent and their mutual interest in this subject.

Norman Hadden, E. A. Bowles, Clarence Elliott, Professor W. T. Stearn were among others and there was also mention of a meeting in London with Reginald Farrer. The question of visiting gardens did not really arise, as he was just as likely to enjoy finding some favourite plant 'on a mountain, or in a hedge or at the side of a road' than to see it incorporated into a planting scheme. Lawrence Johnston's garden at Hidcote was an exception—he enjoyed going there, 'but', Mrs Hampton wrote, 'I don't think he much cared for looking at gardens "Open on Sunday". He *dis*liked herbaceous borders.'

He had an interest in studying the unexplained and like a blind person he sometimes saw not only what could not be seen, but also what is felt and smelt, which may have accounted for his appreciation of scent in flowers. His sense of curiosity was an integral part of his character not something idle, and never impertinent. In the preface to his book *The Curious Gardener* he writes:

> The word 'curious' in the title is intended in its older meanings, which are given in The New Oxford English Dictionary as: careful, studious, attentive, fastidious, ingenious, eager to learn, taking the interest of a connoisseur in any branch of art.

'. . . taking the interest of a connoisseur in any branch of art'. This seems to me to describe exactly Jason Hill's way of life during his retirement. He was knowledgeable about, and interested in so many 'branches of art' to which he could at last give time and thought. These interests emerged in his letters to friends and in his serious reading and writing. His reading, apart from that on gardening subjects, was seldom undertaken in translation, and must have involved a knowledge of several languages.

Here he is congratulating a friend on a magazine article:

> What a very good article . . . you have written about Elders! My wife read it this morning while she was drinking her early morning tea in the kitchen and then brought it upstairs and read it to me. I hope that you will make something out of the heart wood of the old Elders, for you will find it as hard and close-grained as Box and as pleasant to work if you have sharp tools. During the war I made myself a shallow wooden spoon to hold over a patient's eye, while you examined the reaction to light of the other.
> I once had a pink-flowered Elder from Smith of Newry. It turned out to be white, of course, but the old man explained that 'the flowers

have a pink flush which, however, is not perceptible'. It is nice to find Irish people being Irish. . . .

Music is suggested as a therapy:

> A few nights ago my wife . . . said 'I wonder where . . . is now.' And next morning there was a letter to tell us: but I am sorry indeed to hear of enteric. Convalescence from it is sometimes, you know, rather slow; so that I hope that you will sit and listen to the wireless and those nice long, lazy slow-playing records that weave their way through symphonies and sonatas.

And here he is noticing birds and cats:

> We have an old thrush in the garden with no tail and the other day I watched it trying to teach a young one to crack snails. An absurd sight, for the old one was dowdy and dumpy, the young one dapper in first full plumage, but apparently quite stupid for he couldn't get the idea at all and the old one soon lost patience and pushed the snail into his back. . . . White cats are quite successful in catching birds, who, I suppose assume that cats are not white and that anything white is not a cat. This is a human line of thought which was applied recently to the lumps of silica glass which lie about in one small area of the Libyan desert. It was said that, because meteorites are never made of silica, they weren't the remains of a meteorite. But they were.

These letters also included, in addition to the receipt for making tansy pudding, one for making hot chocolate (which must be drunk as soon as it is ready).

Introducing his family by letter to a new friend, he writes (of his wife):

> Dulcie's real name is 'Lucy Madeleine', but she was re-named in childhood. I call her 'Dusha'. Did I tell you that we have 4 daughters—Jillian, Ursula, Nicola and Josephine and lots and lots of grandchildren. I am 72 and enjoy life, especially since I retired as I have always disliked work. I am very fond of good food and wine with my meals; that's all there is about me.

(No mention, of course, of his arthritis.)

One of his great loves was for 'old' roses. Having some favourites of my own I naturally turn to the index of *The Curious Gardener* to see what I can find there and am delighted to see quite a long entry on what is for me a 'special' rose, 'Blairii No. 2', which is climbing over our front door.

> The uncouth name 'Blairii No. 2' conceals a characteristic period rose, large and flat, with a vivid pink centre and a paler margin; it is a climber and rather slow to start, but it should be given plenty of time

and room in which to develop, for it will grow to enormous size and flower with astonishing abundance in old age. It is very fragrant, with a sweet, 'old rose' scent combined with a hint of true musk. It was raised by Blair in 1845, and the only notice that I can find of a 'Blairii No. 1' is in a catalogue of A. Paul & Son for 1845, in which 'Blairii' is described simply as 'bright rose' and 'Blairii No. 2' as 'blush pink', and both are listed at the standard price of 2/6d.

Now we come to quotations from pieces of journalism—from *The Garden* and the *Manchester Guardian* referring to rock gardens, and from an article in *Nineteenth Century*, and from a lecture given to the RHS, both on 'The Scent of Flowers'. This last serves as an introduction to a serious subject for study, and also an immeasurably enjoyable one.

'Fashions in Gardening' *The Garden* 6 December 1924

On the garden, more than elsewhere, it must be difficult to impose a fashion from without, for sooner or later the gardener's real preferences make themselves felt in that struggle for existence of which every garden is the theatre, and schemes which do not quite coincide with the owner's personal taste are gradually, perhaps unconsciously, modified. . . . It will seem significant, for example, that the rise of the informal, or natural, garden and the revolt against carpet bedding coincided with a growing tendency to admire the wilder kind of scenery, a tendency that was beginning to drive people farther and farther afield on their holidays, and it will be noticed that this coincided with the spread of urban conditions of life and with the drift of the population towards the towns.

With the informal garden came the rock garden, which soon acquired so strong an independent life and popularity that it may be taken as the most marked development of the general movement, just as the attraction of the high Alps is the most extreme reaction against the town. The rock garden, in its most austere form, has perhaps a special attraction for us because of its contrast with the lush exuberance of much of the English countryside. . . .

'A Shingle or A Sand Garden' *Manchester Guardian* 28 June 1929

We take holidays in the mountains and we build rock gardens at home probably for one and the same reason—that is, we want to create as complete a change as possible from the regular lines of bricks and mortar in which we spend most of our lives.

'The Scent of Flowers' *Journal of the Royal Horticultural Society* Vol. LIV Part I 1919 Read 17 July 1928

There is some disagreement about the scent of the Hawthorn; the poets have praised it, but to most of us there is a very disagreeable smell of stale fish mixed with its sweetness. This was evident, apparently, to the professionally attuned noses of the fish porters in

France, for they used to have a superstition that if they put down their load under a May tree in flower the fish would go bad. . . .

The scent of the Elder is about the best that I have met among the fly-flowers; at a distance it has a pleasant, vinuous quality that vaguely suggests champagne, but at close quarters it has that blackcurrant smell which easily deepens into a smell of cats, and when very strong it suggests a hot and perspiring crowd. The oil distilled from the flowers has none of these unpleasant qualities, but something of the bouquet of a muscat wine, and the elder tree has enjoyed in the past a certain clandestine association with the wine trade.

On the whole we, as gardeners, owe little to the flies for the flowers that they have created; but our debt is rather greater when we come to the bees, although with them scent seems to play a subordinate role, not attracting them, as it does the flies, but merely guiding them. We get the impression, in fact, as we look at the bee-flowers, that the bee is not particular about the quality of the scent or, indeed, whether the flower is scented or not, but it prefers its flowers to be in broad, easily accessible and conspicuous masses, and its general predilections are those of many gardeners. I may add, without prejudice, that the bee is partially colour blind.

Some of the bee-flowers are scentless, as, for example, the Borage family, the Aconites and the Foxgloves, and we are entitled to assume, I think, that if they are scentless to ourselves, they are scentless also to the bee; for Von Frisch has shown, in a series of very ingenious experiments, that the bee's sense of smell is curiously like our own. They pick up smells from about the same distance as we do, and they confuse scents that we find difficult to distinguish.

Many of the bee-flowers, as we might expect, are honey-scented: the Clovers, the Lime tree, and many of the heaths. . . .

The flowers fertilized by moths are in a very different category. Unlike the bee-flowers they are nearly always fragrant, with a scent of distinct and usually elaborate character; unlike the fly-flowers, their scent is almost invariably pleasant to ourselves, though sometimes we may find it rather too sweet for our taste. Typical moth-flowers are the great white Evening Primrose (*Oenothera eximia*), Honeysuckle, Jasmine, Tobacco Plant, and many of the true Lilies. . . .

In spite of the careful work that has been done on flower-pollination, the relation between the flower and its visitor is sometimes quite obscure. The flowers of the sweet violet, for example, are seldom if ever fertilized by insects, and the scent gives us no clue, for it occurs in widely separated types of flower. We find it in *Iris reticulata*, the White Banksian Rose, *Asparagus tenuifolius*, and the Crab Apple *Pyrus coronaria* and, I believe, in one of the Orchids; there is a violet element, too, in Mignonette and in *Acacia Farnesiana*. And, if I may be allowed to turn aside from the scent of flowers, there is a distinct note of violet, or more precisely of Orris, in 'the excellent cordial smell of strawberry leaves dying,' as Bacon called it. I mention this scent because some people have said that it is a myth, while Lady Ludlow in Mrs Gaskell's story hinted that the power of smelling it was confined to a few of the oldest and most aristocratic families. Neither of these views is correct, but the scent is confined to the leaves of the wild strawberry and its relatives the Alpine and Hautbois, so that people who fail to perceive it in the garden hybrids need not write themselves off as hopelessly plebeian. ...

As it would be difficult to give an impression of the scope of Jason Hill's knowledge by trying to describe his writing, it seems best to quote directly from it. The following are selections from some of his books and letters. The first of these are from chapters IX and X of *The Scent of Flowers and Leaves, Its Purpose and Relation to Man*. Chapter IX is entitled 'Our Appreciation of Scent':

Our appreciation of scent is relatively simple, for it has never been elaborated into an art, and the olfactory impressions have never been used seriously as a means of expressing our emotions and ideas. Yet, so far as the writer is aware, no theory has been put forward which explains satisfactorily why we like that group of scents that we call sweet.

It simplifies the question to use the word 'sweet' rather than 'pleasant'; for many scents, such as the scent of newly baked bread and of the earth after rain, are pleasant but are not 'sweet' in the more definite sense in which we use this word of the scent of Jasmine and Syringa. ...

We have seen that the Heavy and Aromatic flower scents have been evolved to match the scents of the moths and butterflies that visit them, and that the scent of the butterflies plays a part in their courtship and serves to stimulate the mating instinct. ...

Havelock Ellis has noted the connection between the natural human scent and perfumes, and there is little doubt but that our appreciation of sweet scents has remote origin in the former. But our appreciation of scent, in the course of its evolution, has left its primitive origin far behind, and the distance travelled is brought home to us by the scent of the tropical orchid *Dendrobium Devonianum*, which has a distinctly human scent mixed with its sweetness, and is said to recall a dance room on a warm evening—a quality that detracts, for our civilised senses, from its fragrance instead of enhancing it. ...

It therefore seems likely that the fruit scents seem sweet to us because they appeal to the same instinct as do the flower scents, though less powerfully—a theory which would explain more adequately why Schiller used the scent of apples and de Maupassant a mixture of ether and strawberries to stimulate their imagination than by supposing that these scents stimulate the instinct of hunger. ...

Chapter X 'Scent in the Garden'

Gardeners have always appreciated the scent of flowers, and nearly the whole range of flower scents will usually be found in the average garden, although the flowers there may not have been selected with any special thought for their fragrance. ...

The scents of flowers do not seem to clash in the open air, perhaps because most of them have several elements in common. There is therefore no need to group them in any special way, except to take care that the more delicate are not overwhelmed by the stronger. But it is well worth while to pay a little attention to the scent of flowers that we plant near the house, so that we may enjoy it as it comes drifting in through the windows on a summer evening or on the first warm day of spring. . . .

Scented leaves in the garden

A few fragrant leaves give out their scent spontaneously, either after a shower, like sweet briar and *Veronica cupressoides* (cedar wood and violet), or under a hot sun, like the cistus family and *Rubus ororatus* (cedar wood and sweet briar, from the magenta hairs that cover the young shoots). But most need to be brushed against or bruised before they give out their scent, and they will naturally be planted within reach of the hand. All gardeners know the value of the erect Lemon Thyme, with its gold and silver varieties, for a formal edging; Lavender Cotton, especially the compact dwarf form sold as *Santolina squarrosa*, and the dwarf Lavenders may be used in the same way. . . .

The Herb Garden

The herb garden of our ancestors may be reproduced without much difficulty, if its literary associations seem to make it worth while. But most of the old herbs were more beautiful in their names—Sweet Cicely, Tansy, and Elecampagne—than in their scent, and the best of them, Lavender, Rosemary and Balm (*Melissa officinalis*) have long migrated to the border. *Alecost* is useful because its mint-scented leaves are almost evergreen, and may be used for mint sauce during the winter. Sweet Marjoram is tender, but easily raised from seed, and smells pleasantly of camphor and cedar wood. Sweet Cicely (*Myrrhis odorata*) has a very homely smell of aniseed, but its sweetness lies in the sugary taste of its leaves. . . .

Spicy Scent

It is sometimes said that the modern Roses are not so fragrant as the old varieties, and it is sometimes suggested that they are even losing their scent, but this is only a very careless criticism, and quite unjustified by facts. For there have always been scentless Roses, though, for this defect, most of them have passed out of memory as well as cultivation, and only those are noticed which appear inevitably among the great number of new varieties that are produced every year. . . .

There are many recipes for pot-pourri; in most of them the proportion of the ingredients is only vaguely indicated, and many include rare balsams not always easily to be identified, but exact directions for making pot-pourri of proved excellence will be found in Miss Jekyll's book 'Home and Garden' (Longmans and Co., 1901).

The scented leaves, especially Lemon Verbena and Monarda, whether alone or in mixture, provide a long-lasting scent if they are slowly dried in the shade, and, to one person at least, there is no pleasanter pot-pourri than a bowl of lavender.

This is a good point to turn to his correspondence on scent with Miss Jekyll. Dated around the years 1927–9, quite recently after his book on flower scent was published, it presents us with a delightful small collection of queries and details of trial runs with various plants, among a group of friends.

In February 1928 Dr Hampton is writing to her about carnations:

I have heard that carnations lose their scent by the sea, but I am afraid that I have no first-hand information about it, and no theory to offer. But I will write to N. G. Hadden at Porlock and I will let you know all that I can find out about it.

He goes on:

It is very interesting that your keen sense of smell can detect London in the N.E. wind at Godalming. . . . As I work here all day I am saturated with the smoke and do not notice it, but I was struck with the difference in the London smell during the coal strike, when a great deal of wood was burnt, especially tarry wooden paving blocks. And there is a corner near St James' Square where I sometimes catch a whiff of very aromatic wood smoke that takes me straight to the country again.

He ends: 'I apologise for writing such a very long letter, but you raised such interesting questions.'

In other letters they explore the possibilities of rough tweed and mistletoe; 'Oak moss reminds me of Harris tweed, which owes its scent to the lichens with which it is dyed', and he thanks her for a sample of mistletoe. He writes:

This is a most interesting observation of yours, and the distribution of the scent is both unexpected and puzzling. I am most interested to hear that this has a scent, for I had never heard of it. I am writing to Mr Bowles about it, for I know that he is interested in Mistletoe. Hadden tells me that, unfortunately, there is no Mistletoe within reach in his neighbourhood; he had not heard of the scentlessness of carnations by the sea, but says that they are scented in his garden (which is about three miles from the sea). I am writing to Mr Douglas of Bookham for further information. With again many thanks for the Mistletoe, yours sincerely, F.A. Hampton.

About a fortnight later Dr Hampton is writing again:

Dear Miss Jekyll, I have been so preoccupied with patients this week that I have not had a moment in which to answer your very kind letter.

. . . Mr Douglas has written to me about the scent of carnations and says: 'We used to take a house year by year in Devonshire at a place about three miles from Brixham, in the garden there was a scarlet clove carnation of unknown parentage. I always admired the strong clove scent and from the garden one could almost toss a biscuit into the sea. It was high up on a cliff and exposed to every wind that blew.' He offers to make further enquiries and I will try to make some observations myself this summer.

In another letter he is concerned about making Miss Jekyll tired with so much writing (she must by now be eighty-five):

It is kind indeed of you to have taken so much trouble and sent me so many notes, which are full of interest and very valuable to me. But my conscience troubles me sometimes that I should give you the occasion of so much writing. . . . I am enclosing a few notes on your notes and I am sending you a few samples of standard scents; these are not intended as examples of particularly pleasant scent, but only as a kind of 'reference library' of smells. If they are of any interest to you I can easily add to them.

I think that it might be interesting to make an extract of the roots of Asarabacca and if I might come and see you a little later on I should like to take some for experiment. My wife is expecting another baby in about a week (our third) so that I shall be rather preoccupied for some time to come. . . .

There is further mention of both the 'reference library' and the asarabacca.

I think that the best way of dealing with the Asarabacca would be to dry the roots (I do not think that the leaves contain any essential oil) and then a little later I would come, if I may, and collect them. I propose to extract them with a volatile solvent and make an alcohol essence. I will add some more specimens of scent-substances to this little collection and send them back to you, so that in time we might form a kind of reference library of scent.

A few months later a report comes in from Dr Hampton on the roots of asarabacca sent to him by Miss Jekyll. '[They] have nearly finished their process of extraction and promise to yield a very pleasant scent, which I will send to you in the form of an alcoholic solution.' He continues:

I am sending you a tin of Lychees in syrup, for, although I expect that you dislike food out of tins as much as I do, the fresh lychees do not reach this country until the middle of the winter and I thought that you might like to try them now since they seem to me to contain something of the Muscat grape flavour, for which Mr Taylor tells me you have been enquiring. . . . Have you noticed a certain dry, Muscat quality in some of the Darjeeling teas? I think that it recalls the wine rather than the fresh fruit. I find, by the way, that the Chinese describe their teas of the Morning type as 'Peach flavoured' which seems to explain the attribution of a 'tea-scent' to the tea roses, since the scent of them recalls the scent of peaches to so many people. . . .

I am afraid that this is a very long letter, but please do not trouble to answer it; I know that the parcels will arrive.

There are also mentions of Reginald Farrer's edelweiss; in June Dr Hampton writes:

I am enclosing some shoots of Farrer's Lemon-scented Edelweiss (Leontopodium Aloysiodora); the essential oil seems to exist on the surface of the leaves, for the smell is obscured if they are crushed. . . .

In November:

I am sending you one or two leaves that I have just picked from the garden, though they may be quite well known to you. 'Mace', I am afraid, hardly deserves its name and the pleasant smell of fresh lemons which comes from the surface of the leaves in Farrer's Edelweiss is very faint at this time of the year. I must also include my apologies for a letter six pages long! Yours sincerely, F.A. Hampton.
ps. I should be very pleased to send you a little book that I wrote on *Flower Scent* if you would care to have it. A post card would bring it.

A note in a later letter refers to this:

I am sending you, very diffidently, a copy of my little book on flower-scent; there are several bad mistakes in it, notably about the scent of Hammamelis mollis and the production of scent by stamens—the last was due to pure ignorance.

These letters came to light through research into Miss Jekyll's garden plans at the University of California, Berkeley, USA.

He also sends her excerpts from his article in volume 106 of *Nineteenth Century* on 'The Sense of Smell in Everyday Life':

For nearly everyone there are smells that recall, often with hallucinatory vividness, some isolated scene from the past, and it will be found, as we might expect, that such scenes are always associated with some emotionally significant experience (for one person, at least, the sour smell of hops recalls the first introduction, as a medical student, to a hospital surrounded with hop warehouses). If we examine the mental process set going by the smell we shall find that the emotion usually comes back first, and is followed, as a rule, almost immediately, by the memory picture. Occasionally it may take some time to recollect the experience with which the smell was originally associated; sometimes, especially if the experience was in any way painful, it eludes us altogether, and we are aware only that certain smells are unaccountably distasteful.

The smell of our surroundings makes up a large part of their character and individuality; we should all miss something from the sea, a pine forest and almost any foreign city, if we suddenly became anosmic, and the German dug-outs would have been less German during the war without their peculiar smell, vaguely suggesting a draper's shop with a certain fusty mousiness. There are outstanding, assertive smells that force themselves upon our attention, but there is an infinite number of others which are equally characteristic and significant, though they usually pass unnoticed. . . . This power of smells to set up an emotional attitude, even when they are not consciously perceived, might possibly repay consideration. . . . A theatre or concert-hall that is redolent of naphthalene lays an unnecessary handicap upon the performers, and, without imitating the ritual use of incense, which is probably more efficacious in banishing evil spirits than is commonly supposed, something might be done to create a genial atmosphere by the use of pleasant-smelling wood, and even a careful choice of floor polish is not altogether beneath consideration.

DANDELION.

37 Two drawings (and opposite) in silverpoint by Cedric Morris from Herbs, Salads and Seasonings *by Jason Hill and X. M. Boulestin*

The next extracts are from *Herbs, Salads and Seasonings*:

The general principles of the cultivation of salad plants are described in all the standard books on gardening, and it has not seemed necessary to do more here than indicate the requirements of those plants that are not very commonly grown—such as Purslane, Sorrel and Corn Salad—in the separate sections devoted to them. But it is, perhaps, not out of place to suggest that we might grow winter salads more commonly in this country than we do at present. Their cultivation involves a little extra work in the garden, but this is well rewarded by a supply of fresh, crisp Endive and Chicory or, with even less trouble, Corn Salad and Dandelion, throughout the winter. . . .

COSTMARY.

As for salads, they are so to speak an evergreen question. Now, more than ever, in England, they have reached the importance of a topical subject, discovered, boomed, discussed, both by scientists and writers of fashion articles. . . .

The scientist, naturally, raves about mineral salts, organic acids, and becomes positively lyrical over the thousand and one vitamins a salad, apparently, has in store for us. So we learn that radishes stimulate by their pungency, that lettuce has soothing properties, while Garlic is a good remedy against insomnia; that we must use vinegar because the acetic acid it contains softens the cellulose in the salad; and oil because it acts as a kind of lubricant and protects the stomach from irritation by the fibre. This is all very complicated, but we may be thankful, at least, that lubricating oil is not recommended.

Whatever attraction the vitamins may have, their presence is a poor inducement to eating salads. We always thought that we ate salads and ate them properly seasoned because they are fresh, wholesome and pleasant to eat. But evidently this is an exotic and old-fashioned point of view. Yet there is no doubt that the nobles and the peasants of the sixteenth century ate salads for the simple reason. . . .

There follows a quotation from Ronsard detailing the gathering of ingredients for a salad and their preparation. Dr Hampton goes on:

Ronsard's advice is good. Indeed he gives us a good recipe for a perfect simple salad, a simple salad being, after all, the best of all, that is, the green salad that is then 'in'—plain, fresh, crisp, seasoned with wine vinegar, olive oil, freshly ground pepper, sea salt and *fines herbes*, served with a roast chicken or a fillet of veal. All the other mixtures, whatever they are and however good they may be, are not *une salade*, but salads of this or salads of that, standing as separate dishes (or falling) on their own merits.

We are more in sympathy with the writers of society notes: it seems that salads have 'come in' again, that hostesses are making a great show of them on their dinner tables, and that 'salade Carmen is the most fashionable this season'.

Fennel
Foeniculum vulgare   N.O. *Umbelliferae*
F. *Fenouil*   G. *Fenchel*
Fennel carries its yellow flowers on graceful, six-foot columns up through a spray of finely divided leaves, yet it is seldom given a place in the garden which its firm and individual beauty of design deserves.

The English cook practically ignores it, yet it was much appreciated in the old days:
'Crabs, Salmon, Lobsters are with Fennel spread
Who never touched that Herb till they were dead.'
This is the Fennel always used in the making of Bortsch; it will grow anywhere, but prefers a deep root-run in full sun. It may be planted either in spring or autumn and will seed itself, sometimes too freely.

Florentine Fennel
Foeniculum dulce (Miller)
Italian   *Finocchio di Firenze*
Sweet Fennel
Foeniculum officinale (Allioni)
Italian   *Carosella*

Costmary
Costmary is known in Lincolnshire as *Sage o'Bedlem*, *Goose-Tongue*

and *French Sage,* and it is there used as a regular ingredient of veal stuffing. It is one of the few old herbs that have been undeservedly neglected, for while its companions the common Tansy, Alexanders, Lovage and Sweet Cicely have disappeared from the kitchen without regret, Costmary has a distinct character and value for which it is well worth re-introduction.

It resembles Sage only in the shape of its leaves, which are smooth, pale grey-green, and have the flavour of mint with a slight, appetising bitterness. As it is very nearly evergreen it provides a useful substitute for Mint, and a few leaves can almost always be gathered during the winter for use in pea soup and mint sauce or for adding a freshness to the dried herbs.

The name 'Costmary' is borrowed partly from Costus, a violet-scented plant from the Himalyas, whose roots were once of almost fabulous value as a perfume, and partly refers to the Virgin Mary, to whom the plant seems to have been dedicated in most European countries. . . .

Dandelion
Leontodon Taraxacum N.O. *Compositae*
F. *Pissenlit.* G. *Löwenzahn*
The English gardener's dislike for Dandelions is almost invincible and it is not easy to get him to grow them, but in France they are thought worthy of careful cultivation and there, improved forms have been produced by selection which closely resemble the Curled and Broad-leaved Endive. In fact, the cultivated forms of Dandelion, if they are well blanched, can scarcely be distinguished from the Endives in the salad bowl and differ from them chiefly in their merit of complete hardiness. If the improved varieties are not to hand we can still obtain an excellent salad from the common or (most of us can add) garden variety, by covering the plants *in situ* with a flower-pot. A better result, which is worth the trouble, will be obtained by lifting them at the end of the autumn and transferring them to boxes of soil in a warm cellar.

The English cook seems to share the gardener's opinion of the Dandelion, for it is hardly ever eaten in England, though it makes a very good winter salad (in some parts of France little pieces of fried bacon are added to it). The French dictionary acknowledges the value of the Dandelion by the definition 'genre de composées qui se mange en salade.'

In a footnote, Dr Hampton adds: 'While feeling in a sentimental mood on a picnic we admired the woods and watched the primroses growing—our chauffeur in the Vendée last spring . . . improved his evening meal by "thoughtfully, carefully, gathering dandelions".'

In the next book, *Wild Foods of Britain,* he writes in Chapter Ten on 'Tisanes':

All the plants which are known to contain caffeine have been used as beverages by the discriminating natives of their habitats and as tea, coffee, chocolate, mate, kola and guarana are exotics, we have no wild substitutes for tea. But French people may be observed in cafes sipping a hot pale amber drink, which is sometimes 'grog' but more often a tisane, and we may do well by occasionally following their example.

The following can be recommended:

Lime Flowers (dried)
About 1 dessertspoonful to a pint of boiling water. Honey flavour.
Elderflowers (dried)
About 3 teaspoonfuls to a pint. Muscat flavour.
I part of dried Elderflowers added to 3 of standard Indian tea converts it into something very like the best Darjeeling or the Elderflowers in a muslin bag may be stored with the tea.
Mint (fresh)
1 part of Spearmint (Garden Mint) with 2 parts of Bergamot (Monarda didyma) or Apple Mint or *Mentha citrata* or dried Woodruff (Asperula odorata) is unexpectedly good.

The tisane should be made in the same way as ordinary tea; sugar and lemon may be added, but not milk.

In the introduction to *The Fragrant Year* by Helen Van P. Wilson and Leonie Bell there are notes referring to Dr Hampton:

> According to F. A. Hampton, author of a delightful book *The Scent of Flowers and Leaves*, published in England in 1925 and now unfortunately out of print, our ancestors 'invented the first antiseptic by pouring balsam into their own wounds, and the old "Friar's Balsam" (an alcoholic solution of gum benzoin and balsam of Peru) still finds a place in the Pharmacopoeia . . .' (pp. 3, 4, 7).

Having, on various occasions, enquired from blind people about their choice of an attractive scent and frequently having their reply of 'a field of beans in flower', I feel this next note seems to confirm their selection.

> Dr Hampton tells of the effect the beanflower had upon him: 'I remember once being in the train beside the open window; I was reading, and quite absorbed in a very interesting book; presently I became aware that my heart was beating and I had my 'beanfield feeling'. I was just saying to myself, 'This book is as exciting as a beanfield,' when I looked out of the window and saw we were passing a beanfield! The effect passed off as soon as we were out of the scent zone, which proved it was not the book. It was a most delightful sensation, and the excitement pleasurable.'
> . . . In his book *In My Vicarage Garden and Elsewhere*, the Rev. Henry Ellacombe, a nineteenth-century student of fragrance, remarks that 'there are, of course, cases of flowers being attractive to more than one family of insects, and there are insects, such as bees, which do not confine themselves to one flower only, but they all work within certain

fixed limits, and there are cases when, if the particular insect does not come, the flower cannot perfect itself. . . .'

Perhaps these excerpts help to complete the portrait of the man but the final word must be said as a personal comment, not only on his erudition, skill and knowledge, but on his character. Mrs Stevens was a neighbour who knew him well for a good many years and I had almost decided to end with her letter:

My first meeting with Dr Hampton stands out very clearly. It was in March, 1953. We were looking for a house in Bampton and the Hamptons' house was on the market. I went to see the house and was taken round by Mrs Hampton. As I was about to leave she asked me to go into the garden and meet her husband. It was a cold but sunny day and Dr Hampton was sitting on a shooting stick, as by this time he was partially crippled with arthritis. I only had a few minutes conversation with him, but it was long enough for me to realise that I had met a rather exceptional and out of the ordinary person.

My experience of life is that one is privileged to know a few outstanding people and on that short list I have no hesitation in placing Dr Hampton very high. In the following years we were to see a good deal of him. In July, 1953, the Hamptons moved into Gate Cottage and we moved into Lime House just across the road.

I knew little about gardening but had always been a wild flower enthusiast with a particular interest in unusual plants. Dr Hampton gave me every encouragement and any little knowledge of plants that I may have acquired I certainly owe to him.

He was essentially a scholar and a plantsman, although his interests extended to many other fields. He had little time for gardening on the grand scale and I watched the making of his own small and very individual garden. It was full of unusual plants and in an enviably short time it became established. He was a frequent visitor to my garden and his help was invaluable as the garden was in the making. In the latter years of his life he was unable even to cross the road and I would visit him at Gate Cottage taking any interesting specimens with me.

On re-reading this letter I realise how very difficult it is to do justice to an extraordinarily perceptive and gifted man who had a rare understanding of plants and people.

16 February 1972. Mrs A. Stevens, Lime Tree House, Bampton.

However, I feel that the last testimony should come from Alice Coats, who knew some of the same problems of life and who kept up her interests and enthusiasms as he did (he had elbow callipers). She writes: 'Even his weeds had distinction. Every subject he touched was rendered fascinating by his humanity, imagination and charm.'

The Hon. Victoria (Vita)
Sackville-West

1892–1962

> ... We dream our dreams.
> What should we be, without our fabulous
>   flowers?
> They are more lovely than known loveliness,
> They are the consummation of a vision
> Seen by rare travellers on Tibetan hills—
> Bitter escarpments cut by knives of wind,
> Eaves of the world, the frightful lonely
>   mountains—
> Or in Yunnan and Sikkim and Nepal
> Or Andes ranges, over all this globe
> Giant in travelled detail, dwarf on maps;
> Forrest and Farrer, Fortune, Kingdon-Ward
> Men that adventured in the lost old valleys,
> Difficult, dangerous ...

V. SACKVILLE-WEST
The Garden

To most gardeners the name of Miss Victoria (Vita) Sackville-West must surely conjure up memories of a winding Kentish lane leading off the Sissinghurst—Biddenden road, with, already in sight, the twin towers of the castle round which the garden has grown to its present size. It would be impertinent to try to assess the value and beauty of this garden about which so much has already been written. However, the *Observer* in its wisdom invited its owner to become their Gardening Correspondent in 1947, and so we have a permanent record of fascinating happenings and plantings, of flower pictures through all the seasons of the years, of experiments and other excitements. These articles, entitled *In Your Garden*, were published in book form in four volumes by Michael Joseph. (I have good reason to remember the publication of the first. My husband had suffered a very serious heart attack— it was incredible that he came through it. Afterwards he said he would like to find a 'special present' for me, and came home in the evening with volume one under his arm.)

A good many years later a selection was made from these essays by her daughter-in-law, Philippa Nicolson, to be published in one volume entitled *V. Sackville-West's Garden Book* (1968). Turning the pages, one is struck more than anything else by the great variety of knowledge and the feeling that one is included in all the ideas—there is something for every gardener. There is, for instance, valuable information about 'old' roses. 'Drunk on roses, I look round and wonder which to recommend.' Miss Sackville-West then describes the characteristics of the Lawrence Johnston rose, formerly known as 'Hidcote Yellow', and also 'Buff Beauty' and 'Nevada', but 'if the yellows are not to your liking' there is *Gallica complicata*, *Alba celestial* and 'Cuisse de Nymphe', 'Honorine de Brabant' and *Rosa mundi*, 'Madame Pierre Oger' and 'Lemon Pillar'. 'Blairi No. 2' is a most exquisite climber.'

Another facet evident in these essays is her affection for a small garden. She describes, with the acres of Sissinghurst behind her, three small gardens in detail:

> The more I see of finely-cared-for gardens, the more do I realize the high importance given to cultivation. The size of the garden has nothing to do with it: twenty acres or one acre or half an acre, it is all the same, so long as the love and knowledge are there.

Much of the success of a garden, perhaps we might say, depends on a use of colour, and this is of course a major consideration in the book. Miss Jekyll talks of 'painting a picture with living plants' and the owner of Sissinghurst describes trying out different schemes and contrasts by cutting a flower from one part of the garden and holding it in position close to a group of a different tone or colour. 'I try effects, picking flowers elsewhere, rather in the way that one makes a flower arrangement in the home.' This is one of those occasions where a notebook comes in handy, and a special paragraph is included on the use and value of such a notebook to jog one's memory when the season of flowering has gone over. The practical goes hand-in-hand with the artistry of the planting and the more difficult pieces of gardening are not glossed over. For instance, the treatment for the Bourbon roses is mentioned to suit their natural way of growing. 'Dead and twiggy wood should be cut out. How easy to say, and how scratchy to do.'

The book is full of delights and surprises, of expressions of joy, and pleasure and occasionally of intense dislike. ('I hate, hate, hate American Pillar' is cancelled out many times by her love for almost all else.) It has the integrity of a natural gardener. Did she inherit this skill of working with the soil, either from her forebears or closer relatives? Perhaps parents? She writes in *Pepita*:

38 Vita Sackville-West with her dog in her garden at Sissinghurst. Behind her is the double-towered gatehouse where she wrote her books and articles

My mother never cared for flowers; she liked them made of paper, or silk, or feathers, or sea-shells, or beads, or painted tin, but the real flower never appealed to her in the least . . . Plants in pots were just the thing to please her, and any flower-merchant with a barrow was sure of a lavish customer. In fact, I think the hawkers of the neighbourhood must have passed the word round to one another, for, whether in London or in Brighton, these floral barrows seemed to stroll within range of her windows with far greater frequency than anywhere else. She would tap on the windowpane, making wild signals to the flower-merchant to stop, which he was only too willing to do; and then would go down to the front door to meet him in any attire. Sometimes . . . she would be fully dressed; but if during the morning, she would go down in her dressing-gown and night-gown, to stand on the doorstep buying the whole barrow-load off him, and finding out the whole of his family life at the same time.

(A revealing paragraph but not seemingly indicative of a talent for growing or caring deeply for plants.)

Another characteristic which emerges from her writing is her humility. For instance, in *Even More For Your Garden*, she writes about scent:

This whole question of scent in plants is one which I do not understand, though no doubt a scientific explanation is available. The warmth of the sun and the humidity of rain and dew account for much, as we all know from observation and experience, but there must be other factors unrevealed to the ignoramus. Why, for instance, does the balsam poplar waft its scent a hundred yards distant sometimes and at other times remain so obstinately scentless and sniff-less as to be imperceptible on the closest approach? These things retain their mystery for me and I am not sure that I want the answer. A little mystery is precious to preserve.

Again, it is some consolation to a writer to read in *Dearest Andrew* of Miss Sackville-West's anxiety when she had suffered a blockage in her writing and had been unable, for a period of some months, to finish the book she was working on at that time (*The Easter Party*, 1953). In December 1950 she had written to her husband, Sir Harold Nicolson:

Darling, I must write you another little note just to say how happy I am writing. It does make the whole difference in life. I just tell you this, because I like sharing things with you. I have been so miserable in the last two or three years, not being able to write; really worried I have been, thinking it was gone from me forever. . . .

Anyone who has struggled over difficult patches of writing, wondering whether the pen, or typewriter, will ever flow again or how one can surmount a particularly obstinate piece of research which it is essential to include, but where or how?—anyone in one or other of these predicaments will understand the feeling of despair which floods one's mind and brain when the words will not come. She goes on:

> I don't mean by this that I think my novel (*The Easter Party*) will be any good—you know that I am not a good novelist—but at any rate it is exciting just doing it. It keeps me alive, living in an imaginary world. Of course I would rather write poetry. Perhaps that also will return to me one day.

How refreshing it is to find someone with poetry like *The Land* and *The Garden* (Heinemann Prize, 1946) behind them, with a novel like *All Passion Spent*, and gardening articles galore to their credit, humbly being grateful when the flow of writing returns after a barren period. Another example of this approach comes in her reaction to Edward Marsh's comments on *The Land* which she sent to him for his criticism, evidently with a good deal of apprehension in mind.

Christopher Hassall, Marsh's biographer, writes:

> Vita Sackville-West sent him *The Land*, and he at once recognised an achievement which made some of the recent Georgians of the pastoral variety look rather like weekend word-spinners. 'I have no doubt,' he wrote, 'you are the best living poet under eighty and it is such a joy to find someone writing the sort of poetry I like so unmistakably and indisputably better than other people write the sort I don't like so much. Nobody in face of such a book could go on making out that the tradition of English poetry is exhausted, and that sense of beauty, rhyme, and metre, must be given up.
>
> 'I read Winter with admiration and pleasure, but (perhaps through not being warmed up) without any great excitement, except over the lovely passage beginning 'Here is no colour'—but Spring is one long enchantment, especially from the 'ghostly orchard' onward, through my old love the Beemaster with the splendid added passages, to a whole series of various miracles, the list of herbs in Gardener, the technical triumph of the Island with its 18 rhymes so managed that the cleverness only enhances the beauty of the poetry—the exquisite Wild Flowers, the sinister and surprising power of Fritillaries—the profound beauty of Spring flowering in the little lyric about the moorhen's nest which I couldn't see to read to the end till I had tried about six times. I do say, Vita, with my hand on my heart, that this is one of the perfect things in English poetry. And as if this were not enough you finish with a poem about the Nightingale which is as lovely and as new as if no one had ever written about it before.—(Here comes one of my few cavils, the fourth stanza has not the simplicity and

limpidity of the rest, I still can't make out the syntax, and therefore the exact meaning.) I can't go on with this catalogue. . . . I don't know how you dare to write prose as good as your poetry, it's almost too much!

The author wrote from Knole, glad that he had found evidence in her work 'that it is still possible to write in the traditional manner, and yet to avoid falling into "pastiche", and that it is possible to eschew the fireworks of today without being too boring' and continued:

> . . . You have fired me to go on with various abortive scraps I've accumulated since last year; hitherto I have been feeling like a very small breakwater in very heavy seas, trying to stem the tide, but now I shall take my scribbling book out to Persia with a bolder heart.

Her confidence was restored until the next time. Closely connected with this feeling of apprehension was the problem of loneliness. Obviously to write one has to work alone, do research alone, make certain decisions alone; this means that the support often obtaining in a good marriage is of special value because it comes, or is available, just when it is needed. This point comes out in a further letter to her friend 'dearest Andrew', when she writes to him after the death of his close companion.

> I think of you often, and wonder how you manage. It must leave such an awful gap, with stabs of memory throughout the day. I think one of the worst things about losing a life's companion like that, is constantly thinking 'Oh, how that would have amused him!' or 'Oh, I must tell him that,' and then remembering that he isn't there to tell. . . . I should miss the physical presence so much, and not being able to tell and have the little jokes one shares in daily life.

Fortunately for Vita Sackville-West, she and her husband were able to build the Sissinghurst garden together. They pooled their ideas and worked out designs, colours, everything. They frequently visited other gardens and a favourite one was Hidcote. A friendship between the Nicolsons and Major Lawrence Johnston developed and an article on the Hidcote garden was written by Vita Sackville-West for the Royal Horticultural Society's *Journal*. She asked her readers:

> Would it be misleading to call Hidcote a cottage garden on the most glorified scale? . . . It resembles a cottage garden, or rather, a series of cottage gardens. . . . No description of Hidcote would be worth anything without mention of the hedges. [For instance] the hedges of copper beech . . . may not inaptly be compared to a Persian carpet,

with their depths of rose-madder and violet, and the tips of young growth as sanguine as a garnet seen against the light. . . . There is just enough topiary to carry out the cottage-garden idea; just enough, and not so much as to recall the elaborate chessmen at Hever Castle or the tortured shapes at Levens Hall. The topiary at Hidcote is in the country tradition of smug broody hens, bumpy doves, and coy peacocks . . . What I should like to impress upon the reader is the luxuriance everywhere; a kind of haphazard luxuriance which of course comes neither by hap nor hazard at all.

The Editor of *Dearest Andrew*, Nancy MacKnight, mentions the gardening concerns of the autumn of 1953:

> In August she and Harold had driven through Scotland, where they saw many famous gardens. They also visited their favorite English garden, Hidcote in Gloucestershire. On their return to Sissinghurst, Harold loyally remarked, 'The garden is looking well, and we prefer it to all those we have seen, with the exception of Hidcote.'

Later on the in the same book, shortly before she died at the beginning of June 1962, she is writing still to her American pen friend.

> I won't write about the state of the world. Neither you nor I can do anything about it, and meanwhile as Voltaire so wisely remarked, 'One must cultivate one's garden', which I suppose means that one must live one's own life and make the best of it and be as charitable as one can in a Christian way to one's neighbours.

In a letter to her husband written during the previous month she uses the same quotation.

> Meanwhile I go on with my futile little occupation. . . . It sometimes seems rather silly, but as Voltaire wisely remarked, *Il faut cultiver notre jardin*. It is really better to have created a *Jardin* which gives pleasure to us as well as to many other people, than for me to go and sit down in Trafalgar Square.

from *The Garden*: 'Winter'

So does the gardener choose a list to hold
Sweet Sultan and Sweet Alyssum that smells
Of sea-cliffs and short turf
Where move the cropping sheep
And sea-gulls waver sprinkled round the steep
Crags that descend into the constant surf;
A list of mignonette and marigold
And other pretty things,
But lest you be romancefully inclined
Thinking that beauty unattended springs
All jilly-jolly from your scatterings,
Let dull instruction here remind
That mignonette is tricky, and demands
Firm soil, and lime, to follow your commands,
Else failure comes, and shows a barren space,
Where you had looked for small but scented spires.

Then all the earth is bright with clean and neat
Stars of the Apennine anemone,
And coloured primrose cousin of the mild
Insipid primrose in the wood's retreat,
And varnished celandine, that golden child
Unwanted of prolific March; then fling
The sterile cherries in a canopy
Translucent branches over and among
The pavement of the flowers, in a wild
Storm of successive blossom, lightly swung,
So lightly it would seem that they took wing
Also, in notes ethereal, and with Spring
Taught us again the sense of being young.

V. Sackville-West

Bibliography

FOREWORD
Russell Page, *The Education of a Gardener* (Collins, London, 1962)

SIR JOSEPH PAXTON
George F. Chadwick, *The Works of Sir Joseph Paxton* (Architectural Press, London, 1961)
Bea Howe, *Lady With Green Fingers* (Country Life, London, 1961)
J. C. Loudon, *Encyclopaedia of Gardening* (1841)
Violet Markham, *Paxton and the Bachelor Duke* (Hodder & Stoughton, London, 1935)
Cecil Woodham Smith, *Florence Nightingale* (Constable, London, 1950)
Handbook to Chatsworth and Hardwick

SAMUEL REYNOLDS HOLE, DEAN OF ROCHESTER
Reynolds Hole, *A Little Tour in Ireland* (Bradbury Agnew, London, 1858)
A Book about Roses, 2nd edn (Blackwood, Edinburgh, 1870)
Hints to Preachers with Sermons and Addresses (Parker, Oxford, 1880)
Nice and Her Neighbours (Sampson Low, London, 1881)
The Memories of Dean Hole (Edward Arnold, London, 1892)
More Memories (Edward Arnold, London, 1894)
Addresses Spoken to Working Men from Pulpit and Platform (Edward Arnold, London, 1894)
A Little Tour in America (Edward Arnold, London, 1895)
Our Gardens (Dent, London, 1899)
Then and Now (Hutchinson, London, 1901)
A Book About the Garden (Edward Arnold, London, 1904)
Betty Massingham, *Turn on the Fountains* (Gollancz, London, 1974)

CANON H. N. ELLACOMBE
Henry N. Ellacombe, *In a Gloucestershire Garden*, 2nd edn (Edward Arnold, London, 1896)
In My Vicarage Garden and Elsewhere (John Lane: The Bodley Head, London, 1901)

Mea Allen, *E. A. Bowles and His Garden* (Faber & Faber, London, 1973)

Arthur W. Hill (ed.), *Henry Nicholson Ellacombe: A Memoir* (Country Life, London, 1919)

William Robinson, *The English Flower Garden*, 5th edn (John Murray, London, 1897)

SHIRLEY HIBBERD

Shirley Hibberd, *Rustic Adornments for Homes of Taste* (Groombridge, London, 1856)

Garden Favourites (Groombridge, London, 1858)

The Rose Book (Groombridge, London, 1864)

Field Flowers (Groombridge, London, 1870)

The Fern Garden (Groombridge, London, 1875)

The Amateur's Kitchen Garden (Groombridge, London, 1877)

The Amateur's Flower Garden (Groombridge, London, 1878)

The Amateur's Greenhouse (Groombridge, London, 1883)

Familiar Garden Flowers (Cassell & Co., London)

The Book of the Aquarium (Groombridge, London)

The Book of the Fresh-Water Aquarium (Groombridge, London)

The Book of the Marine Aquarium (Groombridge, London)

The Town Garden (Groombridge, London)

Profitable Gardening (Groombridge, London)

Brambles and Bay Leaves (Groombridge, London)

The Ivy (Groombridge, London)

Charles H. Curtis and W. Gibson, *The Book of Topiary* (John Lane: The Bodley Head, London, 1904)

Ted Humphris, *Garden Glory* (Collins, London, 1965)

Gertrude Jekyll, *Home and Garden* (Longman, London, 1900)

THE REVD C. WOLLEY DOD

C. Wolley Dod, articles from *Gardeners' Chronicle*, *Gardening Illustrated* and *The Garden*

E. A. Bowles, *My Garden in Spring*, 5th edn (T. C. & E. C. Jack, London, 1914)

Edward A. Bunyard, *Old Garden Roses* (Country Life, London, 1936)

Reginald Farrer, *My Rock Garden*, 6th impression (Edward Arnold, London, 1920)

Richard Gorer, *The Development of Garden Flowers* (Eyre & Spottiswoode, London, 1970)

Gertrude Jekyll, *Wood and Garden* (Longman, London, 1899)
William Robinson, *The English Flower Garden*, 5th edn (John
  Murray, London, 1897)

MRS MARIA THERESA EARLE
Mrs C. W. Earle, *Pot-Pourri from a Surrey Garden* (Smith, Elder
  & Co., London, 1897)
  More Pot-Pourri from a Surrey Garden, 3rd impression (Smith,
    Elder & Co., London, 1899)
  A Third Pot-Pourri (Smith, Elder & Co., London, 1903)
  Memoirs and Memories (Smith, Elder & Co., London, 1911)
Sir Josiah Conder, *The Flowers of Japan and the Art of Floral
  Arrangement* (Sampson Low, London, 1892, and Tokyo)
Gertrude Jekyll, *Wood and Garden* (Longman, London, 1899)
Jane Loudon, *The Lady's Country Companion*
William Robinson, *The English Flower Garden* (John Murray,
  London, 1897)

WILLIAM ROBINSON
William Robinson, *Gleanings from French Gardens* (Frederick
  Warne & Co., London, 1868)
  The Parks, Promenades and Gardens of Paris (John Murray,
    London, 1869)
  The Wild Garden (John Murray, London, 1870); 4th edn with
    Introduction by Robin Lane Fox (reissued by The Scholar
    Press, London, 1977)
  Alpine Flowers for English Gardens (John Murray, London,
    1870)
  God's Acre Beautiful (John Murray, London, 1882)
  Garden Design (John Murray, London, 1892)
  The English Flower Garden, 5th edn (John Murray, London,
    1897); revised and edited by Roy Hay (John Murray,
    London, 1956)
  The Garden Beautiful (John Murray, London, 1907)
  Gravetye Manor (John Murray, London, 1911)
  The Virgin's Bower (John Murray, London, 1912)
  Home Landscapes (John Murray, London, 1914)
  My Wood Fires and Their Story (Country Life, London, 1917)
  Wood Fires (John Murray, London, 1924)
  Cremation and Urn-Burial (Cassell & Co., London)
  Hardy Flowers (John Murray, London, 1883)

The Sub-Tropical Garden (John Murray, London, 1871)

Reginald Blomfield, *The Formal garden* (Macmillan, London, 1892)

Ralph Dutton, *The English Garden* (Batsford, London, 1950)

Miles Hadfield, *Pioneers in Gardening*

Reynolds Hole, *Our Gardens* (Dent, London, 1899)

Gertrude Jekyll, *Colour in the Flower Garden* (Country Life, London, 1908)

J. C. Loudon, *Arboretum* (1838)

Betty Massingham, 'William Robinson: A Portrait' (Garden History Society, 1979)

John Ruskin, *Unto This Last* (1862)

> *Proserpina* (1875–6)
> *Praeterita* (1885–9)

Selby, *British Forest Trees*

Articles from *Gardening Illustrated* and *The Garden*

Miss Gertrude Jekyll

Gertrude Jekyll, *Wood and Garden* (Longman, London, 1899)

Home and Garden (Longman, London, 1900)

Lilies for English Gardens (Country Life, London, 1901)

Wall and Water gardens (Country Life, London, 1901)

with Edward Mawley, *Roses for English Gardens* (Country Life, London, 1902)

Old West Surrey (Longman, London, 1904), facsimile (Kohler & Coombes, Dorking, 1978); expanded as *Old English Household Life* (Batsford, London, 1925)

Some English Gardens, after drawings by George S. Elgood, R. I. (Longman, London, 1904); 4th edn (1906)

Flower Decoration in the House (Country Life, London, 1907)

Colour in the Flower Garden (Country Life, London, 1908); 3rd edn entitled *Colour Schemes for the Flower Garden* (1914)

Children and Gardens (Country Life, London, 1908)

with Lawrence Weaver, *Gardens for Small Country Houses* (Country Life, London, 1912); 6th edn (1927)

with Christopher Hussey, *Garden Ornament* (Country Life, London, 1918); 2nd edn (1927)

A Gardener's Testament (Country Life, London, 1937)

Reginald Blomfield, *The Formal Garden* (Macmillan, London, 1892)

Miles Hadfield, *Pioneers in Gardening*

C. A. Johns, *Flowers of the Field*
Betty Massingham, *Miss Jekyll—Portrait of a Great Gardener* (Country Life, London, 1966)
Russell Page, *The Education of a Gardener* (Collins, London, 1962)
Sir George Sitwell, *On the Making of Gardens*, new edn (Duckworth, London, 1951)

MISS ELLEN ANN WILLMOTT
Ellen Willmott, *Warley Garden in Spring and Summer*, dedicated to 'my sister' (1909)
> *The Genus Rosa*, with drawings by Alfred Parsons (John Murray, London, 1914)
Gertrude Jekyll, *Children and Gardens* (Country Life, London, 1908)
Audrey le Lièvre, *Miss Willmott of Warley Place* (Faber & Faber, London, 1980)

MRS FRANCIS (LOUISA) KING
Louisa King, *The Well-Considered Garden* (Charles Scribner's Sons, New York, 1915) rev. edn 1922
> *Pages from a Garden Notebook* (Charles Scribner's Sons, New York, 1921)
> *Chronicles of the Garden* (Charles Scribner's Sons, New York, 1925)
> *The Beginner's Garden* (Charles Scribner's Sons, New York, 1927)
> with John Fothergill, *The Gardener's Colour Book* (1929)
> *From a New Garden* (Alfred A. Knopf, New York, 1930)
> *The Flower Garden Day by Day*
> *Variety in the Little Garden*
Alice Morse Earle, *Old Time Gardens*, 1st edn (1908); reprint (Gale Research Co., Detroit, 1968)
Gertrude Jekyll, *Wall and Water Gardens* (Country Life, London, 1901)
Jane Loudon, *Gardening for Ladies* (John Murray, London, 1852)
J. C. Loudon, *Encyclopaedia of Gardening* (1841)
Eleanour Sinclair Rohde, *The Story of the Garden* (Medici Society, London, 1932)

E. A. BOWLES
E. A. Bowles, *My Garden in Spring*, Preface by Reginald Farrer, 5th edn (T. C. & E. C. Jack, London, 1914)

Mea Allen, *E. A. Bowles and His Garden at Myddleton House (1865–1954)* (Faber & Faber, London, 1973)

Reginald Farrer, *Among the Hills* (Headley Bros, 1911)

Louisa King, *The Well-Considered Garden* (Charles Scribner's Sons, New York, 1915)

W. T. Stearn, 'E. A. Bowles (1865–1954), the Man and His Garden', (*RHS Journal*, July, August 1955, vol. LXXX, parts 7 and 8)

VISCOUNTESS WOLSELEY

Viscountess Wolseley, *Gardening for Women* (1908)

  In a College Garden (1916)

  Women and the Land (Chatto & Windus, London, 1916)

  Gardens, Their Form and Design (Edward Arnold, London, 1919)

  Smaller Manor Houses of Sussex, illustrated from photographs specially taken under the author's supervision

  Some Sussex Byways, with eight plates in colour by Garnet R. Wolseley, A.R.A.

  Sussex in the Past, with eight plates in colour by Garnet R. Wolseley, A.R.A.

Sir George Arthur (ed.), *The Letters of Lord and Lady Wolseley 1870–1911* (Heinemann, London, 1922)

Alfred Austin, *Soliloquies in Song* (Macmillan, London, 1882)

Gertrude Jekyll, *Gardens for Small Country Houses* (Country Life, London, 1912)

Sir F. Maurice and Sir George Arthur, *The Life of Lord Wolseley*

Marjory Pegram, *The Wolseley Heritage*

William Robinson, *The English Flower Garden* (John Murray, London, 1897)

THE REVD WILLIAM KEBLE MARTIN

William Keble Martin, *The Concise British Flora in Colour* (Ebury Press and Michael Joseph, London, 1965)

  Over the Hills (Michael Joseph, London, 1968)

REGINALD FARRER

Reginald Farrer, *The Garden of Asia* (Methuen, London, 1904)

  My Rock Garden (Edward Arnold, London, 1907)

  Alpines and Bog Plants (Edward Arnold, London, 1908)

  In a Yorkshire Garden (Edward Arnold, London, 1909)

Among the Hills (Headley Bros, 1911)
The Rock Garden (T. Nelson & T. C. Jack, London, 1912)
'Lecture on Jane Austen', *Quarterly Review* (John Murray, London, 1917)
On the Eaves of the World, two vols. (Edward Arnold, London, 1917)
The Rainbow Bridge (Edward Arnold, London, 1921)
E. A. Bowles, *My Garden in Spring*, Preface by Reginald Farrer (T. C. & E. C. Jack, London, 1914)
E. H. M. Cox, *Farrer's Last Journey* (Dulau & Co., 1926)
Plant Hunting in China (Scientific Book Guild, 1945)
Wang Gungwa, *China and the World since 1949* (Macmillan, London, 1977)
Heinrich Harrer, *Seven Years in Tibet* (Rupert Hart-Davis, London, 1953)
Sir L. E. Jones, *An Edwardian Youth* (Macmillan, London, 1956)
Frank Kingdon-Ward, *Pilgrimage for Plants* (Harrap, London, 1960)
William Robinson, *The English Flower Garden* (John Murray, London, 1897)
Osbert Sitwell, *Great Morning* (Macmillan, London, 1948)
Noble Essences (Macmillan, London, 1950)

ELEANOUR SINCLAIR ROHDE
Eleanour Sinclair Rohde, *A Garden of Herbs* (Medici Society, London, 1920)
The Old English Herbals (Medici Society, London, 1922)
The Story of the Garden (Medici Society, London, 1932)
Herbs and Herb Gardening (Medici Society, London, 1936)
Shakespeare's Wild Flowers (Medici Society, London, 1935)
The Scented Garden (Medici Society, London, 1931)
Sir Hugh Platt, *Delights for Ladies* (1582)

DR F. A. HAMPTON (JASON HILL)
Jason Hill, *The Scent of Flowers and Leaves* (Dulau & Co., 1925)
with X. M. Boulestin, *Herbs, Salads and Seasonings* (Heinemann, London, 1930)
The Curious Gardener (Faber & Faber, London, 1932)
Wild Floods of Britain (A. & C. Black, London, 1939)
The Contemplative Gardener (Faber & Faber, London, 1940)

Henry N. Ellacombe, *In My Vicarage Garden* (John Lane: The Bodley Head, London, 1901)
Helen Van P. Wilson and Leonie Bell, *The Fragrant Year* (Dent, London, 1951)

VICTORIA (VITA) SACKVILLE-WEST
V. Sackville-West, *Pepita* (Hogarth Press, London, 1937)
The Garden (Michael Joseph, London, 1946)
The Heir (The Richards Press, London, reissued 1949)
All Passion Spent (Chatto & Windus, London, 1950)
In Your Garden (Michael Joseph, London, 1951)
In Your Garden Again (Michael Joseph, London, 1953)
The Easter Party (Michael Joseph, London, 1953)
More For Your Garden (Michael Joseph, London, 1955)
Even More For Your garden (Michael Joseph, London, 1958)
V. Sackville-West's Garden Book (Michael Joseph, London, 1968)
Christopher Hassall, *Edward Marsh—a Biography* (Longman, London, 1959)
Nancy Macknight, *Dearest Andrew* (Michael Joseph, London, 1959)
Articles from the *Observer* and the *RHS Journal*

Index

Devonshire, Duke of, 21, 24
Dod, T. C., 68
Dodd, Miss, 168
Dodgson, Charles (Lewis
    Carroll), 181
D'Ombrain, H., 95
Douglas, Mr, 223–4
Downing, Andrew Jackson, 139,
    149
Drumthwacket, 145

Earle, Alice Morse, 146
Earle, C. W., 75–6
Earle, George, 76
Earle, Maria Theresa, 74–87
Earle, Ralph, 76
Eaton Hall, 113
Edge Hall, 67, 68–73, 133, 191
Ellacombe, Emily Aprilla, 46
Ellacombe, Henry Nicholson,
    44–53, 54, 69, 85, 93, 95, 115,
    131, 133–4, 150, 151–2, 156,
    157, 230
Ellicombe, Elizabeth, 45
Ellicombe, H. T., 44–5
Ellicombe, Jane, 45
Elliott, Clarence, 217
Elmhurst, Illinois, 140
Elwes, H. T., 151
Evelyn, John, 137
Ewing, Mrs, 45

Falkner, Harold, 120–1, 126
Farrand, Beatrix, 119, 139
Farrer, J. A., 188
Farrer, Reginald, 67, 108, 153,
    156, 157, 175, 188–200, 205,
    206, 216, 217, 225
Fell, John, 98
Fish, Margery, 212
Fisher, Mark, 99
Folly Farm, Sulhamstead, 124
Forbes and Tate, 122
Fothergill, John, 148

Garden Club of America, 148
Gatty family, 45
George III, King, 53
George, Ernest, 98
Gerard, John, 202
Gibbs, Vicary, 210, 211
Gibson, W., 66
Glasnevin, 89
Gledstone Hall, 146
Glynde Place, 167–72
Glynde School for Lady
    Gardeners, 168–72, 176
Goode, Stephen, 99
Gosse, Edmund, 164
Gosselin, Joshua, 187
Gravetye, 89, 95, 96–108, 120,
    164–6
Greater Dixter, 126
Guiccioli, Countess, 79

Hadden, N. G., 216, 217
Hakluyt, Richard, 204
Hampton, Dr F. A., 205, 212–31
Hanbury, Lady, 176
Hanbury, Sir Thomas, 133, 137
Hassall, Christopher, 236–7
Haymes, Miss, 168
Hestercombe, 117, 124, 129–30
Hibberd, Shirley, 38, 54–66, 85
Hidcote, 237–8
Hill, Arthur W., 50
Hill, Jason, *see* Dr Hampton
Hill, Octavia, 112, 166
Hill, Oliver, 122
Hilton, John, 33
Hilton, Mary Elizabeth, 33
Hole, Caroline, 32–7
Hole, Samuel Reynolds, 26–43,
    51, 57, 85, 90, 92, 93, 95, 97,
    102, 106, 107, 113, 115, 168,
    202
Holmes, Oliver Wendell, 93
Hooker, Sir Joseph, 50, 88
Hudson, E. H., 117, 120, 124
Humphris, Ted, 56

Index of Plants

Acacia farnesiana, 220
achilleas, 145
aconites, 208, 220
Alecost, 222
alkanet, 63
Allium schoenoprasum, 63
Alpine primulas, 157
anchusa, 208, 209, 210
Anchusa italica, 209; A. officinalis, 63
androsaces, 72
anemones, 48, 153
Anemone blanda, 151, 157
Anethum [Foeniculum vulgare], 63; A.
  graveolens, 63
angelica, 63, 207, 208
anise, 63, 209
apricots, 'Moorpark', 56
arabis, 144
Araucaria imbricata, 103
Archangelica officinalis, 63
Artemisia dracunculus, 63; A. vulgaris
  [A. absinthium], 63
asarabacca, 224
Asparagus tenuifolius, 220
Asperula odorata, 230
Asplenium septentrionale, 183–4
aubretias, 144, 165

balm, 63, 64, 210, 222
balsam, 222, 230
bamboo, 48
bastard dittany, 209
bay, 127
beanflowers, 230
beech-fern, 49
Berberis darwini, 144
bergamot, 208, 209, 230
bloodroot, 158
borage, 63, 64, 210, 220
Borago officinalis, 63
broom, Mount Etna, 156
buckbeam, 92
bugloss, 63
burnet, 63, 64
Butcher's broom, 155
buttercups, 48

Calendula officinalis, 63
calceolarias, 166
Camassia esculenta, 132

camomile, 209, 210
Campanula latifolia, 69; C.
  pyramidalis, 143
carnations, 127, 209, 223, 224
catalpa, 47
chervil, 63, 64, 210
chicory, 227
Chimonanthus fragrans, 206
chives, 63, 64, 210
Choerophyllum, 63
cistus, 222
Citrus trifoliata, 151
clary, 63, 64, 209, 210
clematis, 166, 174
Clematis campaniflora, 104; C. florida,
  105; C. languinosa, 104–5
clover, 220
colchicums, 153
columbines, 145, 216
copper beech, 237
coriander, 227
corn salad, 227
costmary, 227, 228–9
cowslips, 156
crocus, 153–4, 160
crown imperials, 144
cumin, 209
cyclamen, 153
Cystopteris fragilis, 49

daisy, 48
dandelions, 48, 226, 227, 229
date-palms, 160
Delphinium chinense, 145
Dendrobium devonianum, 221
dill, 63, 64, 208, 209

edelweiss, Farrer's, 225
elder, 217, 220, 229, 230
elecampane, 208, 222
endive, 227, 229
eucalyptus, 160
evening primroses, 156, 220

fennel, 63, 64, 208, 228
ferns, 56, 59–61
feverfew, 145
Foeniculum dulce, 228; F. officinale,
  228; F. vulgare, 63, 228
forget-me-nots, 144

foxgloves, 69, 210, 220
fritillaries, 236
Fuchsia, 62, 70; *F. fraseri*, 70; *F. riccartonii*, 70
fumitory, 48

Galanthus elwesii, 153; *G. ikariae*, 50; *G. imperati*, 50
gardenias, 127
garlic, 227
Gentiana farreri, 193; *G. verna*, 71
geranium, 166; oak-leaf, 49
glory of the snow, 191

Hammamelis mollis, 225
harebell, tufted, 98
heartsease, 160
heaths, 220
hepaticas, 153
herb Bennet, 209
herbs, 62–5, 201, 207–10, 216
Herniaria glabra, 165
heuchera, 144
hollyhocks, 212
honesty, 126–7, 220
hops, 160, 225
horehound, 63, 209
hyacinths, 145
hyssop, 63
Hyssopus officinalis, 63

Iris reticulata, 220
ivy, 56, 58

Japanese anemones, 145
japonica, 156
jasmine, 127, 220, 221
Jasminum polyanthum, 156

lavender, 63, 64–5, 202, 208, 209, 210, 222
Lavendula spica, 63, 209; *L. vera*, 209
lemon verbena, 223
Leontodon taraxacum [*Taraxacum officinale*], 229
Leontopodium aloysiodora, 225
lettuce, 227
lilies, 145, 220
lily of the valley, 127
lime, 220, 229, 230
Linaria reticulata, 70
Lobelia, 70
London pride, 126
lovage, 208, 229

Lytherum salicaria, 69

madonna lilies, 209
marigolds, 63, 208, 209, 210
marjoram, 63, 222
Marrubium vulgare, 63
meadowsweet, 209, 210
Melissa officinalis, 63, 222
Mentha citrata, 230; *M. rotundifolia*, 63; *M. spicata*, 63
Mexican blackbean, 208
Michauxia campanuloides, 70
mignonette, 160, 206–7, 220
mint, 52, 207, 209, 229, 230; apple, 63, 230; fairy, 98; spear, 63, 65, 230; woolly, 63, 65
mistletoe, 223
monarda, 223
Monarda didyma, 230
mullein, 210
Myrrhis odorata, 222
myrtle, 52

Nandina domestica, 48, 51
narcissi, 70, 99, 153

oak-fern, 49
Ocimum basilicum, 63
Ocymym basilicum [*Ocimum basilicum*], 63
Oenothera eximia, 220
Omphalodes lucilla, 71, 191
orach, 208, 209
Origanum hereacleoticum, 63; *O. majorana*, 63; *O onites*, 63

pansies, 127
Parottia persica, 51–2
parsley, Hamburg, 207, 208
pears, 108
pennyroyal, 207
peonies, 145, 216
phlox, 145, 156
Physalis alkekengi, 48
Pimpinella anisum, 63
pinks, 126, 127, 151
Polemonium caeruleum, 181
Polygonum cuspidatum, 69; *P. japonica*, 72; *P. sieboldi*, 72
Portulacca oleracea, 63; *P. sativa*, 63
potatoes, 55
Potentilla anserma, 48
Poterium sanguisorba [*Sanguisorba minor*], 63
primroses, 209

✣ *Index of Plants* ✣

Primula bowlesii, 157; *P. capitata*,
71; *P. florindae*, 205
purslane, 63, 208, 227
Pyrus coronaria, 220

radishes, 227
rhododendrons, 98, 114
rock-cress, 145
Rosa, 26–43, 46, 57, 131–2, 137,
202–3; *R. alba celestial*, 233; *R.*
'American Pillar', 233; *R. banksiae*,
26, 47–8, 57, 220; *R.* 'Blairii
No. 2', 57, 122, 218–19, 233; *R.*
'Buff Beauty', 233; *R.* 'Cuisse de
Nymph', 233; *R.* 'Dorothy
Perkins', 132, 202; *R. gallica*, 203;
R. g. complicata, 233; *R.* 'Garland',
122; *R.* 'Gloire de Dijon', 41, 57;
R. 'Hidcote Yellow', 233; *R.*
'Honorine de Brabant', 233; *R.*
'Janet's Pride', 72; *R.* 'Julia
Mannering', 72; *R.* 'Madame
Alfred Carrière', 122; *R.* 'Madame
Pierre Oger', 202; *R.* 'Meg
Merrilees', 72; *R. mundi*, 233; *R.*
'Nevada', 233; *R.* 'Paul's
Himalyan Musk', 28; *R.* 'Paul's
Lemon Pillar', 28, 233; *R.* 'Paul's
Scarlet', 28, 29; *R. pomifera
duplex*, 73; *R.* 'Reynolds Hole',
43; *R.* 'Souvenir de Malmaison',
48, 57; *R.* 'Stanwell Perpetual',
202; *R. sulphurea*, 202; *R.
wichuraiana*, 202; *R.* 'Yellow
Provence', 202; *R.* 'Zephirine
Drouhin', 122, 202
Rosmarinus officinalis, 63, 65, 177,
204, 210
rosemary, 63, 65, 204, 209, 210
Rubus odoratus, 222
rue, 63, 65, 204
Ruta graveolens, 63, 204

sage, 63, 209, 210
Salvia officinalis, 63, 210; *S. patens*,
70; *S. sclarea* (formerly *S.
turkestanica*), 63, 210
Sanguinaria canadensis, 158
Sanguisorba minor, 63
santolina, 209, 210
Santolina squarrosa, 222
Saxifraga wolley-dod, 71
saxifrages, 71, 183
Sempervivum comollei, 51

Senecio pulcher, 70
Serratula, 184
Sibthorpia, 184
snowdrops, 156
Solanum nigrum, 184
sorrel, 227
southernwood, 210
speedwell, creeping, 98
Spiraea aruncus, 74
strawberries, 86, 220–1
succory, 208
sunflowers, 70
sweet basil, 63, 64
sweet briar, 52, 72, 126, 209, 210, 222
sweet cicely, 208, 222, 229
sweet peas, 151, 160
sweet william, 145
syringa, 221

tansy, 210, 216, 222, 229
tarragon, 63
thrift, 126
thyme, 52, 63, 98, 127, 209, 223
Thymus azureus, 63; *T. corsicus*, 63;
T. serpyllum, 63; *T. vulgaris*, 63;
T. v. variegatus, 63
toadflax, 48
tobacco plant, 220
Traqium anisum [*Pimpinella anisum*], 63
Tulipa 'Clara Butt', 144; *T.* 'La
Merveille', 143; *T.* 'Rosamund',
144; *T.* 'Thomas Moore', 143; *T.*
'White Swan', 143

Umbellularia californica, 156

valerian, 52, 210
Veronica cupressoides, 222
Viburnum farreri (formerly *V.
fragrans*), 156, 205, 206
Victoria regina, 22, 23
vines, 166
violets, 156, 206, 220

wallflowers, 126, 144, 160, 206
water-lily, 92; Amazon, 22, 23
Wellingtonia gigantea, 103
wellingtonias, 98, 103
willow, cardinal, 98
winter cherry, 48, 209
winter jasmine, 97
winter savory, 209
woad, 208
woodruff, 230
wormwood, 63